HISTORICAL DICTIONARIES OF ANCIENT CIVILIZATIONS AND HISTORICAL ERAS
Series editor: Jon Woronoff

Historical Dictionary
of Medieval India

Iqtidar Alam Khan

*Historical Dictionaries of Ancient Civilizations
and Historical Eras, No. 20*

The Scarecrow Press, Inc.
Lanham, Maryland • Toronto • Plymouth, UK
2008

SCARECROW PRESS, INC.

Published in the United States of America
by Scarecrow Press, Inc.
A wholly owned subsidary of
The Rowman & Littlefield Publishing Group, Inc.
4501 Forbes Boulevard, Suite 200, Lanham, Maryland 20706
www.scarecrowpress.com

Estover Road
Plymouth PL6 7PY
United Kingdom

British Library Cataloguing in Publication Information Available

Library of Congress Cataloging-in-Publication Data
Khan, Iqtidar Alam.
  Historical dictionary of medieval India / Iqtidar Alam Khan.
    p. cm. — (Historical dictionaries of ancient civilizations and historical eras ;
no. 20)
  Includes bibliographical references.
  ISBN-13: 978-0-8108-5503-8 (cloth : alk. paper)
  ISBN-10: 0-8108-5503-8 (cloth : alk. paper)
  1. India—History—1000–1526—Dictionaries. I. Title.
DS457.K46 2008
954.0203–dc22   2007046226

∞™ The paper used in this publication meets the minimum requirements of
American National Standard for Information Sciences—Permanence of Paper
for Printed Library Materials, ANSI/NISO Z39.48-1992.
Manufactured in the United States of America.

to

Kamo

who sustains me in the twilight of my life

Contents

Editor's Foreword

The *Historical Dictionary of Medieval India* deals with a crucial formative period of what is already one of the world's biggest countries and, over recent decades, one that has added economic, political, and social clout to its size and numbers. So it is important to know India's history, and this not only for Indians and others on the subcontinent but for all of us. Admittedly, this volume deals with an early period, namely and roughly the period between 1000 and 1526; however, this book is not just to inform us about what happened so many centuries ago but also to remind us of old sores that have not yet healed and old problems that will not readily go away. Indeed, more broadly, it helps us to put into context what some feel will be the greatest quandary—and also conflict—of the 21st century: the reputed "clash of civilizations." What is happening today is not even as jarring as the clashes that took place in medieval India, not so much among Indians (who did not exist yet) but among the many earlier kingdoms and states that would merge into India, and even more decisively, between the Hindus, Buddhists, Muslims, and Christian West.

This is an extremely tangled web, one that can only be untangled with considerable effort, and then only partially. So it is very helpful to have this handy guide, which—while not following every last strand—at least gives us a good look at many of the crucial details and an impressive overall view. This is done, first, in a chronology, without which it would be extremely difficult to follow events both over time and across the then-existing borders. The introduction extrapolates the main currents and trends, and offers a comprehensible context. But the most important section is the dictionary, with a large number of entries on specific persons, places and events, institutions and customs—mainly political, but also social, religious, and cultural. The bibliography comes at the end of the book, but should be the start of further studies for those who are interested.

This volume was written by someone with exceptional credentials for the task. Iqtidar Alam Khan was a teacher of history at Aligarh Muslim University from 1957 to 1994, and also for some time chairman of the department and, later, dean. During his long career as a teacher, he has engaged in considerable research into different aspects of the medieval Indian history as well as those of the Mughal Empire and most recently the application of gunpowder. As a researcher, his career has been even longer; he published his latest book, *Gunpowder and Firearms: Warfare in Medieval India*, just a few years ago, and has since been working on the present historical dictionary. Thanks to his encyclopedic knowledge, his keen interest in the many subjects touched upon here, and an ability to sum up the overall situation and spell out the many details, he has provided a welcome introduction to a period that, as noted, is far more relevant than one may think.

Jon Woronoff
Series Editor

Preface

For this historical dictionary, the themes for entries have been selected largely on the basis of the importance given to them in the major writings on the period, from the pens of Mohammad Habib, Tara Chand, R. C. Majumdar, H. C. Ray, Ishwari Prasad, T. Mahalingam, A. B. M. Habibullah, Romila Thapar, Haroon Khan Sherwani, Simon Digby, and Peter Jackson. Naturally, a balance had to be maintained between persons and institutions as well as between political, social, and religious aspects. Broadly, the treatment has been restricted to the medieval period of Indian history (1000–1526) with a focus on the Delhi sultanate, 1206–1526, even when the regions concerned lay outside the limits of the Delhi sultanate.

It remains for me to record my thanks: to the staff of the library of the Department of History, Aligarh Muslim University, for the help and courtesy extended to me throughout the preparation of this volume; to Faiz Habib for drawing a map; to Muneeruddin Khan for preparing the press copy; and to Shireen Moosvi, secretary, Aligarh Historians Society, for providing all possible facilities.

Note on Transliteration

When transliterating Indian names or terms, in most instances, spellings already in wide use are preferred. For other Persian terms, I have largely followed the spellings in F. Steingass' *Persian-English Dictionary* but without diacritics. The only diacritics retained are the raised comma and inverted comma representing *alif-hamza* and *ain* respectively. For Sanskrit words of the same nature, again the standard transliteration system in use in the *Epigraphia Indica* is adopted but without diacritics.

INDIA IN THE FOURTEENTH CENTURY

Boundary of the Delhi Sultanate, 1325 ————

Regional dynasties thus   *YADAVAS*

KM 100 0   100 200 300 K.M

Chronology

This chronology of the medieval period of Indian history begins with Mahmud of Ghazni's victory over the Hindu Shahi ruler Jaipal in 1001 and ends with Babur's victory over Rana Sanga in 1527. Events recorded include accessions and demises of important rulers, wars and battles of far-reaching consequences, as well as the rise of new states and the changes of dynasties within them. The deaths of important literary and religious figures such as Alberuni, Shaikh Nizam al-Din Auliya, Amir Khusrau, Ramanuja, Ramanand, and Kabir are also recorded. For the periods 1000 to 1200 and 1400 to 1527, events pertaining to developments in different states are specifically identified, while in the chronology of the period 1200 to 1400, most of the events listed pertain to developments within the Delhi sultanate. A few entries for this period refer to events in other contemporary states and specify the regions and ruling clans concerned.

1001   Mahmud of Ghazni defeated Jaipal Shahi, originally of Kabul.

1002   Ganda, the Chandella ruler of Jejakabhukti, came to the throne.

1003   Didda, queen and virtual ruler of Kashmir, died.

1009   Mahmud defeated the Hindu Shahi ruler.

1010   Mahmud occupied Multan and massacred Karmathians there.

1011   Mahmud raided Thanesar.

1013   Mahmud captured the Hindu Shahi stronghold Nandana.

1014   Chola ruler Rajaraja I died.

1015   Mahmud invaded Kashmir.

1018 Mahmud raided Mathura and Kanauj; Pratihara ruler Rajapala submitted to Mahmud.

1019 Mahmud raided Kalinjar.

1021 Rajendra Chola I extended his sway up to Gangese in Bengal. Samantasena rose to prominence in Bengal.

1022 Mahmud again invaded Kalinjar.

1025 Rajendra Chola led an expedition against Shrivijaya in Southeast Asia. Demolition of Somnath temple by Mahmud of Ghazni.

1030 Death of Mahmud of Ghazni.

1031 Accession of Mas'ud in the Ghaznavid Empire. Bhimadeva Chaulukya of Gujarat wrested Mt. Abu from the Paramaras.

1036 Majdud, son of Sultan Mas'ud, the Ghaznavid ruler, appointed to Lahore.

1038 Mas'ud captured Hansi.

1042 Mas'ud, the Ghaznavid ruler, assassinated.

1044 Chola ruler Rajendra I died.

1048 Abu Rehan Alberuni died. Ghaznavid ruler Ma'udud died.

1060 Ghaznavid ruler Khusrau Shah died. Paramara ruler Raja Bhoj defeated by an alliance of Lata, Chedis, and Chaulukyas.

1064 Karna succeeded Bhimadeva Chaulukya in Gujarat.

1070 Kulottunga I ascended the throne in the Chola Empire.

1085 Gahadavala ruler Chandradeva came to rule at Benaras.

1090 Chandella ruler Kirttivarman repulsed an attack on Kalinjar by the Ghaznavid governor of the Punjab.

1094 Karna succeeded by Jayasimha (entitled Siddharaja) in the Chaulukya kingdom of Gujarat.

1095 Vijayasena's accession in Bengal.

1100 The Kashmiri chronicler Kalhana born.

1112 Govindchandra Gahadavala came to the throne at Kanauj.

1118 Kulottunga I succeeded by Vikrama in the Chola Empire.

1137 Ramanuja died.

1145 Kumarapala ascended throne in the Chaulukya kingdom of Gujarat.

c. 1150 Prithviraja Chahamana II forced the Tomaras of Delhi to acknowledge his overlordship.

1162 Vallalasena occupied Gaud in Bengal.

1164 Kumarapala Chaulukya of Gujarat converted to Jainism.

1167 Visaladeva Chahamana ousted the Ghaznavids from Hansi.

1169 Prithviraja Chahamana III defeated Chandellas of Jejakabhukti. Vallalasena, ruler of Bengal, completed his book *Danasara*.

1173 Jaichandra ascended the throne in the Gahadavala kingdom of Kanauj.

1175 Lakshmanasena succeeded to the throne in Bengal.

1178 Chaulukyas of Gujarat defeated Muhammad Ghauri near Mt. Abu.

1183–1192 Lakshmanasena extended his territory up to Boddh-Gaya.

1186 Last Ghaznavid ruler, Khusrau Shah, expelled from Lahore by Muhammad Ghauri.

1191 Prithviraja Chahamana III defeated Muhammad Ghauri at Tarain.

1192 Prithviraja Chahamana III defeated and killed at Tarain.

1193 Gahadavala ruler Jaichandra defeated and killed by Muhammad Ghauri at Chanwar. Delhi occupied by the Ghaurids. Historian Minjah Siraj Juzjani, author of *Tabaqat-i Nasari*, born.

1197 Qutb al-Din Aibek raided Gujarat, then ruled by Chaulukya ruler Bhima II. Buddhist monastery at Nalanda destroyed during a raid by Muhammad bin Bakhtiyar Khalji.

1203 Qutb al-Din Aibek conquered Kalinjar. Parmardi Chandella killed.

1204 Muhammad bin Bakhtiyar Khalji occupied Nadia in Bengal.

1206 Muhammad Ghauri assassinated and Qutb al-Din Aibek became the ruler of Ghaurid territories in India. Last Sena ruler, Lakshmansena, died.

1210 Qutb al-Din Aibek died at Lahore.

1211 Shams al-Din Iltutmish's accession as the sultan of Delhi

1216 Taj al-Din Yildiz defeated and killed by Iltutmish.

1221 Chingez Khan's coming up to the river Indus.

1228 Iltutmish recognized as the sultan of India by the Abbasid caliph. Annexation of Sind to Delhi sultanate after the suppression of Nasir al-Din Qubacha.

1231 Jalal al-Din Mingbarni died in Iran.

1236 Iltutmish died. Raziya Sultan ascended the throne. Shaikh Moin al-Din Chishti died.

1237 Nur al-Din Turk, accused of having Karmathian leanings, killed in a riot inside the main mosque of Delhi.

1240 Raziya Sultan and her husband, Ikhtiyar al Din Altunia, defeated and killed.

1246 Nasir al-Din Mahmud's accession.

1252 Balban ousted from the position of *na'ib*.

1254 Balban regained his position at Nasir ul-Din Mahmud's court.

1262 Shaikh Baha al-Din Zakarya Suhrawardi died.

1265 Shaikh Farid al-Din Ganj-shikr died.

1266 Sultan Nasir al-Din Mahmud died and Ghiyas al-Din Balban ascended the throne in the Delhi sultanate.

1270 Nusrat al-Din Sanjar Sher Khan, Balban's cousin, poisoned.

1276 Shaikh Hamid al-Din Nagauri died.

1281 Bughra Khan appointed by Balban to Lakhnauti.

1286 Prince Muhammad killed in a skirmish with the Mongols. Balban died.

1290 Establishment of Khalji dynasty at Delhi by Jalal al-Din Firuz Khalji. Malik Chajju's revolt.

1292 Sidi Maula put to death for conspiring against Khalji rule.

1294 'Ali Garshasp (later Sultan 'Ala al-Din Khalji), governor of Kara, attacked Deogir.

1296 Sultan Jalal al-Din Khalji murdered and 'Ala al-Din Khalji ascended the throne.

1297 Gujarat annexed to the Delhi sultanate.

1298 Mongols led by Kutlugh Khan repulsed.

1300 Rukn al-Din Kaika'us, son of Bughra Khan, died at Lakhnauti.

1301 Akat Khan, a nephew of 'Ala al-Din Khalji, tried unsuccessfully to assassinate the sultan. Haji Maula, in collaboration with nobles of the old regime, tried to capture power at Delhi but was killed in fighting. Conquest of Ranthambhor by 'Ala al-Din Khalji.

1303 Conquest of Chitor by 'Ala al-Din Khalji.

1305 Annexation of Malwa to Delhi sultanate.

1310–1311 Malik Kafur's campaign in south India.

1316 'Ala al-Din Khalji died. Malik Kafur killed by *paiks.* Qutb al-Din Khalji ascended the throne.

1320 Qutb al-Din Mubarak Khalji killed. Khusrau Shah overthrown. Ghiyas al-Din Tughlaq ascended the throne.

1325 Ghiyas al-Din Tughlaq's death. Shaikh Nizam al-Din Auliya's death. Amir Khusrau's death. Muhammad bin Tughlaq's accession.

1327 Transfer of the capital to Daulatabad. Mongols led by Tarmashirin repulsed.

1328 Baha al-Din Garshasp executed.

1329 Issuance of a token currency.

1333   Ibn Battuta reached Delhi.

1335   Shaikh Rukn al-Din Suhrawardi died.

1336   Establishment of Vijayanagar Empire.

1337   Amir Hasan Sijzi died.

1339   Jalal al-Din Ahsan Shah, sultan of Madurai, died.

1339–1341   Temporary capital at Swargadwari.

1340   Embassy to Abbasid caliph then residing at Cairo.

1340–1341   Revolt by 'Ain ul-Mulk in Awadh.

1342   Shah Mir, founder of the sultanate of Kashmir, died.

1342–1347   Revolts by nobles in Multan, Gujarat, Malwa, and Deccan.

1347   Establishment of Bahmani kingdom.

1351   Muhammad bin Tughlaq's death. Firuz Shah Tughlaq's accession. Khwaja Jahan Ahmad bin Ayaz put to death by Firuz Shah.

1352   Establishment of Ilyas Shahi dynasty in Bengal.

1355   Vijayanagar ruler Hari Hara died.

1356   Shaikh Nasir al-Din Mahmud Chiragh Dehli died.

c. 1357   Historian Ziya' Barani died.

1359   'Ala al-Din Hasan Shah Bahmani died.

1377   Vijayanagar ruler Bukka I died.

1378   'Ala al-Din Bahmani II died. 'Imad al-Mulk Bashir, the *'ariz-i mamalik*, died.

1388   Firuz Shah Tughlaq died.

1394   Mahmud Shah Tughlaq ascended the throne.

1398   Timur's invasion.

1399   Malik Sarwar, founder of Sharqi dynasty, died. Malik Raja Faruqi, founder of the kingdom of Khandesh, died.

1400 Ibrahim Shah Sharqi ascended the throne.

1401 Dilawar Khan Ghauri declared sultan of Malwa.

1403 Tatar Khan, son of Zafar Khan, declared himself independent ruler of Gujarat.

1404 Ruler of Vijayanagar Harihara II died. Deva Raya I succeeded to Vijayanagar throne. Mahmud Khalji's accession to the throne in Malwa.

1407 Zafar Khan declared himself sultan of Gujarat with the title Muzaffar Shah. War between Bahmani kingdom and Vijayanagar.

1411 Muzaffar Shah I of Gujarat died. Accession of Sultan Ahmad Shah I in Gujarat.

1412 Mahmud Shah Tughlaq, last emperor of the line, died.

1414 Khizr Khan, founder of the Saiyid dynasty, established his control at Delhi.

1415 Raja Ganesh captured power in the kingdom of Bengal.

1417 Kashmiri ruler Sikander Shah died.

1418 Raja Ganesh died and succeeded by his son.

1420 Italian traveler Nicolao Conti arrived at Vijayanagar. Firuz Shah Bahmani beaten back by Vijayanagar forces.

1421 Saiyid ruler Khizr Khan died.

1422 Firuz Shah Bahmani died.

1429 Bahmani capital shifted from Gulbarga to Bidar.

1432 Sultan Hoshang Shah of Malwa died.

1433 Sisodiya ruler Rana Kumbha ascended the throne in Mewar.

1434 Second Saiyid ruler of Delhi, Mubarak Shah, died.

1435 Sultan Ahmad Shah Bahmani died.

1437 Saiyid ruler of Delhi, Muhammad Shah, married his daughter to Ibrahim Sharqi's son. Rana Kumbha defeated Mahmud Khalji of Malwa at Sarangpur. Kumbha built a victory tower at Chitor.

1440   Sultan Ibrahim Sharqi died.

1442   'Abd ul-Razzaq came to Vijayanagar. Restoration of Ilyas Shahi dynasty in Bengal.

1448   Ramanand the *bhakti*, saint, died.

1449   Deva Raya II of Vijayanagar died.

1453   Mahmud Gavan joined Bahmani service.

1458   Rathor chief Raja Jodha founded Jodhpur in Marwar. Sultan Husian Sharqi ascended the throne.

1459   Rukn al-Din Barbak Shah's accession in Bengal. Mahmud Begarha ascended the throne in Gujarat.

1466   Murder of Khwaja-e Jahan and end of regency in the Bahmani kingdom. Rise of Mahmud Gavan to power. Conflict between the Bahmanis and the sultanate of Malwa.

1473   Mahmud Gavan's reforms in the Bahmani kingdom. Sultan Zain al-'Abidin of Kashmir died.

1474   Shams al-Din Yusuf ascended the throne in Bengal.

1476   Last ruler of Saiyid dynasty, 'Ala al-Din 'Alam Shah, died at Badaun.

1481   Mahmud Gavan executed.

1482   Shihab al-Din Mahmud ascended the throne in Bahmani kingdom.

1484   Mahmud Begarha annexed Champanir.

1486   Chaitanya born. Uprising in Telingana and conflict between Bahmanis and Vijayanagar.

c. 1487   Rise of a new dynasty under Narasimha Saluva in Viajayanagar.

1489   Sultan Bahlul Lodi died. Raja Jodha of Marwar died.

1492   Bhakt Kabir Das died.

1493   'Ala al-Din Husain Shah, founder of the Saiyid dynasty of Bengal, ascended the throne.

1498 Vasco da Gama reached Calicut.

1505 Ousted sultan of Jaunpur, Husain Shah Sharqi, died.

1508 Portuguese defeated by a joint naval force of Mamluks and several Indian states near Chaul.

1509 Accession of Krishna Deva Raya in Vijayanagar.

1513 Gujarat sultan, Mahmud Begarha, died.

1517 Demise of Sikandar Lodi and accession of Ibrahim Lodi. Rana Sanga went to help Medni Rai in Malwa.

1519 'Ala al-Din Husain Shah of Bengal died.

1520 'Azam Humayun and several other senior nobles of Ibrahim Lodi killed in a contrived explosion. Rana Sanga advanced up to Ahmadabad.

1524 Muzaffar Shah II of Gujarat besieged Chitor.

1525 Rana Sanga defeated a Lodi detachment at Ghalote.

1526 Babur defeated and killed Ibrahim Lodi at Panipat.

1527 Rana Sanga and allies defeated by Babur at Kanwa.

Introduction

The medieval period of Indian history is difficult to define clearly. It may be perceived as the long phase of India's transition from the ancient to the immediately precolonial times (which some historians regard as India's early modern age). The latter period would naturally be imagined commencing from Vasco da Gama's voyage around the Cape of Good Hope in 1498, or, alternatively, the establishment of the Mughal Empire (1526). The renewed Islamic advance into north India, roughly after the year 1000 and leading to the rise of the Delhi sultanate (1206), can be held to mark in political and cultural terms the beginning of the medieval period.

What is characterized by many historians as "Indian feudalism" appears to have reached its high mark around 1000, by which time there came into vogue in several of the Hindu principalities of north India the practice of making secular hereditary grants to kinsmen of the rulers as well as to high officials and vassals. These were in addition to grants made for the maintenance of temples and priests that had continued since the early centuries of the Christian era. The tendency to create secular grants was particularly marked among the Chandellas of Jejakabhukti, Paramaras of Malwa, and Chahamanas of Ajmer. The peasants under these conditions, though increasingly subjugated as a consequence of the hereditary control of grantees over land, were still far from being reduced to serfdom. They essentially remained small producers who were not entirely immune to fluctuations in the market demand for agricultural products. Urban centers, shrinking since the decline of the Gupta Empire, also started reviving, particularly in northwestern India around this time.

There was also a general revival of foreign commerce, which is attested by Arab geographers' accounts and reinforced by Marco Polo as well as Chola epigraphs. This revival in turn gave a fillip to the export of items like hemp and sugar, stimulating small-scale production, including that by peasants cultivating cash crops. On the whole, by the beginning of 11th century, the agrarian economy in many parts of India appears to have reached a point where a considerable social surplus was available for appropriation by local potentates controlling land, making them more resourceful and assertive.

The rise of a new warrior class represented by *rautas* (*rawats*) or Rajput cavalrymen was a development of far-reaching significance of this period. By the seventh century, charioteers of the ancient period began to give way to cavalry belonging to newly risen warrior clans as the armed servitors of Hindu rulers in north India. Such a development must have been greatly aided by the arrival of the concave saddle and the use of a primitive wooden stirrup that enabled a mounted warrior to charge with a lance or sword. Contributing significantly to political fragmentation and decentralization of political authority within existing state systems, the *rawat* cavalrymen tended to add a new layer of superior right holders in the rural society in north India. They were to survive often as *khots* and *muqaddams* in the Delhi sultanate, described to us as chewing betel leaf and riding horses in *Tarikh-i Firuz Shahi* by Ziya' Barani.[1]

The early years of the 11th century also witnessed renewed interaction between Islam and Hindu civilizations after a gap of about 275 years since the Arab conquest of Sind and southern Punjab early in the eighth century. This renewed expansion laid the pattern of subsequent Islamic penetration of the Indian subcontinent. The nature of Ghaznavid authority in the Punjab until 1186 was not apparently very different from that of the Delhi sultanate during the 13th century. As was the case with the *iqta'* system of the Delhi sultanate, an arrangement making it possible to appropriate a large part of the agrarian surplus and use it for the maintenance of a town-based war machine had precedents in the administration of the Punjab and Sind annexed to the Ghaznavid Empire in the 11th century. An important feature of this arrangement was the incorporation of a large body of Hindu hereditary chiefs in the state structure. The Ghaznavid sultans resorted to large-scale enslavement of ordinary inhabitants captured during raids into the territories of Hindu rulers, but they also recruited Hindu soldiers and commanders as mercenaries.

This led to the emergence of a large body of troops, cavalry as well as infantrymen, within the Ghaznavid army who were Hindus commanded by their own leaders (*muqaddams*). These Hindu soldiers and other state personnel lived at Ghazni and Lahore in their separate quarters where they freely observed their social and religious rituals. The widow of a deceased Hindu resident of Ghazni is reported by a contemporary to have performed sati publicly. Masud's military commander, Tilak, following the custom of Hindu rulers (*rais*), installed a kettle drum at the gate of his mansion at Lahore. The presence of troops identified by Abu Rehan Alberuni as Kanaras (those hailing from Karnataka) suggests that not all the Indian military personnel in the Ghaznavid army were inducted through enslavement or as levies contributed by subjugated chiefs. Evidently, some of the Hindu warrior groups from distant regions of the Indian subcontinent were recruited as mercenaries.

The raids by Mahmud, however, did generate, as Alberuni testifies, strong resentment against Muslims among Indians who had to face the brunt of his savagery in northwestern India. References in some of the Gahadavala and Chahamana inscriptions to a "*Turukshka danda*," a tax on Muslims or for meeting expenses on defense against raids by them, support this impression. But textual and epigraphical evidence also suggests the presence of Muslim settlements in many of the territories controlled by Hindu princes during the 11th and 12th centuries, which shows that ordinary Muslims were not harmed. Similarly, despite Alberuni's assertion of Hindu hostility to Muslims, he himself refers to his free discourses with Brahmans, who in time became anxious to learn about the new discoveries of science that went beyond their own books.

Alberuni himself responded to a desire in circles of the scholarly world of Islam to obtain an accurate knowledge of Indian sciences and Hindu beliefs and customs. He tried to satisfy this quest in a magisterial work, *Kitab al-Hind* (Alberuni's India, translated by E. C. Sachau). On the Indian side during the same period, curiosity to understand the Greek concepts of astronomy preserved in early Islamic writings was quite manifest. This emerges not only from what Alberuni tells us about Brahman scholars reciprocating his curiosity about their scientific knowledge and beliefs but also from the appearance in Sanskrit of astrological works entitled *Tazika-nilakanthi* (Arab Astrology) composed around this time. The Sanskrit legend on the Ghaznavid *tankas*, for example, illustrates an attempt to interpret Islamic concepts for a Hindu audience: V. S. Agarwal cites, in this context, the rendering of the word "*allah*" as "*avyakta*" (invisible one). According to him in "The Sanskrit Legend on the Bilingual Tankas of Mahmud Ghazni," this "happy rendering" shows a "genuine understanding of each other's philosophical concepts" on the part of Hindu and Muslim scholars brought together under Ghaznavid tutelage.[2] The attitude of sympathetic appreciation of Indian culture and philosophy survived on the Muslim side in the writings of Amir Khusrau as well as in the recorded conversations of some of the Chishti Sufis of the 13th and 14th centuries.

The establishment and consolidation of the Delhi sultanate (1206–1236) was no doubt linked to the military superiority that the Ghaurids enjoyed over their Hindu adversaries. They had easier access to superior-quality Central Asian warhorses and were already using the iron horseshoe not yet used in India. Their greater expertise in the use of the iron stirrup possibly enabled them to resort to the use of mounted archers against the mounted lancers of their opponents to good effect. This initial military advantage was enhanced by their success in building a state structure that extracted a very large part of surplus through the working of an assignment or *iqta'* system.

The establishment of the Delhi sultanate led to important economic changes. The growth of a cash nexus coexisting with the *iqta'* system and the imposition of tax-rent (set at half the value of produce) over a very large area in the beginning of the 14th century perhaps represented the most significant of these changes. These, in turn, led to a considerable expansion of internal trade, drawing food grains and other agricultural products to the towns and so leading simultaneously to a new spurt of urban growth. Numismatic evidence of the period also suggests the prevalence of brisk commerce, India's favorable balance in overseas trade leading to the inflow of gold and silver in large quantities. Both the expansion of commerce and accompanying urban growth were partly facilitated by the introduction of crafts based on new technological devices and skills like papermaking, the spinning wheel, sericulture, and liquor distillation introduced from abroad. The new archuate (involving use of the arch) building technique not only accelerated building activity but also gave rise to the subsidiary crafts of brick making and manufacture of lime mortar. This new building technique transformed the architectural scene of urban settlements in most places outside Assam, Orissa, and peninsular India. Apparently, the use of force was necessary in some—indeed, many—instances. Slave labor could be employed at the new crafts. Large-scale enslavement in times of war and natural calamities gave rise to a brisk slave market at Delhi.

The Delhi sultans, like their Arab and Ghaznavid predecessors in Sind and the Punjab, came to treat the Hindus of the conquered territories as *zimmis*, who, according to Islamic political theory, would enjoy the status of protected people on payment of *jiziya*, a poll tax. At the same time, the impossible task of calculating and realizing *jiziya* from the vast Hindu population was circumvented by calling the land revenue realized from the predominantly Hindu rural sector *khiraj-o-jiziya* (tribute and poll tax). Until the mid-14th century, none of the sultans tried to impose the *jiziya* outside the towns. Firuz Shah Tughlaq (1351–1388) did try to impose the *jiziya* as a poll tax on all Hindus, including the Brahmans, hitherto exempt, and this led to a strong protest by the Hindus of Delhi. In all probability, this measure petered out in Firuz Shah's own lifetime. Subsequently, the *jiziya* was never properly levied in the Delhi sultanate or in any one of the successor states.

The Delhi sultans, despite the religious bigotry of some of them, were generally obliged to be quite tolerant toward the public display of Hindu rites in the towns and localities controlled by the sultans, including the capital city of Delhi. Sultan Jalal al-Din Firuz Khalji (1290–1296) is quoted by Ziya' Barani in *Tarikh-i Firuz Shahi* as having complained that crowds of Hindu men and women daily "pass under the walls" of his palace, "beating drums and blowing their trumpets, proceeding to the Jamuna, where they worship idols and perform acts of *kufr* (infidelity)," without his being able to check them.[3] Barani himself describes how in the 13th century, the Hindu Multanis and Shahs of Delhi had accumulated abundant wealth by lending to the nobles of the Delhi sultanate against drafts on their assignments. These prosperous Hindus had also built for themselves a large number of new temples in the territory controlled by the sultans. Firuz Shah Tughlaq (1351–1388) sought to remove some of these temples on the basis that these were built without the formal permission of the authorities.

By the end of the 13th century, the top crust of military officers in the Delhi sultanate, initially dominated by the sultan's Turkish slaves and the freeborn Tajik (Persian-speaking) officers, came to include—in addition to a number of Ghaurid aristocrats—men belonging to such ethnic groups as the Khaljis, Qaraunas (Turks serving under the Mongols), and more importantly, Indian converts to Islam. These Indian converts were looked down upon by others as upstarts and intruders. By 1253, the Indian Muslims had come to acquire a position where one of their leading representatives, 'Imad al-Din Rehan, managed to outmaneuver, for a brief interlude, the slave nobles at the court of Nasir al-Din Mahmud Shah (1246–1266). Under the Khalji and Tughlaq sultans, the Indians became still more visible in the nobility. Writing around 1356, Ziya' Barani gives vent to his resentment over their rise by referring to many of them as belonging to different menial castes (*baghban*/gardener, *khammar*/distiller, *mali*/gardener, *naddaf*/cotton-dresser, etc.), being both Hindus and Muslims.

Inclusion of many Hindus in the nobility, apparently, flowed from the clout gained by Hindu guards (*paiks*) whose special task was to protect the person of the sultan. Prompt intervention of the *paiks* had prevented an assassination attempt by one of 'Ala al-Din Khalji's nephews to capture the throne in 1301. It was again with the support of commanders of *paiks* belonging to the Parwari warrior clan (many of them Hindus) that Khusrau Khan ruled as a sultan for several months, after having assassinated Qutb al-Din Mubarak Shah Khalji in 1320. Hindu officers belonging to the category of financiers managing land revenue became prominent under Muhammad bin Tughlaq (1325–1351). Some of them, like Bhiran Rai, the *mutasarrif* (auditor) of Gulbarga in 1340, became the target of disaffected nobles resisting Muhammad bin Tughlaq.

The changes in the composition of the nobility were accompanied by a process of conflict and accommodation with Hindu local chiefs within the power structure of the Delhi sultanate at different levels. The creation of a new layer of rural intermediaries identified by Ibn Battuta (1333–1344) as *chaudhuris*, each one of whom exercised jurisdiction over a nominal group of 100 villages, may be taken to mark a stage in this process. The *chaudhuris*, remunerated through revenue-free land grants, continued to be a part of the fiscal administration of the countryside not only in the Delhi sultanate but in the Mughal Empire as well. Contrary to his reputation as a sultan who treated Hindus harshly, Firuz

Shah Tughlaq (1351–1388) extended unprecedented concessions to hereditary chiefs who were mostly Hindus. In his proclamation on the eve of his march to Bengal (1354), Firuz Shah gave an assurance to the local chiefs of the region "beyond the Kosi" (in *Insha-i Mahru* by 'Ain al-Din 'Abdu-llah bin Mahru) that the revenue demand for the current year would be remitted.[4] He also promised to reduce burdensome taxes and to stick to the settlement, possibly favorable to the chiefs, made by the then-ruler of Bengal, Haji Ilyas Shams al-Din Bhankara (1341–1358). Partly corroborating this information, Barani also hints at the reconciliation of chiefs who were in rebellion for many years during Muhammad bin Tughlaq's reign (1325–1351).

The new literary trends in Persian writing produced in India as well as in those of the Indian languages including Sanskrit, during the 14th and 15th centuries, often reflect an acute awareness of India as a distinct cultural and political entity in which elements identified with Islamic presence are perceived as acceptable components. The long patriotic passages in the *Nuh-sipihr* (Nine Heavens) of Amir Khusrau are the most striking illustration of this trend. Norms of chivalry and social correctness highlighted by Vidyapati Thakkura in *Purusha-Pariksha* (The Test of a Man; 1412–1416) projected a ruling-class culture free of religious rancor. In one of the stories narrated by Vidyapati, the heroic exploits of two Rajput warriors in the service of Muhammad bin Tughlaq are extolled for having defeated and killed a Mongol chief referred to as *Kaphara* (*kafir*, infidel).

The same period also witnessed the spread of Sufic doctrines among Indian Muslims; the most influential of them was the teachings of the Chishti Sufis. As revealed by Nizam al-Din Auliya's conversations recorded by his disciple Hasan Sijzi, these doctrines not only leaned toward greater tolerance for unorthodox attitudes and practices but also spoke of the Chishtis' appreciation of some of the beliefs and practices of the Hindu yogis they met frequently. As Muhammad Habib opined in *Politics and Society during the Early Medieval Period*, "converting non-Muslims was no part of the mission of Chishti sufis"; claims suggesting that particular Muslim communities were converted by early Chishti saints, according to him, are later inventions.[5] The impact of Chishti teachings, however, contributed significantly to molding the popular Islamic beliefs and practices in a major part of the subcontinent. The rise of devotional cults within Brahmanic Hinduism during the same period was a parallel development that contributed to blunting the clash of religious doctrines. This process was further strengthened by the emergence of the nonadulatory *nirguna bhakti* cults identified with Kabir, Nanak, and others during the 15th and 16th centuries.

By the end of the 14th century, the Delhi sultanate had come to acquire a reputation for amicable relations between Hindus and Muslims, so that Sharf al-Din 'Ali Yazdi, the chronicler of Timur, was prompted to describe the Muslims opposing Timur in his expedition (1398), as "Hindus," "faithless ones," "faithless Hindus," "hypocrites."[6] Massacres of such Muslims were therefore implicitly held to be justified because of their association with Hindus.

The situation during the 15th century, in most of the regions controlled by states succeeding the Delhi sultanate, was not very different. One significant development of the 14th and 15th centuries was, of course, the emergence of regional Hindu powers, such as the Sisodiyas of Mewar, the Gajapatis of Orissa, and the Vijayanagar Empire, who frequently fought with their Muslim neighbors over territorial disputes, which tended to create a false impression of an ongoing conflict between Hindu and Muslim powers for supremacy. Recurring clashes of Mewar with the sultanates of Gujarat and Malwa until the first quarter of the 16th century contributed to such an impression. A continuous state of war between the Bahmanis and Vijayanagar, which was obviously rooted in their conflicting ambitions over the Raichur Doab, was another conflict of the period, in the course of which much religious bigotry was displayed on both sides. That the element of religious divide in interstate conflicts of the 15th century was often a superficial matter is shown by the claim of Rana Kumbha of Mewar in one of his inscriptions that he was a "Hindu sultan" (*Hindu suratrana*) and his putting the name Allah in Arabic characters on the top layers of his Victory Tower. The Vijayanagara emperors for long used the title "sultan over Hindu rayas" (*Hindu raya suratrana*) and also kept in their employ a large contingent of Muslim horsemen, who were provided all facilities to perform their religious rites. The Bahmanis on their part incorporated in their ruling apparatus Hindu chiefs. Indeed, they promoted south Indian Brahmans in their central government on such a scale that it gave rise to a tradition that the founder of the dynasty was originally a Hindu brought up and trained by a Brahman.

In other successor states of the 15th century, too, the trend of accommodating Hindu local chiefs in the state structure at different levels and their growing power and influence was as manifest as it had been in the Delhi sultanate during the 14th century. Strong *zamindar* support to Sharqi rule was indicated by the widespread resistance offered by the local chiefs of the Gangetic Plain to the Lodi takeover of Jaunpur in 1489. Many of these chiefs in the end had to be accommodated in the Lodi service. The prominent role played by Purbia Rajput soldiers and their captains, led by Medini Rai under Mahmud Khalji (1518) of Malwa, is well known. The authority wielded by some of the Hindu chiefs under Ilyas Shahis in Bengal, which led to the capture of power by one of them, Raja Ganesh (1415–1418), again points to a similar situation.

Rushbrook Williams has surely misread this situation when he suggests that in the beginning of 16th century, Hindu and Muslim powers in India were arrayed against each other for a final showdown. According to him in *An Empire Builder of the Sixteenth Century*, "The Rajput confederacy led by Mewar was almost ready to seize the empire which lay within its grasp."[7] As discussed, India of the 15th century was a rather bewildering mosaic of regional powers, many of them ruled by Hindu warrior clans. Each one of these powers imagined itself a successor of the Delhi sultanate in the region it controlled and also had the tendency to accommodate within its structure cultural and religious groups other than those represented by the ruling clans. It was symptomatic of this situation that an alliance of Indian powers cutting across the religious divide confronted Babur at Kanwa under Rana Sanga's command in 1527. Out of the supposed total strength of 100,000 troops who fought at Kanwa against Babur, it must be remembered, the number of Muslims was put at 22,000 (12,000 Mewatis, and 10,000 Afghans).

NOTES

1. Ziya' Barani. *Tarikh-i Firuz Shahi*. Ed. Saiyid Ahmad Khan, Calcutta: Asiatic Society of Bengal, 1860–2, 288.
   2. "The Sanskrit Legend on the Bilingual Tankas of Mahmud Ghazni." *Journal of Numismatic Society of India* 5 (1943): 155–61.

3. Ziya' Barani. *Tarikh-i Firuz Shahi*. 216–17.
4. 'Ain al-Din 'Abdu-llah bin Mahru. *Insha-i Mahru*. Ed. and tr. S. A. Rashid, Lahore: 1965, 17.
5. Muhammad Habib. *Politics and Society during the Early Medieval Period*. Ed. K. A. Nizami, Vol. 1, New Delhi: 1974, 368.
6. Sharfuddin 'Ali Yazdi. *Zafarnama*, Vol. 2, Calcutta: Asiatic Society of Bengal, 1888, 74, 123, 138, 144.
7. Rushbrook Williams. *An Empire Builder of the Sixteenth Century*. Delhi: S. Chand, n.d., 18.

THE DICTIONARY

– A –

'ABD AL-HAMID GHAZNAVI. While serving as a clerk in the **Delhi sultanate** during **Muhammad bin Tughlaq**'s reign (1325–1351), he commenced compiling *Dastur al-albab*, a Persian text that furnishes valuable information on the subject of taxation. This book was completed by 'Abd al-Hamid during **Firuz Shah Tughlaq**'s reign (1351–1388) in 1364–1365. Like other Muslim theorists of the Delhi sultanate, 'Abd al-Hamid characterizes the Hindu subjects as *zimmis*, that is, subjugated people from whom a poll tax (*jiziya*) could be collected.

'ABD ALLAH AJODHANI, MIYAN. He was a respected doctor of Islamic law in the **Delhi sultanate** during the second half of the 15th century. When the **Lodi** prince Nizam Khan (later Sultan **Sikandar Lodi**, 1489–1517) was contemplating interfering with the religious practices of Hindus at Thanesar, 'Abd Allah Ajodhani objected to his plans, telling him firmly that Islam did not permit such interference. Nizam Khan was greatly irritated by this stand of 'Abd Allah Ajodhani and accused him of siding with nonbelievers.

'ABD AL-QUDDUS GANGOHI, SHAIKH (1456–1537). 'Abd al-Quddus was born at Rudauli (District Barabanki, Uttar Pradesh). His father, Shaikh Ism'ail, was a theologian who traced his ancestry to the famous doctor of Islamic law Imam Abu Hanifa (d. 768). 'Abd al-Quddus himself was drawn to **Sufism**, which led to his attaching himself to the **Chishti** hospice established at Rudauli by Shaikh Ahmad 'Abd al-Haq (d. 1474). He migrated to Shahabad in 1491 and from there shifted to Gangoh (District Saharanpur, Uttar Pradesh) at the time of Babur's invasion (1526). At Shahabad, 'Umar Khan Sarwani, an important noble of the Lodi Empire, became his patron. He also cultivated close relations with the Timurid ruler Humayun (1530–1556). In his early youth, 'Abd al-Quddus wrote a treatise, *Rushd-nama* (The Book of Piety), that seeks to reconcile the teachings of Gorakh-nath with Chishti Sufism.

'ABD AL-RAZZAQ, KAMAL AL-DIN (1413–1482). 'Abd al-Razzaq's father, Jalal al-Din Samarqandi, held the position of *qazi* (judge) and *imam* (leader in prayers) in the service of the Timurid ruler Mirza Shah Rukh (1405–1448). 'Abd al-Razzaq was enrolled in Mirza Shah Rukh's service in 1437–1438 and was sent to India as an envoy of the Timurid court in 1441. There he visited the Zamorin of Calicut and the ruler of Vijayanagar during 1441–1444. 'Abd al-Razzaq came to Vijayanagar in 1442 during Deva Raya's reign (1421–1449). On his return to Herat in 1444, he wrote *Matala'-i sa'dan wa-majm'-i bahrain* (Ascends of the Auspicious and Concourse of Oceans), which recorded the experiences of his journey to India in the second volume.

ABU BAKR SHAH (?–1390). Abu Bakr was a grandson of Firuz Shah Tughlaq and figured prominently in the contest for the throne after the sultan's death in 1388. He occupied the throne in 1389 after putting to death Firuz Shah's immediate successor, Ghiyas al-Din. In this coup d'état, Abu Bakr had the support of the large body of his grandfather's slaves present at Delhi. He was soon challenged by his uncle Muhammad Shah, who enjoyed wide support among the nobles and local chiefs outside Delhi. In 1390, Abu Bakr was finally driven away toward Alwar, where he died before the end of the year.

ACHYUTA DEVA RAYA (?–1542). A ruler of Vijayanagar who belonged to the second dynasty established by Narsingha Saluva in 1486. He was the brother and successor of the celebrated ruler Krishna Deva Raya (1509–1529). Achyuta Deva Raya began occupying the throne in 1530 and continued to rule down to 1542. He lost the frontier fortresses of Mudgal and Raichur recovered by Krishna Deva Raya from the 'Adil Shahi sultan of Bijapur after a fierce struggle. In 1535–1536, 'Adil Shah was emboldened to invade Vijayanagar and departed from there only after receiving a heavy tribute. During Achyuta Raya's reign, a large number of grants were made to temples by the nobles. Many inscriptions pertaining to these grants have survived in different parts of southern India.

'ADIL KHAN FARUQI II (?–1491). Faruqi ruler of Khandesh who succeeded his father Mubarak Khan Faruqi in 1456. 'Adil Khan consolidated the Khandesh kingdom by subjugating local chiefs. He founded the town of Burhanpur, which became the capital of his kingdom. Khandesh was invaded by Sultan **Mahmud Begarha** of Gujarat in 1488–1489, forcing 'Adil Khan to submit and pay tribute. Subsequently, he ruled over Khandesh in peace until 1491.

AFGHANS. A tribal people inhabiting the trans-Indus hilly tract whose cultural identity is shaped by the literary flavor of Pushto, an Indo-Aryan dialect, and also by their tribal customs, which were often modified by a fierce attachment to Sunni Islam. Ghiyas al-Din **Balban** (1266–1286) is known to have established Afghan garrisons around **Delhi** and in many places along the Ganges River. Afghan chiefs first came to be included among minor nobles under the **Tughlaqs** (1320–1412). Afghans joined the revolt of *amiran-i sada* against **Muhammad bin Tughlaq** in 1342. Many Afghan clans settled in the Punjab during Tughlaq rule. After capturing power at Delhi in 1451, **Bahlul Lodi** encouraged the settlement of Afghan clans in different parts of north India. An Afghan population grew in Bihar during **Sikandar Lodi**'s reign.

'AFIF, SHAMS-I SIRAJ (1351–?). The author of *Tarikh-i Firuz Shahi* was a descendant of Malik Sa'd ul-Mulk Shahab 'Afif, an important revenue official during **Ghiyas al-Din Tughlaq**'s reign (1320–1325). He appears to have written a history of the **Tughlaq dynasty** some time after **Timur**'s invasion (1398). An account of **Firuz Shah Tughlaq** (1351–1388) has survived from that work under the title *Tarikh-i Firuz Shahi* (History of Firuz Shah).

AGNIKULA. A status of belonging to the "Fire Family" enjoyed by four leading **Rajput** clans, namely the **Pratiharas** (or Pariharas), **Chahamanas** (or Chauhans), **Chaulukyas** (or Solankis), and **Paramaras** (or Pawars). They are supposed to be descendants of a mythical figure who arose out of a vast sacrificial fire pit near Mount Abu in Rajasthan.

AGRA. This important town (one of the capitals of the Mughal Empire during the 16th and 17th centuries) was founded by the **Lodi** ruler **Sikandar Shah** (1489–1517). It served as the army headquarters of the Lodi Empire to exercise effective control over neighboring tracts in Rajputana and central parts of Gangetic **Doab**. Sikandar Lodi also built a palace there in 1495, a part of which, now known as *Barahdari*, survives near Sikandara. Many of the large number of buildings erected by Sikandar Lodi were possibly destroyed in the devastating earthquake of 1504.

AGRAHARA **GRANTS.** The earliest mention of these grants is to be found in the context of Harsha's administration (606–646) where salaries of the officials were often paid through revenue-free land grants. The *agrahara* grants were restricted to Brahmans, which indicated their privileged position. Often an entire village of Brahmans would enjoy a grant of this nature, which under the **Cholas** (10th to 13th centuries) came to be called *brahmadeya*. Although the ruler had the authority to resume these grants, generally the recipients were allowed to hold them in perpetuity. The *agrahara* grants, like those given to secular functionaries in lieu of salaries or as rewards for service, tended to weaken the authority of the king by creating new intermediaries.

AHMAD BIN AYAZ, KHWAJA JAHAN (?–1351). He served as a superintendent of buildings toward the end of **Ghiyas al-Din Tughlaq**'s reign (1320–1325) and was accused by **Ibn Battuta** of engineering the collapse of a newly constructed building that caused Ghiyas al-Din Tughlaq's death in 1325. On **Muhammad bin Tughlaq**'s accession in the same year, Ahmad bin Ayaz was promoted to the position of **wazir**. Ahmad bin Ayaz not only survived Muhammad bin Tughlaq's repressive policy toward nobles but also appears to have improved his position during the latter's reign (1325–1351). At the time of Muhammad bin Tughlaq's death in 1351, Ahmad bin Ayaz, then entitled Khwaja Jahan, was looking after the sultanate's ruling establishment at **Delhi**. During the brief tussle for succession that followed, he put up one of the deceased **sultan**'s sons as the new king but was eventually outmaneuvered. After **Firuz Shah Tughlaq**'s accession, Ahmad bin Ayaz was put to death.

AHMAD CHAP, MALIK. A **Khalji** officer who rose to prominence during the reign of **Sultan Muiz al-Din Kaiqubad** (1287–1290), Ahmad Chap was related to Firuz Khalji (later Sultan **Jalal al-Din Firuz**, 1290–1296). He was appointed to a high position in the central administration after the capture of power by the Khalji nobles in the **Delhi sultanate**. Ahmad Chap was one of the advisors of Jalal al-Din Firuz Khalji and he vainly urged the latter to be harsh with the disgruntled nobles of the previous regime and to distrust his ambitious nephew and son-in-law 'Ali Garshasp (later Sultan **'Ala al-Din Khalji**). In 1296, while proceeding to **Kara** for a meeting with 'Ali Garshasp, Sultan Jalal al-Din left Ahmad Chap in command of the main army. After the assassination of the **sultan** at Kara and proclamation of 'Ali Garshasp's accession with the title Sultan 'Ala al-Din Khalji, Ahmad Chap joined the nobles loyal to the family of the deceased king at **Delhi**. From there, he, along with Jalal al-Din's son Rukn al-Din, escaped to **Multan**. Eventually, Ahmad Chap was captured and blinded on Sultan 'Ala al-Din Khalji's orders.

AHMAD SHAH BAHMANI (?–1435). He was one of the younger brothers of Sultan Taj al-Din **Firuz Shah Bahmani** (1397–1422) and became influential on account of his important role in wars against **Vijayanagar**. Following Firuz Shah's defeat at Pangal at the hands of Vijayanagar forces in 1420, he became a de facto ruler, which led to his formally ascending the throne in 1422. He forced the Vijayanagar ruler **Deva Raya** to pay tribute to him and also subjugated the Raja of **Warangal** in **Telingana** (1424). Sultan Ahmad Shah inflicted a crushing defeat on **Hoshang Shah** of Malwa (1429). Following this victory, he laid the foundation of **Bidar** and shifted his capital from **Gulbarga** to this new township. His policy of securing his northern frontier entangled him in hostilities with the sultanate of Gajarat during 1430–1432, which ended only after the Bahmanis withdrew from Baglana and Mahim. Ahmad Shah died in 1435, leaving the **Bahmani kingdom** in a state of turmoil due to renewed rebellion of the chiefs of Telingana and heightened tensions within the nobility between the immigrants (*afaqis*) and old settlers (*dakhanis*).

AHMAD SHAH, SHIHAB AL-DIN (?–1442). A grandson of the first sultan of Gujarat **Muzaffar Shah** (1407–1410), he came to the throne in 1411. Suspected of having poisoned his grandfather, his accession was opposed by one of his uncles. He overcame this challenge by creating a division in the ranks of his adversaries. In 1413, Ahmad Shah founded **Ahmadabad** on the bank of the Sabarmati River and shifted his capital from **Naharwala** to this new township. The following year (1414), he suppressed disgruntled nobles led by Shah Malik who were supported by several powerful local chiefs, as well as by Sultan **Hoshang** of Malwa.

Ahmad Shah got involved in a prolonged conflict with the sultanate of Khandesh and the **Bahmani kingdom** in 1430, which led to frustrating the Bahmanis' designs on Mahim and Baglana (1432). In 1437, after having suppressed the **Rajput** chiefs on the northern periphery of Gujarat, Ahmad Shah forced the **Sisodiya** ruler of **Mewar** to pay tribute. The following year (1438), he intervened in the tussle for succession in Malwa on the side of Sultan Hoshang's sons and against **Mahmud Khalji** but was forced to withdraw because of a pestilence. He died on 12 August 1442. Side by side with disciplining the nobility and suppressing the hereditary chiefs, Ahmad Shah built a credible army organization identified with a system of land-grants-cum-cash payments. While inducting many non-Muslims in the nobility, Ahmad Shah on the whole deployed an attitude of religious intolerance by imposing discriminatory *jiziya* and also by destroying several temples during his military campaigns.

AHMADABAD. On the left bank of the Sabarmati River in Gujarat, it was founded by Sultan **Ahmad Shah** (1411–1442) as his new capital. **Sultans** of Gujarat built numerous mosques and palaces at Ahmadabad; some of these were built with materials taken from Hindu temples. The carved stonework and exquisite lattices of the windows of these buildings are universally admired. Some of these features were later incorporated in the Mughal architecture. Ahmadabad also became famous for its accomplished weavers. It grew into a prosperous city with a large population that approached an estimated 900,000 during the 17th century.

AHOMS. A Sino-Tibetan hill tribe, possibly an offshoot of the great Tai or Shan race, that spread from what is now Thailand and Myanmar. After settling in the Brahmputra valley, many of them married women from the local Bodo tribes. Most of them gradually adopted Hindu beliefs and customs, although many continued to designate themselves Tai or Thai, literally "of celestial origin." The Ahom rulers, designated as *svargadeos* (kings from heaven), controlled in their palmy days the whole tract from Brahmputra to the Karatoya River. There is a strong case that this region is named Assam after Ahoms.

AHSAN SHAH, JALAL AL-DIN (?–1339). He was originally **Muhammad bin Tughlaq**'s governor of the **Ma'bar** tract. Taking advantage of the **sultan**'s preoccupations at **Delhi**, he raised the standard of revolt at Madurai and assumed royal titles in 1333–1334. An army sent by Muhammad bin Tughlaq against him was destroyed by pestilence (1335). Ahsan continued to rule over Madurai until his death in 1339. His last successor was overthrown by the **Vijayanagar** forces in 1377.

AIBEK, QUTB AL-DIN (?–1210). A slave of the **Ghaurid** prince Mu'izz al-Din **Muhammad** and appointed by him to administer conquered territories in India after the overthrow of **Prithviraja III** in the second battle of **Tarain** (1192). Aibak occupied **Delhi**, which had held out for some time after Prithviraja's defeat, and made it his seat of power. He obtained from Mu'izz al-Din "a letter of manumission together with paraphernalia of royalty and an authority to rule over Hindustan." On Mu'izz al-Din's death in 1206, Aibak is reported to have formally proclaimed himself an independent **sultan**, but this is not confirmed by surviving coins. He disarmed opposition to his acquisition of sovereign status within the Ghaurid Empire by marrying a daughter of Taj al-Din **Yildiz**, who was Mu'izz al-Din's successor at Ghazni. He further consolidated his position by giving in marriage his sister and daughter, respectively, to two fellow slave officers, Nasir al-Din **Qubacha** (commandant of **Multan**) and Shams al-Din

Iltutmish (commandant of Baran [modern Bulandshahr]). Aibak also succeeded in securing the allegiance of Ali bin Mardan, who had seized power in Bengal. On the whole, Qutb al-Din Aibak was successful in keeping the defeated Hindu chiefs in India under control and also asserting his independence of the Mu'izz al-Din's successor at Ghazni. He died at **Lahore** in 1210 from an accident while playing *chaugan*, or polo.

'AINU I-MULK MAHRU (?–1362). Originally known as 'Abdullah Muhammad Sharif, son of Amir Mahru, he was serving as a military officer under **Muhammad bin Tughlaq**; at the time of the latter's death, he was stationed at **Multan** (1351). By then, he had earned the title *'Ainu i-Mulk.* Mahru came to **Delhi** with **Firuz Shah Tughlaq** in the same year and was appointed to the office of *mushrif-i mamalik* (a high office in the central treasury). Because he could not get on well with **Khan-i Jahan Maqbul**, the **wazir**, the **sultan** appointed him governor of Multan and **Bhakkar**. Mahru died in 1362 at Multan, leaving behind a large collection of letters entitled *Insha-i Mahru* (Letters of Mahru).

'AIN UL-MULK MULTANI. He was stationed at **Multan** at the time Ghazi Malik (later **Ghiyas al-Din Tughlaq**) marched out after removing **Khusrau Shah** (1320). 'Ain ul-Mulk rose to a high position in the nobility under **Muhammad bin Tughlaq** (1325–1351). In 1340–1341, as governor of **Awadh**, he is reported to have rendered valuable services during the time the **sultan** was at **Swargadwari**, his temporary capital on the Ganges River and where the **sultan** had shifted on account of an acute famine at **Delhi**. When ordered to be transferred from Awadh to the **Deccan** in 1341, he was greatly perturbed and he revolted. Muhammad bin Tughlaq marched out from Swargadwari, and engaged and captured 'Ain ul-Mulk near **Kanauj**. He was reinstated in the sultan's service after a short spell of imprisonment. His new job was that of the superintendent of royal gardens. 'Ain ul-Mulk apparently served his whimsical master for the remaining part of his life in this comparatively insignificant position.

AITEGIN, IKHTIYAR AL-DIN (?–1240). Along with many other dignitaries, he took an oath of allegiance to **Bahram Shah** (1240–1242) while **Raziya Sultan** (1236–1240) was campaigning in the Punjab against the rebellious governor of **Lahore** (1240). Bahram Shah appointed him viceroy (*na'ib*), which indicates his high standing among slave nobles who had brought about Raziya's ouster. A few months later, Aitegin tried to assume some of the royal prerogatives. Such actions were resented by Bahram Shah, who had him killed (1240).

AJMER. Capital of the **Chahamana** kingdom of Sambhar, which dominated the territory constituting the present-day state of Rajasthan until 1192. After their victory over **Prithviraja III** in 1192, the **Ghaurids** occupied **Ranthambhor** but Ajmer was restored to the Chahamanas. Ajmer was annexed to the Ghaurid Empire in India during **Qutb al-Din Aibek**'s rule. Under **Iltutmish** (1211–1236), it was an *iqta'* that covered the entire territory of the erstwhile Chahamana kingdom. In the early phase of Ghaurid occupation, a monastery of **Chishti Sufis** was established at Ajmer. The founder of the Chishti order in India, **Mu'in al-Din Chishti**, lies buried there. His tomb came to be venerated by a large number of Muslims as well as Hindus. Subsequently, Ajmer was important mainly as a center of Sufic inspiration.

AKAT KHAN SULAIMAN SHAH (?–1301). One of Sultan **'Ala al-Din Khalji**'s favorite nephews, Akat Khan was appointed by the sultan to the office of *wakil-i dar* after the latter seized the throne in 1296. Akat Khan is known to have played an important role in the defeat of the **Mongol** horde led by Qutlugh Khwaja at Kili (near **Delhi**) in 1298. In 1301, Akat Khan and his neo-Muslim Mongol retainers made an attempt to assassinate 'Ala al-Din Khalji, then encamped at Dilpat, a short distance from Delhi. Prompt action by *paiks* in attendance on the **sultan** saved his life. While trying to flee from that spot after the failed attempt, Akat Khan was overtaken by *paiks* and beheaded.

'ALA AL-DIN 'ALAM SHAH (?–1476). A **sultan** of the **Saiyid dynasty** who came to the throne of **Delhi** on the death of his father, Sultan Muhammad Shah (1434–1445). Faced with the general defiance of the central authority by the nobles and the impertinence of the ministers running the central government, he went to Badaun in 1448 and expressed a desire to stay there permanently. The nobles at Delhi rose against ministers loyal to the **sultan** and summoned the **Afghan** chief **Bahlul Lodi** from the Punjab to assume the reins of the government. Bahlul Lodi, even after formally proclaiming himself a sultan, did not disturb 'Ala al-Din 'Alam Shah in Badaun. 'Ala al-Din continued to govern Badaun and the surrounding territory until the time of his death in 1476.

'ALA AL-DIN 'ALI AJODHANI, SHAIKH. The son of Ahmad Sabir, he was included among the prominent disciples of Shaikh **Farid al-Din Mas'ud Ganj-shikar**. He, along with Shaikh **Nizam al-Din Auliya**, is reported to have predicted **Firuz Shah Tughlaq**'s sovereignty (1351–1388). His son Shaikh Mu'iz al-Din was appointed governor of Gujarat by **Muhammad bin Tughlaq** (1325–1351) for controlling the situation there but was killed by the insurgents. 'Ala al-Din 'Ali is credited with founding the *Sabariya* branch of the **Chishti Sufic** order. 'Ala al-Din 'Ali's grave at Kalyar (in District Saharanpur, Uttar Pradesh) is widely venerated by common people of the region.

'ALA AL-DIN II, BAHMANI (?–1378). 'Ala al-Din II Bahmani was known during his princehood days as Mujahid. On the death of his father, **Muhammad Shah Bahmani**, in 1375 Mujahid became the **sultan**. During the whole of his short reign (1375–1378), 'Ala al-Din II was engrossed in a fierce war with **Vijayanagar**, which was precipitated by **Bukka**'s demand on the new sultan to hand over to him the Raichur Doab. An invasion of Vijayanagar by 'Ala al-Din was countered by Bukka by resorting to dispersed resistance. Eventually, 'Ala al-Din was forced to withdraw, fighting his way back. The Bahmani forces were badly mauled in a pitched battle fought close to Vijayanagar. During his retreat, the sultan was assassinated by his cousin Daud on 16 April 1378. *See also* BAHMANI KINGDOM.

'ALA AL-DIN HASAN SHAH BAHMANI (?–1359). The founder of the **Bahmani kingdom**, **Hasan Gangu** was one of **Muhammad bin Tughlaq**'s officers who revolted in the **Deccan** in 1347. The rebels put up Hasan Gangu as the king with the title 'Ala-al Din Hasan Shah Bahmani on 13 August 1347. He claimed descent from the Persian monarch Bahman bin Isfandyar. There is a parallel tradition recorded in the 17th century that assigns him a Hindu origin. The Bahmani practice of appointing Brahmans as their ministers is explained with reference to this tradition. 'Ala al-Din Hasan Shah chose **Gulbarga** as his capital. He divided his kingdom into territorial divisions called *tarafs*. Soon his sway extended from east of **Daulatabad** to Bhongir, and from the Wainganga River in the north to Krishna in the south. Before his death in 1359, 'Ala al-Din Hasan Shah nominated his son Muhammad to the throne. *See also* MUHAMMAD SHAH BAHMANI.

'ALA AL-DIN HUSAIN SHAH (?–1519). Founder of the Saiyid dynasty of Bengal who came to the throne in 1493 and ruled until 1519. 'Ala al-Din Husain Shah captured the throne by removing from power an Abyssinian slave who had set himself up as the **sultan** after assassinating the last ruler of the Ilyas Shahi dynasty, Nasir al-Din Mahmud (1490–1491). He disbanded the *paiks* and Abyssinian slaves who were responsible for the continuing instability in the kingdom of Bengal during the 15th century. The old frontiers of Bengal were restored under 'Ala al-Din Husain, who shifted his capital to Ekdala. Taking advantage of the fall of the **Sharqi** kingdom of **Jaunpur** (1479), 'Ala al-Din extended his sway over parts of Bihar, which came to be sealed under the nonaggression agreement of 1495 concluded between him and the **Lodi** military authorities in Bihar. Under the peaceful and enlightened rule of Ala al-Din Husain Shah, there was a general flowering of the creative genius of medieval Bengal. The Bengali language made tremendous advances, and Hindus came to have a fairly liberal share in the administration and state patronage. For his liberality, 'Ala al-Din Husain Shah came to be called by Hindus an incarnation of Krishna. He is also credited with extending patronage to **Chaitanya**.

'ALA AL-DIN JANI. A Turkish noble of Qutb al-Din **Aibak** (1206–1210) who belonged to a ruling family of Central Asia and who sided with **Iltutmish (1211–1236)** in the latter's tussle with Aibek's son Aram Shah for succession. Iltutmish assigned him **Lakhnauti** with quasi royal status in 1230. Having been expelled from Lakhnauti by the **Khalji** officers, 'Ala al-Din Jani diminished in Iltutmish's favor and was subsequently made to serve in a distinctly less glamorous capacity at **Lahore** in the northwest. He figured prominently on the side of the powerful slave officers (***chihilganis***) in the factional tussle among nobles during the reigns of Rukn al-Din **Firuz** (1236) and **Raziya Sultan** (1236–1240). 'Ala al-Din Jani's son Qilich Khan Mas'ud was promoted to the rulership of Lakhnauti during the time **Balban** ran the central administration as viceroy (***na'ib***) of Sultan Nasir al-Din **Mahmud Shah** (1246–1266) and remained in that position until 1252.

'ALA AL-DIN KHALJI (?–1316). He was the second in line of the **Khalji dynasty** established by his uncle **Jalal al-Din Firuz Shah Khalji** (1290–1296) in the **Delhi sultanate**. 'Ala al-Din rose to prominence in the service of his uncle. As governor of **Kara**, he raided Deogir (later **Daulatabad**), the capital of the **Yadava** kingdom, in 1294 and collected a large treasure from there as tribute. He occupied the throne in 1296 after assassinating Jalal al-Din Firuz and ruled until 1316. 'Ala al-Din's reign marked the highest point of the Delhi sultanate's political power in terms of the area firmly administered and the authority exercised by the **sultan** over the nobles as well as hereditary chiefs and other local authorities.

His success in throwing back with great violence repeated **Mongol** invasions of the years 1298–1303 was indicative of the increased military prowess of the Delhi sultanate. The same was also manifested by the annexation of Gujarat (1297) and capture of the famous strongholds **Ranthambhor** (1302) and **Chitor** (1303) in eastern Rajasthan. These military successes were followed, in 1303–1311, by the submission of the whole of the **Deccan** as well as a large part of southern India up to **Dorasamudra** (modern Mysore) and the Coromandal coast.

To check the fraudulent practices of nobles maintaining military contingents, a new rule was created. It provided for the maintenance of descriptive rolls of horses and horsemen in the central office looking after military organization and for the occasional muster of contingents. The salaries of the troopers paid according to a prescribed scale were barely sufficient for meeting their needs. Soldiers were compensated for these meager salaries by market regulations aimed at keeping the prices of essential commodities very low. State granaries supplied food grains to grocery shops for distribution in urban centers at fixed prices.

The land revenue came to be assessed at the rate of one half of the produce and was calculated on the basis of the measurement of land under different crops. Revenue was realized from the cultivator soon after harvest, obliging the farmer to sell his produce at prevailing prices to grain merchants (*banjaras*) deputed by the central government for bringing grains to state granaries. 'Ala al-Din was remembered in the Delhi sultanate for his market regulations long after his death in 1316.

'ALA AL-DIN MAS'UD SHAH (?–1117). The **Ghaznavid** ruler who came to the throne in 1098 and succeeded Sultan Maudud, a grandson of Sultan **Mahmud of Ghazni**. He married a sister of Saljuq Sultan Sanjar. Mas'ud is reported to have led an expedition into the Gangetic region and is also credited with appointing Husain, son of Sam, to the principality of Ghaur. *See also* GHAURIDS.

'ALAI DARWAZA. Southern gateway of the *Quwwat ul-Islam/Qubbat ul-Islam* mosque at **Delhi** built by **'Ala al-Din Khalji** (1296–1316). It is the earliest surviving building of the Delhi **sultans** that displays a true arch and semicircular dome. It is also noted for its stonework and arabesque decoration.

A'LA UL-MULK, QAZI. An uncle of the historian Ziya' **Barani** who had served in the entourage of Malik 'Ali Garshasp (later Sultan **'Ala al-Din Khalji**, 1296–1316) in **Kara** and **Awadh** until 1296. He was summoned to **Delhi** to become a commandant (*kotwal*) after 'Ala al-Din had established his control there. A'la ul-Mulk is reported to have advised the new **sultan** to confiscate elephants, horses, and wealth possessed by the Hindu local chiefs. To 'Ala al-Din's question if it was advisable for him to establish a new religion, A'la ul-Mulk firmly retorted, "The prophetic office has never appertained to kings, and never will, as long as the world lasts."

ALBERUNI, ABU REHAN (973–1048). A native of Khiva who joined **Mahmud of Ghazni**'s service in 1017 when he was about 45 years of age. During his stay of 10 years in the **Ghaznavid** Empire, Alberuni was frequently moving between Ghazni, **Multan**, and **Lahore**. This enabled him to collect valuable information on the Hindu religion and associated sciences as well as sociopolitical institutions of 11th-century India. This information is presented in Alberuni's celebrated work, *Kitab al-Hind* (Describing India). Alberuni's description of India is important because it represents an attempt to study Hinduism by a highly cultivated Islamic mind of the era when the dogmatism of post-Ghazali (d. 1112) orthodoxy had not yet become a dominant tendency in the Islamic intellectual tradition. It is also an important source and provides insights about the impact of Mahmud's plundering raids into northwestern India.

ALBUQUERQUE (1453–1515). On reaching the Malabar coast in 1498, the Portuguese had established their factories (trading stations-cum-fortresses) in places like **Calicut** and Cannore. In 1508, Albuquerque was appointed governor of Portuguese possessions in the East. He conquered Goa in 1510 as a part of the larger scheme to place the Portuguese in a commanding position on the eastern seaboard. Albuquerque subsequently completed this drive by establishing Portuguese naval stations at Malacca (1511) and Hurmuz (1515). He died in 1515. Albuquerque's short term of governorship at Goa (1510–1515) was marred by the brutal treatment of the Muslim component of the local population.

ALLAHKHAND. A Hindi poem ascribed to Jagnayak, the 12th-century poet who was a contemporary of **Chandbardai** (author of *Prithvirajarasau*). *Allahkhand* describes in stirring language the deeds of love and war of Allah and Udal, two brave Paramara warriors of Mahoba.

ALP GHAZI. *See* IKHTIYAR AL-DIN ALP GHAZI.

ALP KHAN (?–1316). Originally called Junaid, he was a brother of Sultan 'Ala al Din Khalji's wife (mother of Prince **Khizr Khan**), who apparently belonged to a family of **Khalji** chiefs. He was entitled Alp Khan by 'Ala al-Din (1296–1316) and was entrusted with the position of the chief of protocol (*amir-i majlis*). Alp Khan held **Multan** as his *iqta'* for some time. From there he was transferred, in 1310, to Gujarat. The **Jain** works praise Alp Khan for permitting the reconstruction of temples destroyed during the Muslim conquest. As a maternal uncle and father-in-law of the heir apparent, he became influential at the court in the latter part of 'Ala al-Din Khalji's reign. During the last few months of 'Ala al-Din's life (1315), a bitter controversy arose between him and **Malik Kafur**, the viceroy (*na'ib*) who suspected Alp Khan of trying to influence the ailing sultan's mind with the help of his sister, the chief wife. Malik Kafur obtained from the dying sultan an order for Alp Khan's execution. Alp Khan and his sister were subsequently executed before 'Ala al-Din died in January 1316, theoretically because they were attempting to poison him.

ALTUNIA, MALIK IKHTIYAR AL-DIN (?–1240). A slave noble of Shams al-Din **Iltutmish** (1211–1236) who served as the commandant of Sirhind during the reign of **Raziya Sultan** (1236–1240). He revolted against her, along with several other Turkish nobles in 1240. This revolt was an outcome of the general resentment over favors shown by Raziya Sultan to Jamal al-Din **Yaqut**, an Abyssinian, serving as master of horses (*amir-i akhur*). After Yaqut was captured and executed by the rebellious nobles, Raziya won Altunia over to her side by marrying him. Subsequently, Altunia fought on Raziya's side against the nobles who had proclaimed her brother Mu'izz al-Din **Bahram Shah** as the new **sultan**. Altunia and Raziya were defeated near **Delhi** in September–October 1240. While fleeing after their defeat, they were captured and put to death by the local chiefs in the territory of Kaithal.

AL-'UMARI (?–1349). Author of the Arabic encyclopedia *Masalik al-absar*. Al-'Umari put together considerable information on India that is mainly gleaned from travel accounts and diplomatic communications.

AMIR 'ALI BARID SHAH (?–1602). The founder of the Barid Shahi dynasty of **Bidar** was the son of a **Bahmani** noble of Turkish origin, Qasim Barid. As suggested by the word *Barid* in his name, Qasim had perhaps served in his early career as a messenger (*barid*) for some time. He eventually rose to the position of chief *wazir* in the **Bahmani kingdom**. On Qasim's death in 1505, this office and the designation Barid were inherited by his son 'Ali. On the death of the last Bahmani Sultan Ahmad Shah (1518–1520), 'Ali Barid became the virtual ruler of Bidar. In 1528, after the surviving scion of the Bahmani dynasty escaped from Bidar to Bijapur, 'Ali Barid declared himself the **sultan** of Bidar with the title Amir 'Ali Barid Shah. He ruled for the next 70 years, that is, until 1601–1602.

AMIR HASAN SIJZI (1254–1337). A noted poet and compiler of *Fawaid al-fawad*, the discourses of the influential **Chishti Sufi** Shaikh **Nizam al-Din Auliya**, and a close friend of **Amir Khusrau** and Ziya' **Barani**. Amir Hasan was born at Badaun. He came to **Delhi** at an early age. While pursuing his studies there, he started composing Persian verses at the age of 13. Getting the job of a personal attendant with Sultan **Balban**'s favorite son, Prince **Muhammad**, he went with the latter to **Multan** around 1280 and stayed there until 1286. In Multan, Amir Hasan first met Amir Khusrau. On Prince Muhammad's death in 1286 during a skirmish with **Mongols** near **Lahore**, Amir Hasan wrote an elegy where he attributes the Mongols' failure to advance into India to the beneficence of Chishti Sufis. Later he joined the service of Sultan **Jalal al-Din Firuz Shah Khalji** (1290–1296). During **'Ala al-Din Khalji's** reign (1296–1316), he rendered military service at **Lakhnauti** and Deogir. While residing at Delhi during the reign of 'Ala al-Din Khalji, Amir Hasan started visiting Shaikh Nizam al-Din and in 1308 became a disciple of the great *shaikh*. Sometime after Nizam al-Din Auliya's demise in 1325, Amir Hasan migrated to **Daulatabad**, where he died on 26 September 1337.

AMIRAN-I SADA. Literally, "commanders of a hundred." They were the members of a military class who served in the provinces during **Muhammad bin Tughlaq**'s reign (1325–1351). They do not seem to have suffered in any significant measure as a consequence of the famine that ravaged **Delhi** and surrounding territories during the 1340s and that caused serious depletion of the central army commanded by the **sultan** himself. The resulting military imbalance within the sultanate contributed to repeated revolts by the *amiran-i sada* in distant provinces like **Multan** (1342), **Daulatabad** (1343), and Gujarat (1343). As an outcome of these revolts, there emerged in the **Deccan** a new sultanate headed by **'Ala al-Din Hasan Shah Bahmani** (1347–1359).

AMIR KHUSRAU (1254–1325). Besides his widely acknowledged contributions to Indian classical music and folk culture of the Hindustani-speaking people, Amir Khusrau is counted among the leading Persian poets of all times and is believed to have given rise to a distinct Indian style in the Persian literary tradition. Born into a family of Turkish emigrants serving the **Delhi sultanate** in the Gangetic **Doab** at Patiali, Khusrau received his early schooling at **Delhi** where he became a disciple of Shaikh **Nizam al-Din Auliya** at a young age. On entering the service of Sultan Ghiyas al-Din **Balban** (1266–1286), Khusrau became a companion of the latter's favorite son, **Muhammad**. During his stay at **Multan** in Prince Muhammad's retinue during 1280–1286, Khusrau earned wide notice as a rising litterateur. It was during this time that he first met **Amir Hasan Sijzi** and the two became lifelong friends.

In 1286, a **Mongol** invading army defeated and killed Prince Muhammad near **Lahore**. Khusrau was carried away as a prisoner, but he soon escaped from Mongol captivity and came to reside at Delhi. There in 1289 he wrote *Qiranus sa'dain*, the famous rhymed story of a meeting between Sultan **Kaiqubad** (1287–1290) and his father, **Bughra Khan**, the governor of **Lakhnauti**.

Sultan **Jalal al-Din Firuz Khalji** (1290–1296) appointed Khusrau to the high military rank of an *amir* and also assigned him the position of the "keeper of the royal Quran." Around this time, he wrote *Miftah al-futuh*, a versified history of Jalal al-Din Firuz's military campaigns. After **'Ala al-Din Khalji** ascended the throne by assassinating Jalal al-Din Firuz (1296), Amir Khusrau did not hesitate to join the new **sultan** as his courtier. The 20 years of 'Ala al-Din Khalji's reign (1296–1316) was the most productive period of Amir Khusrau's life. During 1298–1300, he completed his well-known romantic versified stories, namely, *Matla' al-anwar*, *Shirin-Khusrau*, *Majnun-Laila*, *A'in-i Sikandari*, and *Hasht bihisht*. Subsequently, he wrote two books in prose; one, *Khazain ul-futuh*, was a history of 'Ala al-Din's military exploits and the other, *'Ijaz-i Khusravi*, was a five-volume work dealing with figures of speech.

From the latter years of Jalal al-Din Firuz Khalji's reign (1290–1296), Khusrau became very close to Shaikh Nizam al-Din

Auliya. One of his long poems of this period, *Nuh sipar*, an account of Sultan **Qutb al-Din Mubarak Shah Khalji**'s reign (1316–1320), reflects a new creative sensitivity. The deeply sympathetic and humane depiction of Indian culture and people in this work is noteworthy. Amir Khusrau died in Delhi in 1325 soon after the passing away of his preceptor, Shaikh Nizam al-Din Auliya.

AMIR KHWURD (?–1369). Author of *Siyar al-auliya*, a collection of biographical notices on **Chishti Sufis** completed during the reign of **Firuz Shah Tughlaq** (1351–1388). Amir Khwurd's grandfather, Muhammad 'Alawi Kirmani, a merchant hailing from Kirman, came into contact with Shaikh **Farid al-Din Ganj-shikar** at Ajodhan and became his disciple. After Shaikh Farid's death in 1265, Muhammad 'Alawi became a close friend of Shaikh **Nizam al-Din Auliya**. Amir Khwurd, who came to India with his grandfather, became a disciple of Nizam al-Din Auliya's successor at **Delhi, Nasir al-Din Chiragh Dehli**, He died at Delhi in 1368 or 1369.

AMIR-I AKHUR. Literally, "commander of horse." This was the designation of the superintendent of the **sultan**'s stables in the **Delhi sultanate**. The office was held by Qutb al-Din **Aibak** prior to his appointment to the conquered territory in India. The same office during the reign of **Raziya Sultan** (1236–1240) was held by an Abyssinian, Jamal al-Din **Yaqut**. Favors shown by Raziya to him sparked off a revolt by the nobles, leading to her ouster and violent death in 1240.

AMIR-I DAD (**Turkish,** *dadbeg*). Officer-in-charge of justice or the public prosecutor or the military justice who, in the **Ghaurid** Empire, sometimes would also command the garrison of a citadel.

AMIR-I HAJIB. Officer-in-charge of the royal court in the **Delhi sultanate** as well as in its predecessor, the **Ghaurid** Empire, who was sometimes referred to by the Turkish designation *barbeg*. He was a military chamberlain who often acted as commander in the field. Until 1281–1282, for example, **Balban**'s *barbeg* (i.e., *amir-i hajib*) shared with Princes **Muhammad** and **Bughra Khan** the responsibility of guarding the northwestern frontier against the **Mongols**.

AMIR-I SHIKAR. The superintendent of the hunt. It was a position of some importance in the **Delhi sultanate**, where hunting was often conceived as a valuable exercise. **Balban** (later Sultan Ghiyas al-Din Balban, 1266–1286) as a slave noble was raised by **Raziya Sultan** (1236–1240) to the office of *amir-i shikar.*

AMUKTAMALYADA. A **Telugu** poem on the art of governance by the **Vijayanagar** ruler **Krishna Deva Raya** (1509–1530) that conveys an acute awareness of the potential wealth to be had from overseas trade. The rulers are advised to improve harbors so as to ensure that elephants and horses of distant lands will not go to the enemies of **Vijayanagar** but would come to its ports.

ANANDPALA (?–1009). A **Hindu Shahi** ruler of **Lahore** who came to the throne in 1001 after his father, Jaipala, committed suicide out of shame for his defeat at the hands of the **Ghaznavids**. In 1004–1005, Sultan **Mahmud** of Ghazni asked Anandpala to give passage and render help to a Ghaznavid expedition against the **Qaramitah** ruler of Mutlan. Anandpala resisted but was defeated. In 1008–1009, Anandpala was again attacked by Sultan Mahmud for sympathizing with Qaramitah. In a pitched battle at Ohind, Anandpala and his allies were defeated by the Ghaznavids, leading to the elimination of the Hindu Shahi principality. This paved the way for Sultan Mahmud's subsequent raids into India.

ANHILWARA. *See* NAHARWALA.

APABRAHMSHA. A Sanskrit word literally meaning "falling down," it denotes a corrupt form of Prakrit, that is, spoken Sanskrit of the post–Vedic Age. It is believed to have originated in the northwestern parts of India. From there it traveled with migrations of people as they scattered and settled in central and western India in the wake of the Hun influx. The **Prakrit** of **Jain** texts, some of which were compiled in the medieval times, was heavily influenced by Apabramsha.

ARANGAL. *See* WARANGAL.

'ARIZ. Officer-in-charge of recruitment to and review of military contingents in the **Delhi sultanate**. The *'ariz* in the central government was called *'ariz-i mumalik* while his field deputy was designated *'ariz-i lashkar*. The *'ariz-i mumalik* had the authority to select or reject aspiring candidates for employment in the central army (*hashm-i qalb*); he also reviewed the contingents brought to muster by the *iqta'* holders. The same system with some variations was in place in the regional sultanates of the 15th century.

ARKALI KHAN. The second son of Sultan **Jalal al-Din Firuz Khalji** (1290–1296), Arkali Khan became notorious for inflicting harsh punishments on persons not reconciled to the seizure of power by the **Khalji** officers led by his father. Arkali Khan became hostile to **Sidi Maula**, an influential dervish favored by his elder brother, Khan-i Khanan. On Sidi Maula's arrest for allegedly plotting to overthrow the Khalji rule, Arkali had him trampled by an elephant in the presence of his father. After Jalal al-Din Firuz Khalji's assassination that led to the seizure of throne by **'Ala al-Din Khalji** (1296–1316), Arkali was arrested and blinded.

ARYUVEDIC. The pre–Islamic-invasion medical practices of India were known by this name. This system continued to be used in India along with the *Yunani* (Greek) medicine introduced from the Islamic world under the Muslim dynasties.

ATALA MASJID. Mosque built by Sultan **Ibrahim Shah Sharqi** (1401–1440) at **Jaunpur**. Built out of materials taken from demolished temples, the *Atala Masjid* is the most interesting and ornate **Sharqi** monument. It represents a curious blending of Hindu and Muslim traditions. The arches are marked by their severe simplicity. These form a link in the evolution of the favorite form under the Mughals.

AUHADI DYNASTY. Nobles belonging to the Auhadi clan controlled **Bayana** during the reign of **Mahmud Shah Tughlaq** (1394–1412). In 1417–1418, the first ruler of the **Saiyid dynasty**, **Khizr Khan**, forced Karim ul-Mulk Auhadi, then controlling Bayana, to submit to **Delhi**. Ten years later (1427–1428), Muhammad Khan Auhadi was ousted from Bayana by Sultan **Mubarak Shah** (1421–1434), but the clan was not uprooted from there. In 1446–1447, Daud Khan Auhadi proclaimed himself a sovereign ruler of Bayana. This short-lived dynasty was finally removed from Bayana by **Sikandar Lodi** in 1491–1492. At Bayana, several buildings constructed by the Auhadis have survived; some of them carry inscriptions.

AWADH. Town on the Sarju River, about 250 kilometers west of **Kanauj**, that *Ramcharitramanas* of Tulsidas (1532–1623) made famous with its Sanskrit name Ayudhya. Annexed to the **Delhi sultanate** in the beginning of 13th century, Awadh came to represent a prestigious *iqta'* under **Iltutmish** (1211–1236). Its location on the route to **Lakhnauti** added to Awadh's strategic importance. **Ziya' Barani** uses the names Awadh and Hindustan interchangeably, which tends to indicate that under the **Tughlaqs** (1320–1412) the entire tract extending northeast of the Ganges up to **Jaunpur** was administered from Awadh. Based on **Nasir al-Din Chiragh Dehli**'s testimony, during the 14th century there existed a large Muslim population at Awadh. In the 15th century, the town of Awadh as well as the entire tract administered from there was a part of the **Sharqi** kingdom.

'AZAM HUMAYUN (?–1520). Ahmad Khan, son of Khan-i Jahan Lodi, was entitled 'Azam Humayun by Sultan **Sikandar Lodi** (1489–1517). In the war of succession that followed Sikandar Lodi's death in 1517, 'Azam Humayun initially sided with Prince Jalal against **Ibrahim Lodi**. Later, having switched sides, he besieged Jalal in the fort of **Gwalior**. Soon after Jalal's elimination, 'Azam Humayun and his sons were removed from service by Ibrahim Lodi. This precipitated a rebellion. In the ensuing struggle, the rebels were defeated and 'Azam Humayun was imprisoned. While in prison, he, along with a number of important nobles suspected of disloyalty by Ibrahim Lodi, died in a contrived explosion (1520).

'AZIZ KHAMMAR (?–1345). One of **Muhammad bin Tughlaq**'s Indian servitors who were stigmatized by **Ziya' Barani** as lowborn. Barani identifies him as a wine merchant (*khammar*). In his early career, 'Aziz worked as the revenue collector of Amroha, in which capacity he is reported to have oppressed the people and also antagonized military leaders stationed there. In 1344, 'Aziz was appointed as the governor of Dhar, which was one of four newly created smaller provinces (*shiqs*) in the **Deccan**. On his arrival at Dhar, 'Aziz executed 80 *amiran-i sada* with the aim of imposing strict discipline in the army, which provoked a rebellion of nobles in the Deccan. When this news reached Gujarat, the *amiran-i sada* stationed there revolted and routed the deputy governor of the province. 'Aziz Khammar, who proceeded to Gujarat to confront the rebels, was captured and put to death by them (1345).

– B –

BABUR (1483–1530). The founder of the Mughal Empire in India, Zaheer al-Din Muhammad Babur was a descendant of **Timur**. He had succeeded his father, Umar Shaikh Mirza, on the throne of Farghana at the age of 11. Having been driven away from Farghana, Babur established himself at Kabul in 1504.

In 1505, he occupied Ghazni and made raids as far as the Indus River. Failing to establish himself at Samarqand with the help of the Safavids in 1512, Babur became more inclined toward extending his sway into the region to the east of the Indus, then ruled by the **Lodis**. In 1519, he succeeded in temporarily occupying parts of the Punjab. Five years latter (1524), Babur undertook another expedition into the Punjab and sacked **Dipalpur** and **Lahore** but had to retreat because the promised cooperation of disaffected Lodi nobles did not materialize. Babur's final invasion of India led to his victory over **Ibrahim Lodi** in the battle of Panipat (1526), which is famous for Babur's effective use of firearms. During his short reign in India (1526–1530), Babur not only overcame the resistance of the Afghan chiefs but also defeated the formidable alliance of other local rulers led by Rana **Sanga** in the battle of Kanwa (1527).

BADR-I CHACH, BADR AL-DIN. A well-known Persian poet of the 14th century hailing from Chach in Turkistan who at **Delhi** was connected with the courts of **Ghiyas al-Din Tughlaq** (1320–1325) and his son **Muhammad bin Tughlaq** (1325–1351). He was in the Deccan with **Qutluqh Khan** in 1345 and went with him to Delhi in that year. Badr left behind a large collection of his poetic compositions, including many odes praising his patrons, which together furnish useful information on the history of the **Delhi sultanate**.

BAHA AL-DIN GARSHASP (?–1328). A nephew of Ghazi Malik (later Sultan **Ghiyas al-Din Tughlaq**, 1320–1325) who, around 1320, was stationed at **Dipalpur** in a subordinate position to his uncle. He joined Ghazi Malik's march on **Delhi** in 1320 to overthrow **Khusrau Shah**. **Muhammad bin Tughlaq** (1325–1351) appointed Garshasp to Sagar (south of **Gulbarga**). His revolt in 1326 was provoked by the **sultan**'s attempt to intensify his authority in the provinces. Pursued by officers loyal to the sultan, Garshasp took refuge in **Dorasamudra** but was eventually handed over by Ballala III to his pursuers in 1328 for execution.

BAHA AL-DIN TOGHRIL. A senior slave of Mu'izz al-Din **Muhammad Ghauri** who was appointed as the commandant of Thangir in 1196 with the instruction to reduce **Gwalior**. He founded Sultankot, which became the nucleus of the township of **Bayana**. At some point following Muizz al-Din's murder in 1206, Toghril briefly styled himself a **sultan** at Bayana. His son-in-law, Arsalan Khan, was later assigned Bayana as *iqta'* on the grounds of his relationship with Toghril.

BAHA AL-DIN ZAKARYA (1183–1262). He was born in a small town near **Multan** in 1182–1183. In his youth, Baha al-Din visited different places in the Islamic world, including Medina, Baghdad, and Bokhara, for higher studies in Islamic subjects. At Baghdad, he became a disciple of Shaikh Shihab al-Din Suhrawardi (d. 1234), on whose behest he established a **Suhrawardiya** monastery (*khanqah*) at Multan. Baha al-Din Zakarya stayed at this monastery in his capacity as the successor of Shihab al-Din Suhrawardi until his death in 1262. His mystic ideology was different from that of the **Chishti Sufis** insofar as he did not practice many of the austerities recommended in that order. He was a stickler about the rules of orthodox *shariah* but did not see any harm in accumulating wealth, nor did he abstain from mixing with men in authority.

BAHADUR NAHIR. A chief of the Meo tribe who inhabited the tract to the southwest of **Delhi** with his headquarters at Alwar. He wielded considerable military clout toward the end of **Firuz Shah Tughlaq**'s reign (1351–1388). Bahadur Nahir is described by a contemporary as the chief of the hills around Delhi. In the tussle for succession that broke out after Firuz Shah Tughlaq's death, Bahadur Nahir was inclined to support **Abu Bakr**, who initially controlled Delhi. After Abu Bakr was dislodged from there, he sought refuge with Nahir at Alwar. Although Bahadur Nahir was not able to protect Abu Bakr, he continued to resist the authority of the new **sultan**. After Delhi was briefly occupied and sacked by **Timur** in 1398, Bahadur Nahir submitted to the invader and was imprisoned. He, along with several prominent nobles of the **Delhi sultanate**, was carried to Samarqand as a captive and was put to death there. Bahadur Nahir's progeny continued to dominate in the Mewat region. Two of his grandsons, Jallu and Qaddu, are known to have defied the **Saiyid** sultans of Delhi during the 1420s.

BAHLUL LODI (?–1489). The first **Lodi sultan** of **Delhi**, he belonged to a family of **Afghans** who were serving under **Khizr Khan** in the Punjab since the beginning of the 15th century. During the reign of **Mubarak Shah** (1421–1434), Bahlul came to control Sirhind, where he commanded a large Afghan contingent. On the retiring of the last Saiyid ruler **'Ala al-Din 'Alam Shah** to Badaun in 1448, Bahlul came to Delhi. In 1451, he proclaimed himself a sultan at Delhi but did not disturb 'Alam Shah in Badaun. After having subdued the nobles and chiefs controlling the **Doab** and the tract round Delhi, Bahlul went to war against the **Sharqi** ruler of **Jaunpur**. This long, drawn-out war eventually led to the annexation of the eastern territories up to Bihar to the Lodi empire. Bahlul Lodi is also credited with reorganizing the **Delhi sultanate**, limiting discordance between its despotic ethos and the tribal susceptibilities of his Afghan followers. He died in 1489, leaving behind an empire extending from the Indus River to the confines of Bihar in the east.

BAHMANI KINGDOM. It originated in a revolt of the nobles of the **Delhi sultanate** leading to the proclamation of **Hasan Gangu** (entitled **'Ala al-Din Hasan Shah Bahmani**) as the **sultan** at **Daulatabad**

in 1347. The Bahmani dynasty founded by Hasan Gangu survived for nearly two centuries; the last scion died in 1538. From their capital **Gulbarga** (shifted to **Bidar** by Ahmad Shah, 1422–1435), the Bahmanis controlled a vast territory in peninsular India that extended from Berar in the north to the Krishna River in the south. This territory was divided into four provinces (*tarafs*) governed by area commanders (*tarafdars*) invested with wide administrative jurisdictions. They were assisted by teams of military officers holding territorial-cum-revenue assignments. These powerful provincial commanders tended to become independent as the central authority grew weak toward the end of the 15th century. In addition to employing a large number of Iranians and other foreigners as nobles (**Mahmud Gavan** being the most illustrious among them), a large number of local notables, including many Brahmans, were appointed to important positions in the Bahmani administration. The association of many Brahmans with the Bahmani state was reflected in the popular tradition ascribing Hasan Gangu's rise to kingship to a prophesy by a Brahman.

The central government in the Bahmani kingdom tended to be a replica of that in the Delhi sultanate with a few distinctive features; one of these was a more elaborate organization of the finance department, which was headed by an expert designated as *amir-i jumla*, and another was an overall functionary (**wazir**-*i kul*) and his assistant (*peshwa*), who together acted as a counterweight to the administrative-cum-military authority of the head of central government (*wakil us-sultanate*). Throughout its existence, the Bahmani kingdom was at war with the **Vijayanagar Empire** over the control of Raichur Doab, which often led to a display of religious frenzy on both sides.

BAHRAM SHAH, SULTAN MUIZZ AL-DAULA (?–1152). The son of the **Ghaznavid** ruler **'Ala al-Din Mas'ud**, he came to the throne in 1117, which was made possible by the removal of his brother Arsalan with the help of Saljuq prince Sanjar. On his rise to kingship, Bahram Shah reestablished the Ghaznavid control in the regions around **Lahore** and **Multan**. Subsequently, a quarrel arose between Bahram Shah and the Shansbani ruler of Ghaur that resulted in the occupation of Ghazni by the **Ghaurids** in 1148. Two years later (1150), Bahram recovered Ghazni. The Ghaurid prince Saif al-Din was captured and fatally tortured. In retaliation, Shaif al-Din's brother 'Ala al-Din Ghauri marched on Ghazni, defeated Bahram, and burned down the town in 1152. Bahram escaped from Ghazni toward his possessions in the Punjab but died on the way. Sultan Bahram is remembered for his patronage of men of letters. The well-known Persian poets Nizami and Hasan Ghaznavi were in his employment. The translation of *Kalila-w-damna* (Fable of Two Jackals) into Persian was an important literary achievement of his reign.

BAHRAM SHAH, SULTAN MU'IZZ AL-DIN (?–1242). After **Raziya Sultan**'s overthrow at the hands of rebelling nobles, **Iltutmish**'s son Bahram was raised to the throne with the title Mu'izz al-Din in 1240, while the administration came to be run by his viceroy (*na'ib*), Malik Ikhtiyar al-Din **Aitegin**. Bahram, not reconciled with this arrangement, had Aitegin assassinated. The next year (1241), a conspiracy was hatched by leading nobles to overthrow the new **sultan** but proved abortive and led to the removal of the suspected conspirators from the important positions they were occupying. Badr al-Din Sanqar Rumi, the *amir-i hajib* implicated in this conspiracy, was executed. In December 1241, **Lahore** was occupied by the **Mongols**. During the expedition launched to recover Lahore, one of the **Tajik** nobles, Khwaja Muhazzab al-Din, conspired to provoke the nobles to revolt en masse. The rebels occupied **Delhi** and killed Bahram.

BAIHAQI, 'ABU'L HAQ (996–1077). The author of *Tarikh-i Baihaqi* (Baihaqi's History), he was the son of Husain Baihaqi, a native of Harisabad in the district of Baihaq in Khurasan. Baihaqi served for several decades in the Correspondence Department (*diwan-i risalat*) of the Ghaznavid central government. While out of employment between 1052 and 1059, he undertook to write *Tarikh-i Baihaqi*, which originally comprised his reminiscences of events from 1018 to 1059. The surviving part of the book mainly deals with the happenings of the reign of Sultan Mas'ud of Ghazni (1030–1041).

BALBAN, GHIYAS AL-DIN (?–1286). One of the slaves of Sultan **Iltutmish** (1211–1236) who ascended the throne in 1266, Balban belonged to the Central Asian Turkish tribe of Ilbaris. The son of a chief commanding 10,000 families, Balban was captured in his early youth by the **Mongols**, who sold him into slavery. His first master, a rich merchant of Basra, sold him at **Delhi** to Iltutmish, who made him a royal attendant belonging to the famous Corps of Forty (*chihilganis*). Although **Raziya Sultan** (1236–1240) had made him the Lord of the Hunt (*amir-i shikar*), Balban eventually joined the disaffected nobles who overthrew her in 1240. Under **Bahram Shah** (1240–1242) and **'Ala al-Din Mas'ud** (1242–1246), as the commandant of Rewari and Hansi, Balban distinguished himself in military operations against the Mongols.

During Nasir al-Din **Mahmud Shah**'s reign (1246–1266), Balban exercised regal powers as *na'ib-i mumlikat*. In 1252, he was removed from this position through a coup d'état masterminded by **Imad al-Din Rehan**, an Indian Muslim, but soon regained his powers when Turkish nobles rallied behind him en masse. As *na'ib-i mumlikat*, Balban conducted successful military campaigns in Sind and Mewat, also against the Mongols. After Nasir al-Din Mahmud's death in 1266, Balban declared himself a **sultan** with the title Ghiyas al-Din. He subsequently harshly treated the chiefs in the **Doab** and **Katehr** regions and curbed the powers and emoluments of the old slave nobles. Many of them were eliminated secretly. He guarded vigorously the northwest frontier against the Mongols, who had succeeded in extending their sway up to **Lahore**.

Balban is credited with establishing his firm control over provincial governors by a policy of blood and iron. The harsh suppression of **Toghril** in Bengal (1279) was one such case. Balban tried to revive the Sasanid notions of kingship to bolster his authority. He was stern and cruel, as well as a great believer in the superiority of noble birth; he did his best to exclude men of common origins from state service.

BALLALASENA (?–1119). A ruler of the **Sena dynasty** of Bengal, who succeeded Vijayasena on the throne in 1108. Ballalasena consolidated the territories inherited from his father. He also promoted arts and literature. Under him, Puranic Brahmanism gained ascendancy in Bengal, which led to caste rigidities. He sent missions to Magadha, Bhutan, Orissa, Nepal, and other locations for the purpose of spreading Brahmanical ideas.

BANIYAS. Communities associated with trade. The Gujarati Baniyas, many of them **Jains**, were found as far as Malabar. **Multanis** and Marwaris established a reputation as merchants in medieval India.

BANJARAS. Petty traders roving in large caravans that were used for transportation by big merchants. Each caravan of Banjaras was headed by a chief, who represented its members before the state authorities. Peddlers with pack animals, they sold their goods from house to house. Banjaras played a crucial role in the medieval Indian economy by carrying large quantities of grains from countryside to towns as well as to distant destinations and port towns for export overseas.

BARANI, ZIYA' AL-DIN (1285–1357?). The author of *Tarikh-i Firuz Shahi* and *Fatawa-i jahandari* (Counsels of Sovereignty) as well as of several theological treatises. His father, Mu'id al-Mulk, had served as a deputy (*na'ib*) to **Arkali Khan**. Barani's uncle, **A'la ul-Mulk**, was appointed by **'Ala al-Din Khalji** as the *kotwal* of **Delhi** in 1296. Sometime later, Mu'id ul-Mulk was appointed by the same **sultan** as the deputy (*na'ib*) and accountant (*khwaja*) of Baran, which explains his son's surname. Barani's maternal grandfather was a middle-ranking military officer (*sipahsalar*) during **Balban**'s reign (1266–1286).

As a theorist and historian of the **Delhi sultanate**, Barani was of the view that the **sultans** were not giving due attention to their exalted office since it was, in fact, the exercise of God's power. He attributes many of the weaknesses of the sultanate to sultans' not adhering to the precepts of Islamic law. He suggested that the suppression of Hindu chiefs was the paramount duty of the sultans and advocated the total exclusion of the Indian converts to Islam from important positions. This he justified in terms of a theory dividing humanity into "highborn" and "lowborn" and attributing the ills of state and society to the rise of lowborn to positions of power.

In his early youth, Barani got acquainted at Delhi with **Amir Hasan Sijzi** and through him **Amir Khusrau**. The three became fast friends; together they were deeply attached to **Nizam al-Din Auliya**. In 1334–1335, **Muhammad bin Tughlaq** (1325–1351) appointed Barani a royal companion (*nadim*), which enabled him to observe the political developments of the last 17 years of his eccentric master's reign from close quarters. On **Firuz Shah Tughlaq**'s accession in 1351, Barani was briefly confined in the fort of Bhatnire, possibly on suspicion of being a party to Khwaja Jahan **Ahmad bin Ayaz**'s abortive move to raise one of the sons of Muhammad bin Tughlaq to the throne. He spent the rest of his life in poverty and neglect at Ghiyaspur, a village near Delhi, where Nizam al-Din Auliya's hospice was located. During this time, Barani wrote *Tarikh-i Firuz Shahi*, which was completed in 1357. Barani died at Ghiyaspur some time after completing this history of the Delhi sultanate that he had wished to present to Firuz Shah Tughlaq but was never able to do so.

BARBAK SHAH, RUKN AL-DIN (?–1474). Second **sultan** of the Ilyas Shahi dynasty of Bengal after its restoration in 1442. Succeeding his father, Nasir al-Din Mahmud Shah, to the throne in 1459, Barbak Shah raised a militia of Abyssinian slaves and also organized a large body of Arab soldiers. This was obviously aimed at reducing the clout of the local *paiks* who had contributed to the seizure of power by **Raja Ganesh** in 1415. The reign of Barbak Shah witnessed a total expansion. Madaran in Orissa and the region up to cis-Karatya in Kamrup were reoccupied. The frontier in the west was extended as far as Purnia and the entire Jesore-Khulna tract in the south was also annexed. Barbak Shah is known for his patronage of Bengali literature. Maledhar Basu, the compiler of *Sri Krishna Bijay* (Victory of Lord Krishna), was entitled Gunaraj Khan and was provided with financial support from Barbak.

BARBEG. See AMIR-I HAJIB.

BARBOSA, DUARTE (?–1521). Was in the service of the Portuguese government in India during 1500–1515, mostly staying at Cochin. He was proficient in **Malayalam** and is reported to have acted as interpreter at **Albuquerque**'s meeting with the ruler of Cannor in 1503. Barbosa returned to Portugal in 1515, where he published his travels that carry interesting information on the Portuguese activities in India and on the situations in Indian coastal states during 1500–1515. This book is available in English translation under the title *The Book of Duarte Barbosa*. In a subsequent voyage undertaken in 1521, Barbosa was killed by a local chief in the Philippines.

BARID. This was an intelligencer or spy in the **Delhi sultanate**. The head of the intelligence department was designated *barid-i mumlik*. The role of *barids* had come to gain particular significance under autocratic **sultans** like **Balban** (1266–1286), **'Ala al-Din Khalji** (1296–1316), and **Muhammad bin Tughlaq** (1325–1351). The father of 'Ali Barid, founder of the Baridi dynasty of **Bidar**, possibly earned this surname on account of having served as an intelligencer at some stage during his early career.

BASHIR, 'IMAD UL-MULK (?–1387). Bashir, a personal slave of **Firuz Shah Tughlaq** (1351–1388) since his days as a prince, was appointed on the latter's accession to the office of *'ariz-i mamalik* and also entitled 'Iamd ul-Mulk. At the same time, he was assigned the *iqta'* of Rapri. Being a favorite of the **sultan**, the central revenue office did not obtain from him the center's share of revenues, which made him fabulously rich. Bashir left behind 13 *kror* (130 million) *tankas*, nearly equal to two years' income of the sultanate. Much of this wealth was accumulated by corrupt means. In his old age, Bashir transferred his duties as *'ariz-i mumalik* to his son Ishaq and also freed his own 4,000 slaves, advancing to each one of them a handsome amount to establish himself as a freeman.

BAYANA. The town grew up round Sultankot, a fort founded by **Baha al-Din Toghril**, who was *muqti'* of the tract southwest of **Mathura** in 1196. In 1259, Bayana and Mathura formed the extensive *iqta'* of **Sher Khan**, **Balban**'s cousin. Bayana came to be ruled by the **Auhadi dynasty** in the 15th century. The Auhadis were ousted from Bayana by the **Lodis** in 1492.

BELUR. An ancient town in the Indian state of Karnataka where some of the finest examples of **Hoyasala** temples have survived.

BENARAS. Same as Kashi and modern Varanasi; it was a well-known pilgrim center of Hindus on the Ganges River east of its junction with Yamuna at Allahabad. Since ancient times, it was known as a center of Brahmanical learning and also for its muslins and other fine clothes. Benaras was plundered by a **Ghaznavid** invading army in 1034. After **Jaichandra Gahadavala** was defeated and killed in

1193, Benaras was annexed to the **Ghaurid** Empire. In the 15th century, Benaras became a center of emerging **bhakti** cults. **Kabir** (1425?–1492) preached at Benaras.

BERAR. Central part of the **Deccan** plateau demarcated roughly from Bastar and Maharastra proper by the Pinganga and Godawari rivers, respectively. It represented the territory of one of the four provinces of the **Bahmani kingdom** that emerged as an independent kingdom toward the end of the 15th century. Berar came to be ruled by the Imad Shahi dynasty established in 1487 by a Bahmani noble, Fath Allah Imad ul-Mulk. *See also TARAF.*

BHAGWADGITA. The "Song Celestial" is a commentary on sacred literature in the spirit of personal devotion or *bhakti* that had become the dynamic force of later Hinduism. It came to be added to the *Mahabharata*, originally a secular epic, in the form of a beautiful poem believed to have been recited by Krishna, an incarnation of Vishnu, to Arjun on the eve of the battle to persuade him to do his duty as a *kshatriya* when he showed a reluctance to fight against his kinsmen. As suggested by Abu Rehan **Alberuni**'s remarks, already by the beginning of the 11th century, this Vaishnav version of Brahmanical faith appears to have become more popular in northwestern India. The *Bhagwadgita* was perceived by Alberuni as the most important religious text of the Hindus, though the version he quotes is not the standard one. *See also* VAISHNAVAS.

BHAKKAR. Town situated south of **Multan** on an island in the Indus River. At the time of **Muhammad Ghauri**'s death (1206), Nasir al-Din **Qubacha** set himself up as an independent king at Uchch and occupied Bhakkar. **Iltutmish** annexed Bhakkar to the **Delhi sultanate** in 1227. Around 1257, Bhakkar, like **Multan** and **Lahore**, had passed under the control of the **Mongols**. Bhakkar came to be effectively ruled from **Delhi** only under the **Tughlaqs** (1320–1388). After **Firuz Shah** (1351–1388), it passed to the control of local authorities.

BHAKTI CULTS. During 500–900, **Jainism** and **Buddhism** gradually gave way in south India to a new form of religious worship represented by the devotional cults of the Tamil saints, which were among the early expression of what later came to be called the *bhakti* movement. From the 14th century onward, the *bhakti* cults became a dynamic force in north India. Insofar as these cults attracted the artisans and professional castes, the *bhakti* movement may be seen as filling the vacuum created by the disappearance of Buddhism. At the same time, some of the **Vaishnava** saints, such as **Ramanuja** and **Vallabha**, have also been associated with the *bhakti* movement. Some of the teachings of *bhakti* cults that were to make a deeper impact on social rather than purely religious ideas were influenced by Islamic mysticism. The Sufic and *bhakti* thought and practice coalesced at various points. The essential belief in the need to unite with God by cultivating divine love and a stress on the necessity of being guided by a preceptor are indicative of this coalescence.

But the mysticism of **Sufis** was not encouraged by all the *bhakti* saints. Many of them belonged to the class of less prosperous cultivators and artisans, in most cases from lower castes. In their teachings, institutionalized religion and objects of worship were attacked, caste disregarded, women were encouraged to join gatherings, and teachings were entirely in the local vernacular languages. **Kabir**'s and **Nanak**'s teachings were the most significant contributions of this nature during the 15th and 16th centuries.

BHARUCH. The same as modern Broach; a Gujrati port town in the Gulf of Cambay. It was annexed to the **Delhi sultanate** after the conquest of Gujarat by **'Ala al-Din Khalji** in 1297. In 1344, the governor of Bharuch, 'Alim ul-Mulk Nizam al-Din, was entrusted with the command of **Daulatabad** by **Muhammad bin Tughlaq** (1325–1351) with the instructions to bring the disgruntled military officers (*amiran-i sada*) of that place to Bharuch under guard. These officers mutinied and arrested 'Alim ul-Mulk, sparking a general revolt. Bharuch became a hotbed of this revolt in Gujarat.

BHASKARACHARYA (1114–?). He is counted among the great Indian astronomers. In mathematics he added the cyclic method, as he calls it, and the combination of old and new methods, which gives integral solutions of $Du^2 + 1 = t$. Bhaskaracharya developed his scientific doctrines in elegant and complex meters that were distinct from those of usual versified statements in Sanskrit.

BHATTA, PADAM. Founder of a school of Sanskrit grammar in Bengal. He is credited with writing a treatise on grammar, *Supadmavyakarana*, in 1375, which became popular in parts of eastern India.

BHIRAN RAI (?–1340). One of the Hindu officials appointed by **Muhammad bin Tughlaq** (1325–1351) to high positions. He was made the auditor (*mutsarrif*) at **Gulbarga** and Kohir was assigned to him as his *iqta'*. In 1340, Bhiran detected large sums of revenue being retained by military officers in the region under his charge. He prevailed upon the governor to let him farm the revenues, undertaking to increase them by 50 percent. Military officers in Gulbarga, led by Ali Shah Khalji, revolted. They seized and killed Bhiran Rai.

BHOGTA. One of the titles of lesser feudatories of the period of **Indian feudalism** (800–1200) that had possibly been in existence since the time of the Guptas (320–500).

BHOJA, RAJA (?–1060). The renowned **Paramara** king who ruled over Malwa from his capital Dhar for 40 years, 1020–1060. He is known in Indian folk tradition as a just king and a great patron of the learned and virtuous. A large number of poets and scholars were connected with his court. Some of Bhoja's own literary works have survived. Bhoja was often at war with the neighboring kingdoms of the Latas, Chedis, and **Chaulukyas**. It was in a struggle against the united forces of the Latas and the Chedis that he ultimately succumbed in 1060.

BHUWA, MIAN. Son of Khwas Khan, he was a *wazir* of Sultan **Sikandar Lodi** (1489–1517) for many years. Sultan **Ibrahim Lodi** (1517–1526) had him removed and imprisoned. He was accused of being in league with Daulat Khan Lodi, who had rebelled in the Punjab. The old *wazir* was put in chains and placed under the charge of one of his erstwhile subordinates. While imprisoned he was killed in a contrived explosion. Mian Bhuwa prepared a treatise in Persian on medicines in which the prescriptions of ancient Indian medicinal texts as well as those of Khurasan and Iran were incorporated. It is popularly known as *Tib-i Sikandari*.

BIDAR. A district town in the state of Karnataka, it was founded by Sultan **Ahmad Shah Bahmani** in 1429. The same sultan shifted the **Bahmani** capital from **Gulbarga** to Bidar. Subsequently, Bidar came to possess important monuments built by Bahmani **sultans** as well as nobles. The college (*madrasa*) built by **Mahmud Gavan** is perhaps the most fascinating of these monuments.

BIHMANDKHANI, MUHAMMAD. Author of *Tarikh-i Muhammadi* (completed in 1434), which is a chronicle of Islamic history down to that of the **Delhi sultanate** and of the rise of the independent kingdom of Kalpi in 1390 as well as its struggle with the neighboring states, including the sultanates of Malwa and **Jaunpur**. Muhammad was the son Malik Bihmand, who rose to prominence in the service of Tughlaq noble Firuz Khan. Firuz Khan's son, Junaid, had assigned to Muhammad the fiscal subdivision (*pargana*) of Chaurasi. During the 1390s, the ruler of Kalpi gave him Erach as a territorial-cum-revenue assignment (*iqta'*). At Erach, Muhammad fought against **Sharqis** and was wounded. Muhammad's short account of **Timur**'s invasion (1398) is important for the anguish he expresses over the sufferings inflicted upon the Indians, Hindus as well as Muslims. He calls Timur "a cunning and mischievous ruler." According to him, the important **Tughlaq** nobles as well as the Hindu chief of Mewat were captured and carried to Samarqand "where they suffered martyrdom."

***BRAHMADEYA* GRANTS.** These were land grants made in perpetuity by Hindu rajas for the support of Brahmans that gave a right to individuals, sometimes to entire communities, to collect taxes on the produce of land and also exercise general control over local resources. Under the **Cholas** the recipients of *brahmadeya* grants were treated as secular landowners where any question of tenure was involved. The pattern of these grants remained unchanged from the Pallava times. This is borne out, for example, by the Anbil grant of Sundara Chola that records the donation of land to Aniruddha Brahmadhiraja.

BUDDHISM. During 900–1300, Buddhism practically disappeared from India; Buddha came to be commonly accepted as an incarnation of Vishnu. The decline of the mercantile communities, on whose support Buddhists generally depended, seems to have led to the receding of Buddhism in most parts of India. The only region where Buddhism held its own down to the 13th century was eastern India, where it had royal patronage. This is borne out by the ruins of a Buddhist monastery at **Nalanda**. In the 13th century, harried by their local opponents in Bengal as well as by the Turks and Afghans, the Buddhists fled and sought refuge in the monasteries of southeast Asia.

BUGHRA KHAN. Second son of Sultan Ghiyas al-Din **Balban** whose original name was Mahmud. He was entitled Bughra Khan after Balban's rise to kingship (1266). Along with his elder brother, **Muhammad**, he was deputed by **Balban** to guard the northwest frontier against **Mongol** raids. Bughra Khan was stationed at Samana. In 1281, he was deputed to govern Bengal virtually as a sovereign. After his brother Muhammad was killed in a skirmish with a Mongol raiding party in 1286, Bughra Khan was recalled to **Delhi** and his father offered him the throne, but instead Bughra Khan quietly left for Bengal. On Balban's death (1286), the nobles—going against the choice of the deceased **sultan**—placed Bughra Khan's son **Kaiqubad** on the throne. From this time onward, Bughra Khan assumed royal status in Bengal with the title Nasir al-Din Muhammad Bughra Khan.

Near the end of Kaiqubad's short reign (1287–1290), Bughra Khan proceeded toward Delhi purportedly with an aim to warn Kaiqubad of the evil designs of some of his ministers. Kaiqubad left Delhi to meet his father in **Awadh**. The two met on the bank of the Sarju River in Awadh. **Amir Khusrau**'s earliest narrative poem *Qiran al-sa'dayn* recounted this meeting of father and son. Some time after the overthrow of Kaiqubad by the Khalji officers in 1290, Bughra Khan abdicated at **Lakhnauti** in favor of his son Rukn al-Din Kaikaus, who died around 1300. Bengal continued to be ruled by the progeny of Bughra Khan until 1324.

BUKKA RAYA I (?–1377). A local prince of Kampila (in the Raichur Doab) who, along with his brother **Harihara**, was taken prisoner by the army of the **Delhi sultanate,** brought to **Delhi**, and converted to Islam. The two brothers were subsequently sent back to the south to restore the **sultan**'s authority there. In 1336, they revolted and reverted to Hinduism. Harihara was crowned the king of Hastinavati (modern Hampi), which then formed the nucleus of what was to become the **Vijayanagar** Empire. Bukka succeeded to the throne of the newly established kingdom in 1356. His reign witnessed the beginning of a long-drawn-out tussle between the **Bahmani kingdom** and Vijayanagar for the control of Raichur Doab. Bukka I is credited with naming his capital Vijayanagar. He is reported to have restored harmony between the **Vaishnavas** and **Jains**. The Vijayanagar Empire was strong and prosperous at the end of his reign (1377).

BUQUBUQ, MALIK. One of the Turkish slave nobles of **Balban**'s reign (1266–1286). As commandant (*muqti*) of Badaun, Malik Buqubuq commanded 4,000 horsemen. Some time after Balban's rise to kingship (1266), Buqubuq's son Qara Beg came to be stationed there as an ordinary assignment holder (*iqtadar*). By then, Malik Buqubuq had ceased to be the commandant of the place. On receiving a report that Malik Buqubuq had killed a personal attendant, Balban had him executed.

BURHAN AL-DIN GHARIB, SHAIKH. A disciple of Shaikh **Nizam al-Din Auliya** who was for some time in charge of the kitchen in the **Chishti** monastery at **Delhi**. He willingly submitted to the austere lifestyle prescribed for the disciples of the great *shaikh*, which is also suggested by his nickname *gharib* (poor, humble). Nizam al-Din Auliya had nominated him as one of his deputies having the authority to enroll disciples. After his preceptor's demise (1325), Burhan al-Din migrated to Deogir (renamed **Daulatabad** by **Muhammad bin Tughlaq**) where he established a Chishti monastery. He is reported to have enrolled many disciples in the **Deccan**. One of his disciples, Shaikh Nizam, is reported to have persuaded Raja Nasir Faruqi (1399–1437) to name the new town the latter founded in Khandesh as Burhanpur in his memory.

– C –

CALICUT. A town that grew up around a complex of palace-cum-fort built by the ruler of a Nediyirippu on the Malabar coast in the 13th century. It came to be called Kozhikode, pronounced "Kalikat" by the

Arabs and "Calicut" by the Europeans. Calicut continued to be ruled by the **Zamorins** until modern times.

CAMBAY. An ancient port town in the Gulf of Cambay, Cambay is mentioned as one of the ports on the west coast as early as the Gupta period (320–500). It is referred to frequently in the accounts of Arab geographers as one of the Indian ports frequented by Arabs. Cambay was an important port of the Gujarat sultanate (1407–1536). Cottons exported from Cambay were renowned in the textile trade for their quality.

CHAHAMANAS. One of the four **Rajput** clans claiming *agnikula* origin, the Chahamanas ruled during 10th century, over a large area in eastern Rajasthan located to the southwest of **Delhi**. Within this region branches of the main clan ruled in adjacent tracts during the 10th to 12th centuries. These were originally feudatories of **Pratiharas**. The Chahamana principality of **Ajmer** became independent of Pratiharas during the 12th century and subjugated the **Tomaras** of Delhi in the second half of the 12th century. Their ruler Prithviraja III was defeated and overthrown by Muizz al-Din **Muhammad Ghauri** in 1192.

CHAITANYA (1486–1533). A Vaishnava saint who propagated the cult of Krishna and Radha in Bengal. He had become a mendicant at the age of 25. According to Chaitanya, mere conventional rites (*karma*) were not sufficient for salvation, which could be attained only by worshipping Hari (Krishna) and singing his praises. Chaitanya promoted the process of incorporating the lay Buddhist society into the Vaishnava fold by opening his creed to everyone irrespective of caste or belief. Chaitanya spent the last 16 years of his life at **Puri**. He was patronized by the Saiyid **sultans** of Bengal.

CHAJJU, MALIK 'ALA AL-DIN MUHAMMAD. He was the son of Sultan Ghiyas al-Din **Balban's** brother **Kishli Khan** and was counted among the powerful nobles of Mu'izz al-Din **Kaiqubad** (1287–1290). Malik Firuz Khalji (later Sultan **Jalal al-Din Firuz Khalji**, 1290–1296) asked him in 1290 to act as the regent of boy king **Kaimurs**, who had been brought to the throne after removing

Kaiqubad, but the offer was refused by Malik Chajju. On Kaimurs' removal, Jalal al-Din Firuz Khalji, while assuming kingship, agreed to Malik Chajju's request for the governorship of **Kara** and also allowed the surviving members of Balban's family to repair to that location.

In the very first year of Jalal al-Din Firuz Khalji's reign (1290–1296), Malik Chajju revolted at Kara. He was joined by Amir Ali Hatim Khan, the governor of **Awadh** and other nobles of the old regime. Responding to Malik Chajju's appeal, a large number of Hindu chiefs of the trans-Gangetic region joined him with their foot soldiers (*paiks*) and archers. Malik Chajju and his allies advanced toward **Delhi** along the left bank of the Ganges River. At Bahlana (near Badaun), an army commanded by Jalal al-Din Firuz Khalji's son **Arkali Khan** forced the rebels to cross to the right side of Ram Ganga. Simultaneously, Jalal al-Din Firuz, crossing the Ganges at Bhojpur (near **Kanauj**), overtook the rebels at Ram Ganga. In the battle that ensued, the rebels were defeated, and many of their leaders were killed or made prisoners. Malik Chajju himself escaped to the territory of rebellious Hindu chiefs but was captured a few days later. Captured rebels were treated very harshly. Many of them were executed or sold into slavery. Malik Chajju disappeared from the political scene after he was imprisoned at **Multan** on this occasion.

CHAKRAVARTIGAL. This high-sounding royal title of the earlier period survived in early medieval India at a more formal plane in the formulas used for describing the royal status of some of the more important Hindu rulers. The title *chakravartigal* (sovereign of the world) of the Chola kings of the period was an equivalent of the northern *chakravartin*.

CHANDBARDAI. The composer of *Prithvirajarasau* who narrates the incidents of this story in early Hindi or Hindivi. The text of his book available now carries apocryphal elements that indicate that it acquired the present form between 1460 and 1675. Whether Chandbardai was a contemporary of **Prithviraja Chahamana III** (1180–1192) is an open question, but the language he uses in some parts of his book does suggest that it was penned in its original form in the 15th century.

CHANDELLAS. Yasovarman Chandella established the power of his clan at Kalinjar, the seat of Jejakabhukti kingdom in the ninth century. The Chandellas became independent of **Kanauj** in the first half of the 10th century. **Ganda Chandella** (999–1025) made common cause with the **Hindu Shahi** ruler **Anandpala** against **Mahmud of Ghazni**. He attacked Rajpala of **Kanauj** and killed him for surrendering before Mahmud. Mahmud forced Ganda to surrender Kalinjar to him in 1023. On **Paramardi Deva**'s accession (1165), Chandellas got involved in a prolonged war with the **Chahamanas** of **Ajmer-Delhi**. Qutb al-Din Aibek put an end to Chandella power by defeating and killing Paramardi in 1202 when he occupied Kalinjar.

CHANDERI. A **Rajput** stronghold in northern Malwa located about 200 kilometers south of **Gwalior** that was controlled by the **Paramaras** at the time of **Muhammad Ghauri**'s invasion (1192). It passed to the control of the **Delhi sultanate** in the beginning of 14th century. By 1312, Chanderi and Erach together constituted a large *iqta'*. After the disintegration of the **Tughlaq** Empire, Chanderi again came to be controlled by the Rajputs. It was annexed to Malwa kingdom in 1515 but was soon occupied by the **Lodis**, who lost it to **Mewar** in 1517.

CHANDI. Consort of Lord Shiva. Her cult had many followers in early medieval Bengal. The first **Pala** ruler Gopala (765–770) was a follower of Chandi's cult. According to legend, the goddess Chandi had given him a club to protect himself against demons.

CHANDIDASA. Bengali poet of the 14th century who wrote extensively on the theme of love between Radha and Krishna. Chandidasa was the greatest exponent of *sahajiya* philosophy, or the philosophy of natural path in which sexual love came to be perceived as a means of salvation.

CHARAI. Grazing tax imposed by '**Ala al-Din Khalji** (1296–1316) that was in addition to the land revenue (*kharaj*). An accompanying assessment was that on dwellings (*sukunat-ghari*).

CHAUDHURI. In the **Delhi sultanate** during 14th century, *muqaddams* and *chaudhuris* represented a new superior emerging rural class. They replaced the old rural aristocracy of *ranas* and *rautas*. In the new hierarchy, *chaudhuris* stood at the top, defined by **Ibn Battuta** as "the chief of infidels" in each *sadi*, a unit of hundred villages that corresponded to the *pargana*.

CHAUHANAS. *See* CHAHAMANAS.

CHAULUKYAS. Same as Solankis. An *agnikula* **Rajput** clan that dominated in early medieval India large parts of Gujarat and the **Deccan** plateau. In 973, Tailapa II, a Chaulukya prince of south India dethroned the last Rashtrakuta ruler Kakka II, laying the foundation of the Chaulukya dynasty of Kalyani. The Chaulukyas of Vengi sometimes also referred to as Eastern Chaulukyas, ruled over Andhra region and a portion of Kalinga. They were defeated and humiliated by the **Chola** ruler **Rajaraja** (985–1016). The Chaulukya dynasty of Kalyani continued to rule over a large part of western **Deccan** down to 1185. The most famous ruler of the dynasty was **Vikramaditya VI** (1076–1126). Bilhana's *Vikramanka-deva-charitra* furnishes a detailed account of his reign.

CHAURAPANCHASHIKA. A collection of erotic poetry of **Govardhana** or Bilhana that introduced the description of erotic scenes and feelings in Sanskrit verses that did not require the disguise of religious theme. Govardhana was patronized by **Lakshamanasena** (1175–1206).

CHETTIS. They were among the better-known merchants and middlemen who operated all over south India since the prime of the **Chola** Empire. Some of them migrated to southeast Asia and continued the family business overseas.

CHIHILGANIS. The Turkish slave officers, each of whom commanded 40 slave subalterns, were called *chihilganis*. They dominated the **Delhi sultanate** during 1236–1266, contributing to the gradual elimination of the persons of noble lineages. The indiscipline and mutual jealousies of the *chihilganis* led to the disorganization and factional fights under **Iltutmish**'s successors (1236–1266). The *chihilganis* were finally eliminated by Ghiyas al-Din **Balban** (1266–1286) who, ironically enough, had emerged from their own ranks.

CHINGEZ KHAN (1155–1227). Chief of the nomadic **Mongol** tribes of the Gobi Desert initially known as Tamujin. He became famous as Chingez (Genghis) Khan after he had established his sovereignty over a large area and many tribes. Pursuing the Khwarazmi prince **Jalal al-Din Mingbarni**, Chingez Khan reached the bank of the Indus River in 1221. **Iltutmish** avoided getting involved in a conflict with Chingez Khan by tactfully refusing to grant asylum to Mingbarni at his court.

CHIRAGH DEHLI, SHAIKH NASIR AL-DIN MAHMUD (?–1356). He was a successor (*khalifa*) of Shaikh **Nizam al-Din Auliya** at **Delhi** who continued to coordinate the activities of the **Chishti order** in India after the passing away of his preceptor in 1325. A collection of his sayings, *Khair ul-majalis* (Beneficent Conversations) compiled by **Hamid Qalandar**, is regarded as a major **Sufic** tract produced in India. Nasir al-Din Chiragh emphasized the confirmation of Sufic doctrines by the Quran and sunna. Like his preceptor, he was quite indifferent toward political authorities. He believed in not reacting to personal harm and violence. Nasir al-Din did not nominate any deputy and willed that all the sacred relics be buried with him in his grave. One of his distinguished disciples was Saiyed Muhammad **Gesudaraz**, who became famous for propagating Sufic ideals in the **Deccan**.

CHISHTI ORDER. Originally established by Khwaja Abu Ishaq (d. 940) at Chisht (in Khurasan), this **Sufic** order was introduced into India by **Mu'in al-Din Chishti** in the 12th century. From the monastery (*khanqah*) established by Mu'in al-Din Chishti at **Ajmer**, the Chishti order's influence spread to **Delhi** and from there to different parts of India during the 13th and 14th centuries. Among those who contributed to the popularity of the Chishti order in India, mention may be made of three distinguished successors of Mu'in al-Din Chishti: **Farid al-Din Mas'ud Ganj-shikr**, **Nizam al-Din Auliya**, and **Nasir**

al-Din Chiragh Dehli. The Sufis of the Chishti order traced their spiritual lineage to 'Ali through Hasan Basari. There has always been a distinct tilt in the preaching of Chishti Sufis toward conceding the spiritual preeminence of 'Ali.

CHITOR. A historic stronghold in southeastern Rajasthan. It emerged as an important military and political center following the establishment of the rule of **Guhila** clan over the territory of **Mewar** during the ninth century. Chitor was made the capital of Mewar by the Guhila ruler Jaitra Singh (1213–1261). In 1303, **'Ala al-Din Khalji** besieged Ratan Sen in the fort of Chitor, forcing him to surrender after a siege of seven months. 'Ala al-Din Khalji placed Chitor under the charge of his officer Malik Shahin after having renamed the place as Khizrabad. This arrangement, however, broke down in 1316. A few years later, **Hammira** (1326–1364) of the **Sisodiya** clan established his rule over Mewar. Under the Sisodiyas, Chitor tended to become a symbol of **Rajput** resistance to the **sultans** of **Delhi**, Malwa, and Gujarat. In 1442, Rana **Kumbha** (1433–1468) succeeded in beating back the Malwa ruler Sultan **Mahmud Khalji**'s assault on Chitor with heavy losses. He had earlier defeated Mahmud Khalji in 1437 and commemorated his success by building a victory tower at Chitor. Another attack on Chitor by the Malwa ruler Nasir-al-Din (1501–1510) was repulsed by Raimal (1473–1508) in 1503.

CHOLAS. They are mentioned as one of the south Indian ruling groups in Asoka's inscriptions (273–233 BCE). The Cholas dominated the east coast of peninsular India from a very early date and were associated with the emergence of **Tamil** culture. The rise of Parantaka Chola (907–955) heralded the emergence of the Cholas as a major power in south India. The next important rulers, **Rajaraja I** (985–1014) and **Rajendra I** (1014–1044), brought about the consolidation of the Chola kingdom, leading to the extension of its control to Malabar and Ceylon. Rajendra I marched up to the Ganges River in the north and also conducted overseas campaigns to protect Indian commercial interests in southeast Asia. By the third quarter of the 12th century, the Chola ascendancy was waning, leading to the **Pandyas** superseding the Cholas as the dominant power of the Tamil country.

Among the early southern states, the Chola kingdom was conspicuous for having a centralized political organization where feudatories were ignored significantly. Chola central authority maintained contact with the cultivators on a wide scale. The high-sounding royal title *chakravartigal* and the cult of God kings of the Chola system defined its absolutist nature. The division of the Chola kingdom into provinces (*mandalam*), each one of them subdivided into districts (*valanadus*), and the presence of other subdivisions (*kurram*, *nadu*, or *kottam*) as well as the autonomy of village level government were some of the distinctive features of the Chola administration.

CONTI, NICOLAO. A Venetian who was in **Vijayanagar** around 1420 and who left an account of that city. On his return from India, Nicolao went to Pope Engenius at Florence craving absolution for having renounced his faith on account of a threat to his wife and children who had accompanied him. This happened when he was passing through Egypt. The detailed statement of his journey, which includes his passage through India, was written down by Poggio Bracciolini and published in his book *Historia de Varietate Fortunae*, Lib. IV.

CUTTAK. Situated north of **Puri** on the bank of the Mahanadi River, Cuttak was the capital of Eastern **Gangas** who ruled over Orissa during the 14th century. In Persian histories, it is often referred to as Katak-Banaras.

– D –

DAKKANI. A form of Hindustani (Hindi/Urdu) carrying the traces of North Indian dialects like Punjabi, Khari-boli, and Braj. It developed in the urban centers of the **Deccan** controlled by the **Bahmanis** and successor sultanates. Most of the surviving Dakkani texts are written in Persian script. The earliest of them, *M'araj al-'ashiqin* (Ascent to Heaven of Devotees), is ascribed to Saiyid Muhammad **Gesudaraz** (d.1422).

DAMARAS. Kashmiri landowners of the 10th century who were in the position of feudal local magnates wielding considerable military clout. They were used by the rulers to control the Tantrin soldiery, who had become very powerful after the deposition of Queen Sugandha in 914.

DAMGHANI, SHAMS AL-DIN (?–1381). A senior noble appointed by **Firuz Shah Tughlaq** (1351–1388) as the governor of Gujarat in 1377. After Damghani failed to collect the amount he had undertaken to collect, he rose in rebellion against the **sultan** in 1380. He soon alienated the mass of the middle-ranking nobles (*amiran-i sada*) stationed in Gujarat on whose support he relied. These nobles, rallying around the royal cause, attacked and killed him in 1381. Damghani's revolt was the only instance of a senior noble rebelling against Firuz Shah Tughlaq. This was in sharp contrast to the situation in **Muhammad bin Tughlaq**'s reign.

DASHAGRAMIKA. A grantee holding the revenue of 10 villages in the **Pala** kingdom of Bengal. This was possibly a reflection of the practice to group villages in units of 10 for the purpose of revenue collection that was prevalent in the **Deccan** during the early medieval period.

DAUD, MULLA. Author of *Chandayan*, a versified narration in Hindvi of the love story of Norak and Chanda completed in 1373 or 1375. Daud presented this work to his patron Jaunashah, who was a noble of **Firuz Shah Tughlaq** (1351–1388).

DAULAT KHAN (?–1414). He was raised by fellow nobles to the throne on the death of **Mahmud Shah Tughlaq** in 1412. Daulat Khan as a ruler was more in the position of the head of a military oligarchy. His position was strengthened when two military leaders, Mubariz Khan and Malik Idris, also opted to support him. Shortly after his rise to rulership, Daulat Khan led an expedition to **Katehr** and received the submission of local chiefs there. But, subsequently, his position was weakened by **Ibrahim Shah Sharqi**'s expansionist drive that led to an advance into Kalpi. Daulat Khan could not take any measures to force Ibrahim Sharqi to withdraw from Kalpi. Taking advantage of this situation, **Khizr Khan**, the governor of **Multan**, advanced upon **Delhi** and forced Daulat Khan to surrender the capital to him on 23 May 1414. Daulat Khan was put to death by Khizr Khan.

DAULAT KHAN LODI (?–1526). He was the governor of **Lahore** at the time of **Sikandar Lodi**'s death (1517) and opposed **Ibrahim Lodi**'s accession; subsequently, he remained alienated. In 1523, Daulat Khan invited **Babur** to advance into the Punjab, and Ibrahim Lodi retaliated by evicting him from **Lahore**. In 1524, Daulat Khan met Babur at **Dipalpur** but soon there was a rift between them over sharing the territory in the Punjab. In 1526, when Babur again advanced into the Punjab, Daulat Khan submitted to him. He died in the same year. Daulat Khan was a man of refined literary taste. His personal library was seized by Babur.

DAULATABAD. Town built by **Muhammad bin Tughlaq** (1325–1351) during 1326–1330 at the site of old Deogir, the capital of the **Yadava** rulers conquered by '**Ala al-Din Khalji** (1296–1316). The court and a large part of the **Delhi** population shifted to Daulatabad on Muhammad bin Tughlaq's orders in 1326–1327. One obvious reason for this transfer was its central location. Some of the contemporaries, however, ascribe to the eccentric **sultan** the motive of causing hardships to the population of Delhi, who were suspected by him of being hostile toward his person. Eventually the new capital was found unsuitable and the court returned to Delhi around 1335–1336.

DAYABHAGA. One of the two systems of Hindu family law regulating the division of land and inheritance since the early medieval period. According to the *dayabhaga* school, it was only on the death of father that a son can claim rights to the property. *See also MITAK-SHARA.*

DEBAL. One of the ports in the Indus delta along the west coast that is frequently referred to in Arab geographers' accounts. In 1182–1183, it was ruled by Sumera princes of Ismaili leanings who were attacked and beaten by Mu'izz al-Din **Muhammad Ghauri**.

Iltutmish received the submission of Chanisar, the prince of Debal, after the suppression of **Qubacha** in 1227. It remained a part of the **Delhi sultanate** until the middle of the 13th century.

DECCAN. The entire tract extending from the valley of the Narbada River south to the Krishna-Tungbhadra Doab is vaguely referred to in the medieval Indian historical texts as the Deccan. In the 11th century, the northern part of the Deccan was controlled by the **Yadavas**, blocking the **Chola** expansion in the northwesterly direction. **Marathi** and **Telugu** were the two dominant languages of the region. The kingdoms of the northern Deccan of the period 700–1200 were in the nature of bridge kingdoms between the north and south. In the northern Deccan, during the Turkish and **Afghan** rule, the influence of Islamic culture found a free field. The **Delhi sultanate**'s failure to hold onto the Deccan led to abandoning the idea of the whole of the subcontinent being administered from one center. After 1347, the Deccan came to be controlled by the **Bahmani** kingdom from its capital first at **Gulbarga** and then **Bidar**.

DELHI. The city of Delhi (styled Dhillika in a Sanskrit inscription dated 1328) was built by the **Tomaras** in the region of Haryana. The Tomara rulers had paid tribute to the **Chahamanas** of Ajmer since the middle of the 12th century. After the defeat of the **Prithviraja Chahamana III** and his allies in the second battle of **Tarain** (1192), a permanent Ghaurid military camp was established near Delhi at Indraprasta (Indrapat). On this occasion, Delhi proper was granted by Mu'izz al-Din **Muhammad Ghauri** to a surviving prince of the Tomara dynasty as a tributary. Sometime later, it passed to Ghaurid control. On **Qutb al-Din Aibak**'s death at Lahore in 1210–1211, the Ghaurid officers present at Delhi invited **Iltutmish**, then commandant of Baran (Bulandshahar), to come and take power in his hands there, which marked the creation of the **Delhi sultanate**.

DELHI SULTANATE. After the defeat of **Prithviraja III** in the second battle of **Tarain** (1192), the territories annexed to the **Ghaurid** Empire in north India came to be administered from **Delhi**. The rise of **Iltutmish** (1211–1236) as the sovereign ruler (**sultan**) of Delhi duly recognized by the Abbasid caliph in 1229 may be treated as the foundation of Delhi sultanate. It was ruled successively by four dynasties. Two of them were founded by slaves, Shams al-Din Iltutmish (accession 1211) and Ghiyas al-Din **Balban** (accession 1266). The **Khaljis** (1290–1320) and **Tughlaqs** (1320–1412) were the other two. During the 14th century, the Delhi sultanate came to control almost the entire Indian subcontinent. It also succeeded in checking the advance into north India of the **Mongol** hordes located in Central Asia and Iran.

To begin with, the nobility of the Delhi sultanate comprised mainly the Persian-speaking **Tajiks** and the Turkish slaves. Among them, the latter were more influential. During the 14th century, there came to be included many nobles not necessarily of Turkish or Tajik origin. Indian coverts to Islam were also accommodated as well as Hindu warrior elements (*rautas*), who had a long tradition of military service. Ziya' **Barani**'s perception of the rise of the "lowborn" under **Muhammad bim Tughlaq** (1325–1351) seems to reflect this tendency.

A system of land assignments and military organization rooted in the institution of *iqta'* contributed to a high degree of centralization within the Delhi sultanate. Two hundred years of its rule gave rise to a distinct cultural tendency revolving around the Persian language that began to interact with traditional Indian to create a genuinely composite culture. The emergence of a large Muslim population was a part of this cultural process.

DEVA RAYA I (?–1419?). The son of **Harihara**, he succeeded to the **Vijayanagar** throne in 1404. He was opposed by one of his brothers, whom he suppressed in 1406. Deva Raya faced repeated invasions by the **Bahmani** sultan **Firuz Shah** (1397–1422), compelling him to give one of his daughters in marriage to the Bahmani ruler. Deva Raya died in 1419.

DEVA RAYA II (?–1449?). A grandson of **Deva Raya I** (1404–1419?), he came to the throne in 1419. He continued the war against the **Bahmanis**, during which **Ahmad Shah Bahmani** (1423–1434) ravaged **Vijayanagar**. Impressed by the performance of the Bahmani cavalry, Deva Raya II recruited into his army a large number of Muslim horsemen, who were allowed full freedom to practice their religion. In 1443, the Bahmanis again inflicted heavy losses upon him, forcing him to agree to pay tribute. During Deva Raya II's reign (1419–1449), Vijayanagar was visited by the Italian Nicolao **Conti**, who had arrived in 1420, and **'Abd al-Razzaq** (1443). Deva Raya II died about 1449.

DEVAL RANI. Love of Deval Rani, a Hindu princess, for a prince of the **Delhi sultanate**, **Khizr Khan**, is celebrated in **Khusrau**'s famous versified story *Deval Rani-Khizr Khan ishqia* (Love Story of Deval Rani and Khizr Khan). Deval Rani was the daughter of Rai Karan **Vaghela**, ruler of Gujarat, by his wife, Kamla Devi who was captured by '**Ala al-Din Khalji** and taken as wife in 1299. In 1306, 'Ala al-Din's forces invaded Gujarat again, this time making a demand for the surrender of Deval Rani. This demand was made on the insistence of Deval Rani's mother who evidently had, by then, come to exercise some influence on 'Ala al-Din. To avoid handing over Deval Rani to 'Ala al-Din's officers, Rai Karan sent his daughter to Ram Chandra of Deogir, but she was pursued into the **Yadava** principality and captured by **Alp Khan**, deputed by the **sultan** for this purpose. She was brought to **Delhi** and given to the care of her mother. During her stay in the sultan's harem with her mother, Deval Rani fell in love with Khizr Khan, the eldest son and heir apparent of 'Ala al-Din. They were married in 1307. From this time until Khizr Khan's imprisonment and execution in 1316, Deval Rani remained with him through thick and thin. After Khizr Khan's execution, she was taken as wife by 'Ala al-Din's successor, Qutb al-Din Mubarak Khalji (1316–1320).

DIDDA (?–1003). She ruled over Kashmir in the second half of the 10th century. Didda's husband, Ksemagupta (950–958), is known to have risen in prominence after his marriage with Didda, who, on her mother's side, was descended from the **Hindu Shahi** kings of Kabul. Didda was a woman of great ability. After Ksemagupta's death in 958, the throne passed to one of his minor sons while Didda became the regent. The nobles who opposed this arrangement were ruthlessly suppressed by Didda. She died in 1003, and the throne passed to her nephew, the ruler of Lohara, who founded a new dynasty.

DIHLIWAL. In the early decades of the establishment of the **Delhi sultanate**, *dihliwal* was an imitation of the bullion coin formerly minted by Hindu rulers at **Delhi**.

DILAWAR KHAN GHAURI (?–1405). A descendant of Mu'izz al-Din Muhammad **Ghauri** who was serving as an officer under **Firuz Shah Tughlaq** (1351–1388). In 1387, Firuz Shah appointed him as the governor of Malwa. Following **Timur**'s invasion (1398), Dilawar Khan, like other provincial governors, took advantage of the confusion in the central government and made himself independent within his own charge. In 1401, he formally declared himself the **sultan** of Malwa and struck coins in his name. He shifted the seat of his power from **Dhar** to **Mandu**, which became the capital of the newly established sultanate of Malwa. Dilawar Khan died in 1405 and was succeeded by his son **Alp Khan** with the title Sultan **Hoshang Shah Ghauri**.

DINAR, MALIK. One of the Indian slaves of **'Ala al-Din Khalji** (1296–1316) who was for some time the **sultan**'s superintendent of elephants (*shihna-i pil*). He survived **Malik Kafur**'s drive against 'Ala al-Din's old nobles during the last illness of the sultan. Malik Kafur sent him to Gujarat in 1315 to control the situation, as the army officers loyal to **Alp Khan** had rebelled on hearing of the latter's execution. Dinar returned from the frontier of Gujarat on hearing of 'Ala al-Din's death (4 January 1316). The next sultan, **Qutb al-Din Mubarak Shah** (1316–1320), married Malik Dinar's daughter and was given the title Zafar Khan by Dinar. He was then appointed governor of Gujarat. After the recall of **'Ain ul-Mulk Multani** from Gujarat, the situation there had gotten out of control, but Malik Dinar and the nobles assisting him there were able to manage. Malik Dinar disappeared from the scene around the time **Ghiyas al-Din Tughlaq** rose to sovereignty (1320) after the overthrow of **Khusrau Shah**.

DIPALPUR. Situated on the right side of the Satlaj River, south of **Lahore**, Dipalpur was an important military outpost on the northwest frontier of the **Delhi sultanate** during the 13th and 14th centuries. It was included in the tract where **'Ala al-Din Khalji** (1296–1316) enforced measurement of land under cultivation. Dipalpur was held as his *iqta'* by Ghazi Malik before he rose to the throne as **Ghiyas al-Din Tughlaq** (1320–1325). **Timur** advanced toward **Delhi** (1398) from the side of Dipalpur. While withdrawing from India, Timur confirmed **Khizr Khan** as the governor of **Multan** and Dipalpur. Under the **Saiyid dynasty** (1414–1451), Dipalpur was held by **Bahlul Lodi** as his *iqta'*.

DOAB. The fertile region between the Yamuna and Ganges Rivers was generally termed Doab in the early histories of **Delhi sultanate**. To them, Doab and **Awadh** together represented the Hindustan of the 13th and 14th centuries. Most of the Doab was *khalisah* during **'Ala al-Din Khalji's** reign (1296–1316). **Ziya' Barani** in this context refers to "the towns (*qasbat*) of Doab," which indicates that by then the number of small urban centers was quite large in the Doab. The revenue collection from the Doab in the late 1360s is calculated at 8,000,000 *tankas*. As early as **Balban**'s time (1266–1286), the *iqta's* of the troops of the central army were concentrated in the Doab. The Doab supplied grain to **Delhi**. In 1332–1334, the failure of grain supply from the Doab led to a severe famine at Delhi that was partly a consequence of local uprisings. These uprisings led to **Muhammad bin Tughlaq**'s campaigns in Baran, Kol, Qanauj, and Dalmau.

DORASAMUDRA. This town was located near modern Mysore. The town of Halebid is believed to be the site of the old Dorasamudra It represented the core of the kingdom of **Hoyasala**, which arose during the first half of the 12th century. The Hoyasalas were then feudatories of the **Chaulukyas**. **Ibn Battuta** visited Dorasamudra. According to him, the Hoyasala king of the place had 20,000 Muslims in his army. Advancing from Deogir, in 1310–1311, toward Dorasamudra, **Malik Kafur** passed through **Telingana** country. In 1311–1312, we are, however, told that the Hindu chiefs of Dorasamudra were forced to submit to the **sultan** of **Delhi**. After his rebellion, **Baha al-Din Garshasp** escaped to Dorasamudra but was handed over by Ballala III to his pursuers in 1327.

– E –

ERKALI KHAN. *See* ARKALI KHAN.

– F –

FAKHR AL-DIN KOTWAL, MALIK UL-UMARA. Fakhr al-Din held the position of the commandant (*kotwal*) of **Delhi** during **Bal-**

ban's reign (1266–1286). He was not on good terms with Balban's eldest son, Prince **Muhammad**. On Balban's death, Fakhr al-Din's party ignored the claims of both **Kaikhusrau** (son of Muhammad) and **Bughra Khan**. They supported the enthronement of Bughra Khan's son **Kaiqubad**. Fakhr al-Din was the first to take the oath of loyalty to the new **sultan**.

Fakhr al-Din was one of the prominent **Tajik** nobles who survived in the **Delhi sultanate** until 1286 in spite of the growing preponderance of the Turkish slaves of the *chihilganis* category. Fakhr al-Din and his father, Jamal al-Din Nishapuri, together occupied the office of *kotwal* of Delhi for about 80 years. Under Mu'izz al-Din Kaiqubad (1287–1290), he was entitled *Khan-i Khurasan*. His nephew and son-in-law, **Nizam al-Din**, became Kaiqubad's *amir-i dad*. Fakhr al-Din died during **Jalal al-Din Firuz Khalji**'s reign (1290–1296). The position of *kotwal* of Delhi vacated by him was filled by **A'la ul-Mulk** after **'Ala ul-Din Khalji**'s accession (1296).

FAKHR AL-DIN MUBARAK SHAH (?–1350). Fakhr al-Din (also known as Fakhra) was in his early career an armor bearer (*salahdar*) of **Muhammad bin Tughlaq**'s adopted brother Bahram Khan. In 1338, on the death of Tatar Khan, who was until then governing Sonargaon for the **sultan** of **Delhi**, Fakhr al-Din declared himself the sovereign ruler of that part of Bengal with the title Mubarak Shah. He also tried to extend his control to **Lakhnauti** but eventually was expelled from there by Husam al-Din (entitled Nizam al-Din), who had been sent from Delhi to deal with this situation. Fakhr al-Din Mubarak Shah continued to rule at Sonargaon until 1350.

FAKHR AL-DIN MUBARAK SHAH FARRUKHI (?–1242). He was one of the **Tajik** nobles who became very powerful during the reign of Mu'izz al-Din **Bahram Shah** (1240–1242). Under his influence, Bahram Shah was contemplating a wholesale removal of the Turkish slave officers from high positions. Getting an inkling of the planned move, they killed Farrukhi in October 1242. He was the last *wazir* with military inclinations in the **Delhi sultanate** until the rise of the **Tughlaq** dynasty in 1320.

FAKHR AL-DIN MUHAMMAD JAUNA. *See* MUHAMMAD BIN TUGHLAQ.

FAKHR-I MUDDABBIR. Author of *Adab al-harb wa'l-shaja'a* (Modes of Warfare and Chivalry), a military-cum-administrative treatise presented to Shams al-Din **Iltutmish** in 1232. In chapter 26, Fakhr-i Muddabbir reviews the principles and practices of Islamic governments regarding their non-Muslim subjects, and lists the restrictions under which these people should live. According to him, their adornment, dress, and deportment ought to be different from those of Muslims. He also lists the categories of people who should pay *jiziya*. Among them are included idol worshipers (*butparastan*). This would suggest that, in Fakhr-i Muddabbir's view, the Hindus in India qualified as tributary subjects (*zimmis*).

On his mother's side, Fakhr-i Muddabbir descended from Amir Bilga-tagin, the father-in-law of Sultan **Mahmud of Ghazni**. Around 1169–1170, he was residing in **Multan**. In his early years, he is known to have prepared genealogical tables that attracted the notice of **Qutb al-Din Aibak** (1206–1210). Fakhr-i Muddabbir wrote *Adab al-harb wa'l-shaja'a* in India at a time when he was quite old. It was possibly his last work.

FARID AL-DIN MAS'UD GANJ-SHIKAR (1175–1265). He was a **Sufi** of the **Chishti order** who established his hospice at Ajodhan (same as Pttan south of **Dipalpur**). As head of the Chishti order in India, Farid al-Din Mas'ud was the third in direct succession to **Mu'in al-Din Chishti**. He had a large following among the common people in northwestern India. With the passage of time, there grew up a legend of Farid as a saint propagating syncretic ideas. Some of the **Punjabi** compositions imbued with the spirit of *bhakti* are to be attributed to him in *Guru Granth Sahib* (Composition of Gurus) compiled by Guru Arjan Dev in 1604.

Farid al-Din, on the one hand, insisted on the strict observance of the commands of the Islamic *shariah* and, on the other, held music parties and had friendly dialogues with Hindu mendicants that would often offend the more dogmatic members of orthodox *'ulama*. He is also reported to have introduced in the Chishti tradition *namaz-i m'akus* (literally, "inverted prayer," i.e., the practice of offering prayers while suspended in an inverted position), clearly suggesting the influence of Hindu yogis. He is also credited with strengthening the Chishti tendency to keep aloof from rulers and not to accept charity from them.

The most illustrious disciple of Farid al-Din Mas'ud was **Nizam al-Din Auliya**, who continued to lead the Chishti order in India from his hospice at Ghiyaspur near **Delhi**.

FAWAID-AL FAWAD **(Consolation of Heart).** A record of **Nizam al-Din Auliya**'s conversations compiled by his disciple **Hasan Sijzi**, a well-known Persian poet of the 14th century. The book consists of five parts in which the record of conversations at 188 sittings, during 1308–1322, is furnished. Several parts of text were revised and corrected by Nizam al-Din Auliya himself, which speaks of the authenticity of the available text.

FEUDALISM. *See* INDIAN FEUDALISM.

FIREARMS. The earliest gunpowder device, as distinct from naphtha-based pyrotechnics, introduced in India from China during the second half of the 13th century, was a rocket called *hawai* (later named *ban*). From the second half of the 14th century, this rocket came to be used as a weapon of war. The use of gunpowder artillery of a primitive type is roughly dateable from 1440, while similar handguns came only toward the end of the 15th century. European and Ottoman cannons and muskets came to India with the Portuguese (1498) and Babur (1526). *See also KAMAN-I RA'D*; ROCKET.

FIRUZ SHAH BAHMANI (?–1422). He ascended the throne at **Gulbarga** in 1397 after two successors of Ghiyas al-Din Muhammad Bahmani (1377–1397) were deposed, one after the other, in the same year. Firuz Shah proved to be one of the ablest rulers of the **Bahmani** dynasty. Resuming war against **Vijayanagar**, Firuz forced the *raya* to give his daughter in marriage to him and to also surrender Bankapur and other western districts as dowry. The war with Vijayanagar was renewed in 1419–1420 when Firuz tried to occupy the fort of Pangal. In this second war, the Bahmanis were defeated in battle and Firuz had to retire to his capital greatly humiliated, which affected his health adversely. He died in 1422, a totally broken man. Firuz Shah Bahmani contributed significantly to adorning his capital Gulbarga with magnificent buildings. He also constructed a fortified palace at Firuzabad on the bank of the Bhima River.

FIRUZ SHAH KHALJI. *See* JALAL AL-DIN FIRUZ SHAH KHALJI.

FIRUZ SHAH, RUKN AL-DIN (?–1236). At the time of **Iltutmish**'s death in 1236, Firuz was his eldest surviving son. He was then holding the prestigious charge of the commandant (*muqti'*) of **Lahore**, which had been given to him by his father only three years earlier. Firuz came to **Delhi** not long before Iltutmish's death and stayed there, which created a wide impression that he was being groomed for succession. Firuz ascended the throne within a few days of Iltutmish's passing away in 1536. The nobles opted to support Firuz's succession, overlooking Iltutmish's behest favoring **Raziya**.

Firuz Shah, a pleasure-loving youth, left the running of the government in the hands of his mother, Shah Tarkhan, who used her authority to ill treat the ladies of Iltutmish's harem. A large number of Iltutmish's nobles, including the all-powerful *wazir* Nizam ul-Mulk **Junaidi**, turned against the new regime, and a state of rebellion prevailed at Delhi as well as in many of the provinces, which ended only with the proclamation of Raziya as the new **sultan**. Rukn al-Din Firuz was captured and put to death in November 1236. A mob of Raziya's supporters stormed the royal palace and seized Shah Tarkhan as well.

FIRUZ SHAH TUGHLAQ (?–1388). He was the son of **Ghiyas al-Din Tughlaq**'s younger brother Sipah-salar Rajab by a **Rajput** wife. Firuz was proclaimed **sultan** by the nobles present in the army at the time of **Muhammad bin Tughlaq**'s death (1351) in Sind during a military campaign. On reaching **Delhi**, Firuz Shah put to death **Ahmad bin Ayaz Khwaja Jahan**, the *wazir* of the deceased sultan, for having placed a young boy of doubtful ancestry on the throne in the intervening period.

Firuz Shah Tughlaq made a demonstrative break with Muhammad bin Tughlaq's repressive policy toward the nobles. By making assignments (*iqta's*) to continue in most cases from fathers to sons, Firuz Shah enhanced the prestige as well as the clout of the nobles within their charges. There was no serious attempt to reassert the imperial authority over the **Deccan**, Bengal, and Sind. This radically eased the tension between the central authority and nobles administering different provinces.

Firuz Shah is remembered for his building of canals and barrages as a part of an attempt to extend agriculture in the famine-prone tract around Delhi. A positive aspect of his attitude of adhering strictly to the Islamic *shariah* was the abolition of barbaric punishments that were often meted out by earlier **sultans** to captured rebels; the abolition of various taxes not permitted by the sacred law was another positive aspect of this policy. But this policy also resulted in an attempt to impose the discriminatory *jiziya* on Hindus living in the towns, which led to protests by sections of the Hindu population of Delhi. Firuz Shah also demolished some of the temples within the **Delhi sultanate** that had purportedly been built during the previous reigns without the formal permission of the sultans. His demolition of ancient temples at Kangra and **Puri** in the course of military campaigns were, in any case, a naked display of religious intolerance and vandalism that had no justification in the Islamic *shariah*. See also *FUTUHAT-I FIRUZ SHAHI*.

FUTUHAT-I FIRUZ SHAHI. What might be called an "official" history is represented by the copy of **Firuz Shah Tughlaq**'s lengthy inscription that has come down to us as *Futuhat-i Firuz Shahi* (Gifts of Firuz Shah). In this text, the **sultan** himself reveals clearly the orthodox Islamic credentials for which he wished to be remembered, namely, the abandonment of harsh punishments, the abolition of unauthorized taxes, the suppression of deviant forms of Islamic practices, the destruction of newly built Hindu temples, the promotion of conversions to Islam, and the foundation of new mosques and schools.

– G –

GAHADAVALAS. Same as Gahawars. They ruled from their capital **Kanauj** over extensive territories in the Gangetic **Doab** during 1090–1193. The Gahadavala dynasty was founded by Chandradeva, who established himself at Kanauj in 1085 and ruled until 1112. The greatest ruler of the dynasty was **Govindachandra** (1112–1155). The last of the Gahadavalas, **Jaichandra** (1170–1193), was defeated and killed by **Muhammad Ghauri**.

GANDA CHANDELLA (?–1025). He was the ruler of Jejakabhukti from 1002 to 1025. Taking offense when Rajapala, who was the **Pratihara** ruler of **Kanauj**, did not offer resistance to a **Ghaznavid** invading army in 1019, Ganda attacked and killed Rajapala. Subsequently, in 1023, **Mahmud of Ghazni** led an expedition to Jejakabhukti that forced Ganda to surrender the fort of Kalinjar.

GANGAS, EASTERN. The Gangas, who belonged to the Brahman caste, came to control the territory along the east coast in the 10th century. The first ruler of the dynasty in Orissa, Anantvarman Cholagonga (1076–1147), established his authority over the whole tract between the Ganges and Godavari. The temple of **Jagannath** at **Puri** was built under his order near the close of the 11th century. In 1244, Toghan Khan, then controlling **Lakhnauti** for the **sultan** of **Delhi**, was defeated in warfare with the Ganga king of Jajnagar. In 1282, **Balban** led a brief campaign into Orissa that reduced the Ganga ruler, Mal Deo, to submission. Until the end of the 14th century, despite occasional setbacks such as **Firuz Shah Tughlaq**'s invasion of 1360, the Gangas remained firmly established in Orissa. But, during the first three decades of the 15th century, their authority tended to weaken under the pressure of neighboring powers. The last ruler of the dynasty, Bhanudeva, was ousted from the throne by one of his ministers, Kapilandra, in 1435.

GANESH, RAJA. *See* RAJA GANESH.

GARSHASP, BAHA AL-DIN. *See* BAHA AL-DIN GARSHASP.

GESUDARAZ, SAIYED MUHAMMAD HUSAINI (1321–1422). Gesudaraz, a disciple of the **Chishti** saint **Nasir al-Din Chiragh**, came to **Gulbarga** from **Delhi** in 1402–1403 and established his hospice in the vicinity of the royal fort. The reigning **sultan**, Taj al-Din **Firuz Shah Bahmani** (1397–1422), began to doubt Gesudaraz' intellectual credentials, which obliged the latter to move away from there. *M'araj-ul 'ashiqeen* (Ascent to Heaven of Devotees), the earliest text written in **Dakkani**, is ascribed to him.

GHALIB KHAN. The son and successor of Malik Qabul Qur'ankhwan, he was with Prince **Muhammad** in his tussle with **Abu Bakr**

for the throne after **Firuz Shah Tughlaq**'s death in 1388. He was exiled by **Ghiyas al-Din Tughlaq Shah II** (Firuz Shah Tughlaq's immediate successor), which deprived him of the *iqta'* at Samana. But the *amiran-i sada* of the area killed Tughlaq Shah's nominee and restored Ghalib Khan in 1389. In 1397, Ghalib Khan was attacked in Samana by Sarang Khan, the governor of **Dipalpur** for **Mahmud Shah** (1394–1412), then controlling **Delhi** and **Siri**. He appealed to **Tattar Khan**, a supporter of Nusrat Shah at Firuzabad, who came and drove Sarang back to **Multan**. The subsequent career of Ghalib Khan is lost in obscurity.

GHAURIDS. The ruling family of Ghaur (the mountainous region east of Herat) that belonged to the Shansbani clan. The Ghaurids had their capital at Firuz Koh, and they emerged as a power to be reckoned with in the early decades of the 12th century. In 1150, the Ghaurid chief, 'Ala al-Din, sacked Ghazni, winning the sobriquet *Jahansoz* (Incendiary). 'Ala al-Din's nephew, Ghiyas al-Din Muhammad bin Sam (1163–1203), installed his younger brother Muizz al-Din **Muhammad Ghauri** at Ghazni in 1173–1174, who subsequently captured **Multan** (1175–1176) and **Lahore** (1186) and defeated and killed **Prithviraja Chahamana III** (1192). The Ghaurid army consisted of the hill people of Ghaur and tribal cavalry from among the **Khaljis**, a nomadic people from the Bust and Zamindawar tract. Ghiyas al-Din also recruited a large number of Turkish slaves, who were promoted to high administrative and military positions outside Ghaur. Following Muizz al-Din's assassination (1206), the Ghaurid Empire ceased to exist; the conquered territories in India came to be ruled by **Qutb al-Din Aibek**, while another slave noble, **Yildiz**, declared himself a **sultan** at Ghazni.

GHAZNAVIDS. The dynasty of Turkish rulers of Ghazni founded by Subuktigin (977–997), who rose to royalty from the position of a slave. In its heyday under **Mahmud of Ghazni** (998–1030), their empire extended from Ray to Isfahan in Persia and up to Hansi in north India. The Ghaznavids are credited with eliminating **Qaramitah** from **Multan** and Mansura. The Ghaznavids were expelled from Ghazni by the Ghaurids in 1152. The last Ghaznavid ruler, **Khusrau Malik**, surrendered **Lahore** to Muizz al-Din **Muhammad Ghauri** in 1186.

GHIYAS AL-DIN MUHAMMAD SHAH. *See* MUHAMMAD BIN TUGHLAQ.

GHIYAS AL-DIN TUGHLAQ SHAH (?–1325). Originally, he was an important military officer belonging to the race of Qarauna (half **Mongol**) Turks. Under the **Khaljis** (1290–1320), he earned the sobriquet Ghazi Malik for his successes against the Mongols. In 1320, Ghazi Malik led a revolt against **Khusrau Shah**, purportedly for the purpose of restoring the primacy of Islam in the **Delhi sultanate**, which had allegedly been undermined by the neo-Muslim supporters of the **sultan**. Many of the senior nobles, however, were reluctant to join Ghazi Malik; some of them even sided with Khusrau Shah. However, Ghazi Malik was actively assisted in this revolt by the **Khokhar** chiefs, who were Hindus. After the overthrow of Khusrau Shah, Ghazi Malik was persuaded by the nobles to ascend the throne with the title Sultan **Ghiyas al-Din Tughlaq Shah**. During his short reign (1320–1325), the territory of **Telingana** was annexed, **Dehli**'s authority was reestablished over **Ma'bar**, and Bengal was subjugated again. On his return from Bengal in 1325, Ghiyas al-Din Tughlaq was killed in the collapse of a pavilion at Delhi.

GHIYAS AL-DIN TUGHLAQ SHAH II (?–1389). Tughlaq Shah was a great-grandson of **Firuz Shah Tughlaq**, whom the **sultan** had selected as the heir apparent in 1376. This was contested by one of the surviving sons, leading to a sharp factional tussle at the court. Eventually, Tughlaq Shah did ascend the throne with the title Sultan Ghiyas al-Din II Tughlaq Shah in 1388. But, five months later (February 1389), he was killed in a rising by *na'ib-wazir* Rukn al-Din Jund, who placed **Abu Bakr**, a grandson of Firuz Shah, on the throne.

GITAGOVINDA. A 12th-century Sanskrit poem written by **Jayadeva** that portrays the love of the **Vaishnava** god Krishna for his consort Radha. This poem heralds the literary trend of explicit erotic descriptions in the Sanskrit literature.

GORAKH-NATH. He lived sometime in the 11th century and was one of the teachers of the Natha sect, a strictly celibate and austere yogic cult. Gorakh-nath preached mainly in the Punjab and other north-western parts of India. The teachings ascribed to him are in **Apabrahmsha** from northwestern India during the 11th to 13th centuries.

GOVARDHANA. The composer of the well-known Sanskrit work *Chaurapanchashika*, he was patronized by **Lakshamansena**. Govardhana was a contemporary of **Jayadeva**, whom he extols as incomparable in erotic descriptions.

GOVINDARAJA TOMARA (?–1192). The **Tomara** ruler of **Delhi** who fought against **Muhammad Ghauri** in the first battle of **Tarain** (1191) as an understudy of **Prithviraja Chahamana**. On this occasion, Tabarhind, originally a part of the Tomara principality, was recovered. In the second battle of Tarain (1192), Govindraja again fought in a subordinate position to the Chahamana ruler. Prithviraja was captured by the Ghaurids, but Govindaraja was killed in the battle.

GOVINDCHANDRA GAHADAVALA (?–1155). The third **Gahadavala** ruler of **Kanauj**, Govindchandra, who succeeded his father, Madanapala, in 1112, is regarded as the greatest ruler of the dynasty because of the large extant of his domains. His rule extended in the east to Patna and south to the frontier of the Kalachuri kingdom.

GUHILA DYNASTY. The Guhila ruling family of **Chitor** remained undisturbed by the **Ghaurid** conquest until the end of the 13th century. It claimed unbroken descent from a solar race. The founder of the dynasty, Bapa Rawal, is credited with repulsing the Arab invasions of Rajputana in the eighth century. His son, Guhila, gave the ruling dynasty its name. The Guhilas were evicted from **Chitor** by 'Ala al-Din Khalji in 1303, but their authority was restored by Rana **Hammir** (1326–1364) of the **Sisodiya** branch of the family. The famous Rana **Kumbha** (1433–1468) and Rana **Sanga** (1508–1527) belonged to the same dynasty.

GULBARGA. It was an important military outpost of the **Delhi sultanate** in the stretch between **Daulatabad** and **Warangal** and was placed by **Muhammad bin Tughlaq** under the fiscal authority of his Hindu officer **Bhiran** sometime around 1345. Gulbarga was the capital of the **Bahmani kingdom** from the very beginning (1347). The capital was shifted from there to **Bidar** by Ahmad Shah Bahmani (1422–1435).

GURJARAS. A Central Asian tribe that in the sixth century came with the Huns and then moved toward the south and west. The **Pratiharas**, a branch of the Gurjaras, subsequently ruled over parts of Rajputana, Malwa, and the Gangetic Plain until the beginning of the 11th century.

GWALIOR. Situated south of the Yamuna River about 100 kilometers southeast of **Bayana**, Gwalior was controlled by the **Pratiharas** at the time of the **Ghaurid** conquest (1192). It was occupied by the Ghaurids in 1201. **Iltutmish** was the commandant of Gwalior under **Qutb al-Din Aibek** (1206–1210). Subsequently, the **Pratiharas** regained Gwalior for a brief span but were driven out by Iltutmish in 1234. For some time, Gwalior was again in the hands of Hindu rebels, who were suppressed by **'Ala al-Din Khalji** (1296–1316). Toward the end of **Firuz Shah Tughlaq**'s reign (1351–1388), Gwalior came to be ruled by the **Tomaras**. Under the **Saiyid dynasty**, the Tomaras of Gwalior paid tribute to **Delhi**. Gwalior was annexed to the **Lodi** Empire by **Ibrahim Lodi** (1517–1526).

– H –

HAJI MAULA (?–1301). Originally, Haji Maula was a slave of **Fakhr al-Din**, the *kotwal* of **Delhi** during the reign of **Jalal al-Din Firuz Khalji** (1290–1296). Haji Maula tried to seize power at the capital while **'Ala al-Din Khalji** was besieging **Ranthambhor** in 1301. He killed the then *kotwal* and placed on the throne 'Alawi, who was distantly related to **Iltutmish**. Some of the nobles of the previous regime came forward to support him. This revolt was soon suppressed by officers loyal to 'Ala al-Din. Haji Maula was killed in the fighting while 'Alawi was captured and executed summarily. The nobles of the previous regime executed on this occasion included two sons of Fakhr al-Din.

HAMID AL-DIN NAGAURI (1192?–1276). Shaikh Hamid al-Din Nagauri, a disciple of Shaikh **Mu'in al-Din Chishti**, was born at **Delhi** around 1192. He spent his life in a small village in the vicinity of Nagaur and subsisted on income from a small plot of land that he tilled. He led the life of a poor peasant, was a strict vegetarian, and conversed in the local dialect. Insofar as he did not observe the congregational Friday prayers or was prepared to recognize the spiritual virtues of a non-Muslim, Hamid al-Din's attitude in religious matters was rather unconventional even far a **Chishti Sufi**.

HAMID AL-DIN, *NA'IB WAKIL-I DAR*. A son of 'Umdat ul-Mulk *'Ala Dabir*, he was given a high position at **'Ala al-Din Khalji**'s court. In 1300, on the occasion of **Akat Khan**'s failed attempt to assassinate 'Ala al-Din near Tilpat, Malik Hamid al-Din advised the **sultan** to pursue the conspirators without delay. Hamid al-Din was *amir-i kohi* (price controller) in 1301, when he challenged the rebels led by **Haji Maula** at **Delhi** and overpowered them. He was one of the prominent nobles summoned by 'Ala al-Din in 1301 for consultations and was later made *na'ib wakil-i dar*. As **Malik Kafur**'s influence at the court grew during 1306–1315, Hamid al-Din and his brother 'Aziz al-Din were removed from the important positions they were holding, leading to their disappearance from the scene.

HAMID QALANDAR. A disciple of Shaikh **Nasir al-Din Chiragh Dehli**, he compiled his preceptor's discourses, entitled *Khayrul-majalis* (Auspicious Conversations) in 1354. Hamid's father was a disciple of Shaikh **Nizam al-Din Auliya**. The nickname *qalandar* (a wandering dervish) was given to Hamid by the great *shaikh* himself. After migrating to the **Deccan** during **Muhammad bin Tughlaq**'s reign (1325–1351), he remained there attached to Shaikh **Burhan al-Din Gharib**. Hamid returned to **Delhi** in 1353 and met Nasir al-Din Chiragh, which led to his compiling *Khayrul-majalis* a year later.

HAMMIRA DEO, RANA (?–1301). The **Chahamana** ruler of **Ranthambhor**, Rana Hammira (a corruption of Arabic *Amir*), was attacked by **'Ala al-Din Khalji** for his refusal to return a fugitive from the **Delhi** court in 1299. After a prolonged siege during which **Nusrat Khan**, one of the commanders deputed by 'Ala al-Din, was killed, the fort of Ranthambhor was defeated. Rana Hammira Deo was captured and put to death (1301). That this conflict was not perceived by many of the participants as a religious war is borne out by the following anecdote recorded by **Nayachandra Suri**. Mir Muhammad Shah, a **Mongol** neo-Muslim who had fought on Hammira's side, was also captured. While interrogating him, 'Ala al-Din asked, "What would you do if I order your wounds to be dressed and spare your life?" Mir Muhammad Shah's reply was, "If I recover from my wounds, I would have thee slain and raise the son of Hammir Deo upon the throne."

HAMMIRA SISODIYA (?–1364). He belonged to the **Sisodiya** branch of the **Guhila** ruling family of **Mewar**. After **Chitor** was occupied by **'Ala al-Din Khalji** (1296–1316), Hammira and his Sisodiya followers organized resistance to force the installation of a scion of the Guhila ruling family but who was soon overthrown. In 1326, Hammira seized power at Chitor. He ruled over Mewar until 1364. Latter rulers of Mewar traced their ancestry through him.

HAMPI. A town in the Bellary district of the state of Karnataka where extensive remains of a **Vijayanagar** city built by **Harihara I** (1336–1355) in 1336 have been found.

HARIHARA I (?–1355). Harihara and his brother **Bukka** were originally in the service of the **Kakatiya** ruler of **Warangal**. Later they joined the ruler of Kampili and, on the annexation of that principality to the **Delhi sultanate**, were taken prisoners and carried to **Delhi**. In 1336, **Muhammad bin Tughlaq** allowed them to return to Kampili, where they started a rebellion. In the course of this rebellion, the city of **Vijayanagar** was founded on the bank of the Tungabhadra River. Within a decade or so, the two brothers established their control over the whole valley of Tungabhadra. This was achieved by carrying on a ceaseless war against the **Bahmani kingdom**, the sultanate of Madurai, as well as against the remnants of the

Hoyasala kingdom. By the time Harihara I died in 1355, the process of assimilation of Hoyasala chiefs in the Vijayanagar Empire and of dismemberment of the Madurai sultanate had been completed. There is no evidence indicating that Harihara I ever assumed royalty, but he was certainly the founder of the first dynasty that ruled in Vijayanagar down to 1487.

HARSHA (?–1101). Ruler of Kashmir belonging to the first Lohara dynasty who came to the throne in 1089. Harsha is remembered as a tyrant who imposed oppressive taxes. He is also reported to have destroyed temples in order to appropriate the wealth hidden there. His numerous acts of oppression and incest made him very unpopular. The outraged nobles attacked and killed him in 1101.

HASAN GANGU. *See* 'ALA AL-DIN HASAN SHAH BAHMANI.

HASAN NIZAMI. He is sometimes also referred to as Sadr al-Din Muhammad bin Hasan al-Nizami. A native of Nishapur, Hasan Nizami appears to have migrated to **Delhi** prior to 1205–1206. He was commissioned in that year to write a record of the deeds of Muizz al-Din **Muhammad Ghauri**. Hasan Nizami wrote *Taj al-ma'asir*, a rhetorical account of the military exploits of Muizz al-Din Muhamad Ghauri, Qutb al-Din **Aibek**, and **Iltutmish**, prior to 1217.

HASAN QARLUQ, SAIF AL-DIN. A Khwarazmi noble whom **Mingbarni** had deputed to control territories west of the Indus River in 1222. As Khwarazmi authority in the region crumbled under **Mongol** pressure, Hasan Qarluq moved out and established himself in lower Sind. After the elimination of **Qubacha** (1227), Hasan Qarluq submitted to **Iltutmish**. He continued to control a considerable territory in the Punjab until 1236. In that year, following Iltutmish's death, he shifted his allegiance to the Mongol authorities who controlled Ghazni and Ghaur. Hasan Qarluq was operating in the region around **Multan** until 1249. He is reported to have eliminated **Kabir Khan Ayaz**, another Turkish freebooter, from there in that year.

HASAN SIJZI, AMIR. *See* AMIR HASAN SIJZI.

HINDU SHAHI DYNASTY. This dynasty was established by Kallar, a Brahman, who was originally a minister of Lagaturman, the last Turkish ruler of Kabul. Kallar occupied the throne after removing Lagaturman. The dynasty established by Kallar was ruling over Kabul and the Punjab when Subuktigin (977–998) became the **sultan** of Ghazni. Subuktigin's contemporary, Jaipala of the Hindu Shahi dynasty, was forced in 991 to accept his overlordship. The last ruler of the line, Trilochanpala, died fighting against **Mahmud**. By the time **Alberuni** was writing *Kitab al-Hind*, the Hindu Shahi dynasty had already been overthrown.

HOSHANG SHAH GHAURI (?–1432). Originally known as **Alp Khan**, he was the son of **Dilawar Khan Ghauri**. Alp Khan succeeded his father on the throne of Malwa in 1405 with the royal title Sultan Hoshang Shah Ghauri. During his reign of 27 years, Hoshang Shah was continuously involved in hostilities with neighboring powers, particularly the sultanate of Gujarat. On one occasion (1407–1408), Sultan **Muzaffar Shah** (1407–1411) of Gujarat was provoked to invade Malwa and chase away Hoshang from his capital **Mandu**. Hoshang died in 1432, leaving the sultanate of Malwa to his son Muhammad Ghauri, who was soon overthrown and the throne seized by one of his nobles, **Mahmud Khalji**.

HOYASALAS. They began as hill chieftains whose main source of revenue was banditry in the hilly tracts of south India. Gradually, the Hoyasalas moved down into the plains and emerged in the first half of the 12th century as a small kingdom that was a feudatory of the **Chaulukyas**. In the 13th century, the core of their kingdom was represented by **Dorasamudra**. Vishnuvardhana, who converted from **Jainism** to **Vaishnavism** under the influence of **Ramanuja**, contributed to the consolidation of Hoyasala rule. The Hoyasalas were overthrown by Muslim invaders from the north during the reign of **Muhammad bin Tughlaq** (1325–1351).

HUN. The popular name of a **Vijayanagar** gold coin called *pratap* that, because it carried the image of a temple, came to be called pagoda by the Europeans. This coin circulated widely in the **Bahmani kingdom** during the 15th century.

HUSAIN SHAH. *See* 'ALA AL-DIN HUSAIN SHAH.

HUSAIN SHAH SHARQI (?–1505). He was the last king of the **Sharqi** dynasty and came to the throne after the demise of Muhammad Shah Sharqi in 1458. Husain Shah got increasingly involved in the struggle among the successors of the **Saiyid dynasty** for the control of the Gangetic **Doab** and its periphery. This brought Husain Shah into a conflict with **Bahlul Lodi**, who defeated him decisively in 1476. Subsequently, Husain Shah was deprived of all his possessions but allowed to linger on for some time at **Jaunpur**. He finally fled to Bihar and died there as a fugitive in 1505.

– I –

IBN BATTUTA (1304–1369?). Abu 'Abdullah Muhammad Ibn Battuta was born in Tangier (Morocco) in 1304 and belonged to a Berber clan settled in that place. After completing his education at the age of 21 (i.e., around 1325), he proceeded to Mecca. From there, Ibn Battuta traveled to India and reached **Delhi** in 1333. At Delhi, he was appointed a *qazi*, in which position he served during the next seven years. During this time, Ibn Battuta accompanied **Muhammad bin Tughlaq** on his different expeditions, including one leading to his prolonged stay at **Swargadwari**. In 1442, on being ordered to proceed to the court of the **Mongol** emperor of China as Muhammad bin Tughlaq's envoy, he traveled from Delhi to Peking via Coromandal, Malabar, and Ceylon. During his return journey, instead of returning to Delhi, he proceeded directly to Tangier. Ibn Battuta is reported to have died in Tangier around 1369 or 1377. His celebrated travelogue, *Tuhfat al-nuzza* or *A Gift to Those Who Contemplate the Wonders of Cities and the Marvels of Traveling* (popularly known as *Rihla* or *Journey*), furnishes interesting information on India, particularly on happenings at Muhammad bin Tughlaq's court between 1433 and 1442.

IBRAHIM LODI (?–1526). Ibrahim, the eldest son of **Sikandar Lodi** (1489–1517), ascended the throne in 1517 without facing opposition. But soon his brother, Jalal Khan, declared himself a king at **Jaunpur**

and the new **sultan** had to resort to harsh measures to suppress him. After this episode, Ibrahim began to assert his absolute powers without paying heed to the tribal feelings of the Afghan nobles, which led to the widespread disaffection of the nobles. **Daulat Khan Lodi**, the governor of the Punjab, invited **Babur** to invade the **Lodi** Empire, and many other senior nobles started openly defying the sultan. Eventually Babur defeated and killed Ibrahim Lodi in the battle of Panipat (1526), which led to the end of the Lodi Empire.

IBRAHIM SHAH SHARQI (?–1440). He succeeded to the throne of **Jaunpur** after the demise of his elder brother, Mubarak Shah Sharqi, in 1401. Ibrahim, who reigned for 40 years, is generally regarded as the most capable **Sharqi sultan.** He extended the frontiers of his empire by annexing **Kanauj**, **Awadh**, and Bihar and is also reported to have besieged **Delhi** twice; on the second occasion (1437), he forced Sultan **Muhammad Shah** to marry his daughter to Ibrahim's son, Muhammad Khan.

IBRAHIM, SULTAN RUKN AL-DIN. Ibrahim, the son of **Jalal al-Din Firuz Khalji** (1290–1296), proclaimed himself a king with the title Rukn al-Din Ibrahim after the assassination of his father by Malik 'Ali Garshasp (who had proclaimed himself Sultan **'Ala al-Din Khalji**) at **Kara** in 1296. When 'Ala al-Din approached **Delhi**, Rukn al-Din came out with his troops to resist him. In the fighting that took place, Rukn al-Din was defeated. 'Ala al-Din succeeded in winning over most of the Khalji nobles by lavish rewards. Ibrahim, along with other members of the deceased **sultan**'s family, escaped to **Multan** but was captured a few months later. He was blinded and thrown into prison.

IKHTIYAR AL-DIN AITEGIN. *See* AITEGIN, IKHTIYAR AL-DIN.

IKHTIYAR AL-DIN ALP GHAZI (?–1290). Alp Ghazi was an offspring of one of the slaves of Ghiyas al-Din **Balban** (1266–1286). At the time of **Kaiqubad**'s overthrow, he was holding a position in Kasrak as its *muqti'*. Alp Ghazi, who had joined Malik **Chajju**'s revolt against **Jalal al-Din Firuz Khalji**, died fighting for him (1290–1291).

IKHTKIYAR AL-DIN DAULAT SHAH. After the death of Nasir al-Din Mahmud (son of **Iltutmish**) at **Lakhnauti** in 1228, the authority there was usurped by Daulat Shah (also known as Bilge Malik), who was formerly an official deputed from **Delhi**. He declared himself a sovereign ruler of the province. Some of the coins struck by him from **Lakhnauti** have survived.

ILTUTMISH, SULTAN SHAMS AL-DIN (?–1236). A scion of an Il-bari noble family of Central Asia, Iltutmish was reportedly sold away by his jealous brothers to a slave merchant who in turn sold him to Qutb al-Din **Aibek**, then a slave officer of Muizz al-Din **Muhammad Ghauri**. Having distinguished himself in a skirmish with **Khokhar** tribesmen, Iltutmish earned manumission from his master. On Qutb al-Din Aibek's death (1210), Iltutmish, then *muqti'* of Baran (modern Bulandshahr), was proclaimed **sultan** at **Delhi**. In 1216, he defeated **Yildiz** who, because he controlled Ghazni, claimed to be the inheritor of Muizz al-Din **Muhammad Ghauri**'s imperial legacy. A decade later (1227), another rival claimant of royal authority, **Qubacha**, who controlled Sind, was eliminated. In 1229, the caliph of Baghdad recognized him as the **sultan** of Delhi. Besides reasserting his authority in provinces, Iltutmish also subjugated the Hindu chieftains of **Ranthambhor** (1226), **Mandu** (1227), and **Ujjain** (1234). Iltutmish had the distinction of saving northwestern parts of India from **Chingez Khan**'s savagery by resorting to clever diplomacy.

ILYAS SHAH, SULTAN SHAMS AL-DIN (?–1357). In the early 1350s, Ilyas Haji, a former retainer of 'Ali Mubarak, the provincial *'ariz*, overthrew Ikhtiyar al-Din Fakhra and proclaimed himself a **sultan** at **Lakhnauti** with the title Sahms al-Din Ilyas Shah. Later he shifted his capital to Pandua. In 1353, **Firuz Shah Tughlaq** mobilized a large army against him but in the end recognized Ilyas Shah's independence. Ilyas Shah is also reported to have made a plundering raid into the territory of Nepal. The dynasty established by him continued to rule Bengal until 1415 when, after a short phase of anarchy, the throne was captured by **Raja Ganesh**.

'IMAD AL-DIN REHAN. Rehan represented an emerging section of Indian Muslim nobles in the **Delhi sultanate**, some of whom had already come to occupy important positions as early as 1252. In that year, he was one of the officers who collaborated with **Kushlu Khan** in securing **Balban**'s dismissal from the office of *na'ib*. In the ensuing reshuffle, Rehan, who at that time was a slave employed in the royal household, became *wakil-i dar*. **Minhaj Siraj**, who had lost the post of chief *qazi*, bitterly denounced Rehan as a baseborn Indian eunuch. After Balban was restored to his old position in 1254, Rehan lost the position of *wakil-i dar*. A year later (1255), Rehan was appointed *muqti'* of Bahraich. His subsequent career is, however, lost in obscurity.

'IMAD UL-MULK BASHIR. *See* BASHIR, 'IMAD UL-MULK.

IN'AM. Any payment in the **Delhi sultanate**, and also in the successor states, not linked to military obligation, often in the form of a revenue-free grant, was called *in'am*. Under the **Lodi dynasty**, Hindu dignitaries were remunerated for their piety and cooperation with the administration through *in'am* grants. *In'am* grants, like other similar grants, were ordinarily neither transferable nor resumable, but the **sultan** had a right to cancel them. Succession to a grant was to be regulated by the order of the sultan rather than the rules of *shariah*.

INDIAN FEUDALISM. The politico-economic system that existed in India during 800–1200 came to be identified by many modern historians as a type of feudalism that, though not identical with the feudal system of western Europe, did include features such as the presence of a peasantry largely tied to the land and the presence of feudatories that collected revenue from land granted to them by the king and maintained military contingents from this income that they were duty-bound to furnish for the service of the king. This system largely collapsed with the rise of the **Delhi sultanate**, which had a tendency toward centralization of resources as well as of political authority.

IQTA'. A tract, varying from a village to an entire province, assigned in the **Delhi sultanate** to a noble in lieu of his cash salary was known as his *iqta'*. Under the *iqta'* system, land itself was not granted but only the revenue from land was assigned in lieu of salaries. The holder of a larger *iqta'* was called *muqti'*, who maintained cavalry troops from the assigned income and was also responsible for law and order within his charge. A trooper holding a village or a part thereof in lieu of his salary was called an *iqtadar*.

In the early phase of the Delhi sultanate, the practice of rotating *iqta's* did not allow the holders to develop claims over them. After the time of **Firuz Shah Tughlaq** (1351–1388), an *iqta'* would often pass from father to his son.

'ISAMI (1311–?). 'Isami, the author of *Futuh us-salatin* (Gifts of the Sultans), was the son of 'Izz ul-Din 'Isami. He was born in 1311, possibly at **Delhi**. The family was forced to migrate from Delhi to **Daulatabad** in 1327 on **Muhammad bin Tughlaq**'s order. 'Isami's father died on the way. During his stay at Daulatabad, 'Isami was disgusted with what he perceived as the misdeeds and tyranny of Muhammad bin Tughlaq (1325–1351). He planned to migrate to Mecca, but only after writing a history of Muslim rule in India. 'Isami completed this book, *Futuh us-slatin*, which he also calls *Shah-nama-i Hind*, in 1350 at a time when Daulatabad had already come to be ruled by **Hasan Gangu**.

'IWAZ KHALJI, SULTAN GHIYAS AL-DIN (?–1230). After 'Ali Mardan was killed by the **Khalji** officers present at **Lakhnauti** (1211), they raised 'Iwaz Khalji to the position of a ruler with the royal title Sultan Ghiyas al-Din. Taking advantage of **Iltutmish**'s preoccupations in the northwest, 'Iwaz extended his sway toward Bihar, Jajnagar, Tirhut, and Kamurp. When Iltutmish marched to Bengal in 1225, Iwaz submitted to him; but as soon as Iltutmish retired from there, 'Iwaz reverted to his earlier defiance of **Delhi**'s authority. Sometime around 1230, while 'Iwaz was busy in investing a small fort in the vicinity of his capital, an army headed by Iltutmish's son, Nasir al-Din Mahmud, the governor of **Awadh**, occupied Lakhnauti. He subsequently captured 'Iwaz and executed him.

– J –

JAGANNATH TEMPLE. Located at **Puri**, it is a fine specimen of the Kalinga style of architecture. It was built at the site of an old Buddhist monastry in the first half of the 12th century. The temple is for the Hindu god Purushottama. The surviving inscriptions suggest that many of the present structures were erected by Anantavarman Chodagonga

Deva (1076–1147). The temple was partly demolished during **Firuz Shah Tughlaq**'s invasion of Orissa in 1360.

JAHANPANAH. In 1326–1327, **Muhammad bin Tughlaq** enclosed the space separating the fort of **Siri** built by 'Ala al-Din Khalji from the old **Delhi** or Qil'a Rai Pithura. This enclosed space came to be known as Jahanpanah. The palace of one thousand pillars (*hazar sutun*) built by 'Ala al-Din Khalji was located within Jahanpanah.

JAICHANDRA (?–1193). **Gahadavala** ruler of **Benaras** and **Kanauj** who came to the throne in 1173. He controlled a vast territory that extended east to Gaya and Patna. There is a belief that he had turned hostile toward **Prithviraja III** because the latter had eloped with his daughter Sanjogta. Tradition also suggests that Jaichandra had encouraged **Muhammad Ghauri** to invade northwestern India ruled by the **Chahamanas**. Jaichandra was defeated and killed by Muhammad Ghauri at Chanwar (40 kilometers east of **Agra**) in 1193.

JAINS. Followers of the creed preached by Mahavira in the fifth century BCE. They rejected the authority of Vedas and exclusive claims of Brahmans. In medieval India, the Jains were to be found in large numbers in Gujarat and Rajputana. In these regions, many of the traders belonging to the **Baniya** caste professed Jainism. **Muhammad bin Tughlaq** (1325–1351) is mentioned in Jain texts as showing favor to Jain scholars. These texts also praise **Alp Khan**, '**Ala al-Din Khalji's** governor of Gujarat, for permitting the reconstruction of temples destroyed during the Muslim conquest.

JALAL AL-DIN AHSAN SHAH. *See* AHSAN SHAH, JALAL AL-DIN.

JALAL AL-DIN FIRUZ SHAH KHALJI (?–1296). Originally known as Firuz Khalji, he rose to prominence at the head of a group of freeborn nobles belonging to the **Khalji** tribe hailing from the lowlands (*garmsir*) of Ghaur. He served under Prince **Muhammad** in **Multan** and held the office of '*ariz* under **Kaiqubad** (1287–1290). In 1290, he rose to the position of **sultan** with the title Jalal al-Din Firuz Shah Khalji on the support of nobles, many of them Khaljis, who had brought about the deposition of Kaiqubad. This change was deeply resented by many Turkish nobles and Hindu chiefs loyal to the house of **Balban** and led first to Malik **Chajju**'s revolt and then to the conspiracy to bring **Sidi Maula**, an influential dervish of **Delhi**, to the throne. Many leading men of the old regime involved in these episodes escaped unpunished, which added to the dissatisfaction of the younger Khalji officers with the manner in which Firuz was running the sultanate. Taking advantage of this situation, Firuz's nephew and son-in-law Malik 'Ali Garshasp assassinated him at **Kara** in 1296 and proclaimed himself as the new sultan with the title 'Ala al-Din Muhammad Shah Khalji. *See also* ALA AL-DIN KHALJI.

JALAL AL-DIN KASHANI. *See* KASHANI, JALAL AL-DIN.

JALAL AL-DIN MINGBARNI. *See* MINGBARNI, JALAL AL-DIN.

JAMAL AL-DIN 'ALI KHALJI. A Khalji noble who rose to prominence during **Balban**'s reign (1266–1286). He served Balban as his personal *hajib* during Nasir al-Din **Mahmud**'s reign (1246–1266). In 1260, Balban had sent him as his personal representative to the **Mongol** court. After his accession, Balban appointed Jamal al-Din 'Ali a deputy to the *amir-i dad*. He again held the same office under **Jalal al-Din Firuz Khalji** (1290–1296). In the 1296 tussle for the throne, he supported Firuz Khalji's sons but was spared by **'Ala al-Din Khalji**. Jamal al-Din remained for some time in the service of 'Ala al-Din Khalji as well.

JANI, 'ALA AL-DIN. *See* 'ALA AL-DIN JANI.

JATS. A local people of Sind and the Punjab who in the eighth century suffered from the many restrictions imposed on them. Jats were to take dogs with them whenever they went outdoors. This practice was confirmed by a caliphal order. By the middle of the 13th century, the Jats had spread to the east of the Beah River and emerged as a large peasant community in that tract.

JAUNPUR. A town on the bank of the Gomti River about 25 kilometers northwest of Varanasi (**Benaras**), it was founded by **Firuz Shah Tughlaq** (1351–1388) in 1359–1360. He named it after his cousin and predecessor, **Muhammad bin Tughlaq** (1325–1351), whose original name was Muhammad Jauna. In the wake of **Timur**'s invasion (1398), Jaunpur emerged as the capital of the **Sharqi dynasty** and controlled the vast territory that extended roughly from **Kanauj** to Bihar. Jaunpur was finally annexed to the **Lodi** Empire when **Sikandar Lodi** (1489–1517) expelled the last ruler of the Sharqi dynasty from there. The town is famous for the monuments representing the Sharqi style of Indo-Muslim architecture. *See also ATALA MASJID*; MALIK SARWAR SULTANUS SHARQ.

JAYADEVA. An important Sanskrit poet of 12th-century Bengal. He was patronized by **Lakshamansena** (1175–1206). Jayadeva's *Gitagovinda* was a landmark in the history of Sanskrit literature as well as of the spread of **Vaishnava** religious beliefs in Bengal.

JITAL. A billon coin introduced by **Iltutmish** in the **Delhi sultanate**. It contained 3.6 grains of silver. A *jital* carried a lower level of silver content than that of the *dihliwal* that it replaced. Forty-eight *jitals* were equal to 1 silver *tanka*.

JIZIYA. A capitation tax imposed in an Islamic state on non-Muslims who possessed scriptures (*ahl-i kitab*). It was in lieu of military service. Originally this applied to Christians and Jews, but later **Zoroastrians** in Iran and Hindus in Sind were also included. In the **Delhi sultanate**, the *jiziya* was not distinguished from the land tax and tribute from chiefs. In **Firuz Shah Tughlaq**'s time (1351–1388), an attempt was made to collect the *jiziya* as a poll tax on Hindus living in urban centers, but the attempt apparently failed.

JODHA, RAJA (?–1489). Son of Rao Ranmal, a scion of the **Rathor** ruling family of **Marwar**, who had joined the service of the ruler of **Mewar** and was murdered by the nobles there in 1438. After the murder of his father, Jodha returned to Marwar. During the next 15 years, he fought to drive away the Mewar troops and brought the whole of Marwar under his control. In 1459, he founded Jodhpur as his new capital. Under Jodha's rule, Marwar emerged as a powerful rival of Mewar. Even **Rana Kumbha**, who was initially hostile, was forced to make peace with Jodha. Subsequently, Kumbha's successor, Rana Udai, settled the boundary of the two principalities by transferring Sanbhar and **Ajmer** to Marwar.

JUNAIDI, NIZAM UL-MULK (?–1236). He rose to the position of **Iltutmish**'s *wazir* from a humble beginning. He participated in Iltutmish's campaign against **Qubacha** (1227) and joined the nobles' move to oust **Rukn al-Din Firuz Shah** (1236), leading to enthronement of **Raziya Sultan** (1236–1240). Janaidi was one of the **Tajik** nobles killed by the Turkish slaves during the aforementioned episode. Nizam ul-Mulk Junaidi is remembered as a patron of literature. Nur al-Din Muhammad Aufi dedicated his famous collection of stories, *Jawami' ul-hikayat* (Encyclopedic Stories) to him.

– K –

KABIR (1425?–1492). The son of a Brahman widow brought up in a Muslim weaver's family at **Benaras**, Kabir became a disciple of **Ramanand** and also associated with **Sufis**. He rejected the idea of caste as well as schools of Brahmanical philosophy and held that there was no religion without *bhakti*; to him piety, asceticism, fasting, and almsgiving were meaningless in the absence of *bhakti*. Kabir's teachings provoked both Hindus and Muslims, but both communities claimed him as their own after his death. His poems composed in both forms of the spoken language of north India—namely, the Sanskritized Hindi and Persianized Rekhta or Urdu—are preserved in a collection entitled *Bijak* (Seed Drill). Some are also preserved in the holy scripture of the Sikhs, *Guru Granth Sahib* (Compositions of Gurus).

KABIR KHAN AYAZ 'IZZ AL-DIN. One of the 25 Shamsi slaves bought by **Iltutmish** from the family of **Yildiz**'s officer Nasir al-Din Aytemur. In Iltutmish's service, Kabir Khan attained the high position of a *muqti'*. Kabir Khan figured prominently in the revolts leading to **Raziya**'s enthronement (1236) and then fall (1240). After his removal from **Lahore** (1240), Kabir Khan moved to **Multan**

and established an independent principality there. His son, Abu Bakr, is reported to have died in the early 1240s while defending this principality against **Hasan Qarluq**.

KAFUR, MALIK, THE *MUHRDAR* (?–1322). Holding the important office of the keeper of the royal seal *(muhrdar)* under **Khusrau Shah**, he fought on the latter's side during the struggle that ensued from the declaration of *jihad* by Ghazi Malik (later **Ghiyas al-Din Tughlaq**) against Khusrau. After Ghiyas al-Din Tughlaq was proclaimed **sultan** (1320), Malik Kafur joined his service and was appointed *wakil-i dar*. In 1322, while accompanying Prince Ulugh Khan (later **Muhammad bin Tughlaq**) during an expedition against **Warangal**, he was executed for his mutinous behavior.

KAFUR HAZARDINARI, MALIK (?–1316). A personal slave of 'Ala al-Din Khalji purchased in Gujarat at the high price of 1,000 dinars, thus the dubbing *hazardinari*. In his early career, he held the office of *barbeg* and is also reported to have fought against the **Mongols** (1306–1307). In 1310, 'Ala al-Din deputed him to command an army mobilized for the purpose of subjugating the south Indian rulers. Malik Kafur forced the rulers of Deogir and **Warangal** to submit to **Delhi** and pay tribute. In his next campaign (1310–1311), he overran the region to the south of the Krishna River, forcing the rulers of **Hoyasala** and **Pandya** dynasties to submit and pay heavy tribute. During 'Ala al-Din's last illness (1315), Malik Kafur became all powerful as the viceroy *(na'ib)*, which led to a clash with the heir apparent, **Khizr Khan**, and the senior nobles supporting him. While Khizr Khan was imprisoned, his supporter, **Alp Khan**, was executed. After 'Ala al-Din's death (January 1316), Malik Kafur tried to install on the throne an infant son of the deceased ruler. He obviously planned to rule in the name of this person, but his ambition was cut short by his assassination a few days later.

KAIKHUSRAU (?–1287?). The son of Prince **Muhammad**, nominated by **Balban** (1266–1286) as heir apparent toward the end of his reign. On Balban's death (1286), setting aside Kaikhusrau's claim, the nobles brought to the throne **Kaiqubad (Bughra Khan**'s son), who was an incompetent and pleasure-loving youth. Kaikhusrau was subsequently murdered.

KAIMURS, SULTAN SHAMS AL-DIN (?–1290?). Kaimurs was the infant son of **Kaiqubad** in whose favor he abdicated in the beginning of 1290. The Khalji officers seized control of the infant **sultan**, and **Jalal al-Din Firuz Khalji**, the *na'ib*, ran the administration for a few months. Around April–May 1290, Kaimurs was removed from the throne, which now came to be occupied by Jalal al-Din Firuz himself.

KAIQUBAD, SULTAN MUIZZ AL-DIN (?–1290). On **Balban**'s death (1286), the nobles brought to the throne Kaiqubad, one of Balban's grandsons, overlooking Kaiqubad's father, **Bughra Khan**, then the commandant of **Lakhnauti**. Kaiqubad proved to be a worthless ruler who wasted his time in drunken orgies. The administration was left in the hands of nobles, leading to sharp factional fights. Bughra Khan had a meeting with Kaiqubad and advised him to remedy this situation, but it was of no avail. Kaiqubad was finally removed from the throne in 1290 by a group of **Khalji** nobles who set up their leader, **Jalal al-Din Firuz Khalji**, as the **sultan**.

KAKATIYA DYNASTY. The Kakatiyas rose to power in the central part of the **Deccan** during the 12th century when the **Chaulukyas** were fast declining. They came to rule over **Telingana** from their capital at **Warangal**. The Kakatiyas were subjugated in 1310 by **'Ala al-Din Khalji**'s general **Malik Kafur**. Their kingdom was eventually annexed to the **Delhi sultanate** in 1321.

KALAHANA (1100?–?). The historian of Kashmir who belonged to a family of learned Brahmans in the employ of King **Harsha** (1089–1101) of Kashmir. Like his father, Kalahana was a devotee of Shiva but was also respectful toward **Buddhism**. He wrote his celebrated work *Rajatarangini* in the middle of the 12th century.

KAMAL AL-DIN GURG (?–1315). He belonged to a family hailing from Kabul. Kamal al-Din was a noble of high standing in 1315, having Jalor as his *iqta'*. **Malik Kafur** deputed him to pacify an officers' revolt in Gujarat following **Alp Khan**'s removal from there. He also collaborated with Malik Kafur in putting Alp Khan to death. Kamal al-Din was killed in Gujarat while conducting military operations the same year.

KAMAN-I RA'D. Literally meaning "lightening bow," this was the generic name that applied to gunpowder-based artillery and handguns used in different parts of India during the second half of the 15th century. According to contemporary descriptions, these were cast in bronze and threw spherical projectiles. *See also* FIREARMS.

KANAUJ. Writing in the second decade of the 11th century, **Abu Rehan Alberuni** describes Kanauj as the sociopolitical center of the Ganga-Yamuna **Doab.** At the beginning of the century, it was the capital of the **Pratihara** kingdom. Its ruler, Rajapala, submitted to **Mahmud of Ghazni** in 1018. By the end of the century, Kanauj came to be ruled by the **Gahadavalas.** The last ruler of that dynasty, **Jaichandra**, was defeated and killed by Muizz al-Din **Muhammad Ghauri** in 1193, and Kanauj was annexed to the **Ghaurid** Empire. Subsequently, Kanauj was always an important *iqta'.* Under **Sikandar Lodi** (1489–1517), the *sarkar* Kanauj yielded around 13.663 million Bahluli *tankas* per annum.

KARA. Situated on the bank of the Ganges River about 56 kilometers west of its confluence with the Yamuna, Kara was already a part of the **Delhi sultanate** under **Iltutmish** (1211–1236). In 1290, at the time of **Jalal al-Din Firuz Khalji**'s accession, Kara was held by Malik **Chajju**, who subsequently revolted and could only be suppressed with some difficulty because he commanded the support of a large number of Hindu chiefs of the region. In 1296, 'Ali Garshasp, then holding Kara as his military charge, assassinatated his uncle, Jalal al-Din Firuz Khalji, who had come to visit him there, and declared himself **sultan** with the title **'Ala al-Din Khalji.** Kara subsequently remained an important *iqta'* and was generally referred to along with **Awadh** as representing the territory of Hindustan within the Delhi sultanate.

KARKHANA. This was a workshop that produced articles required for the royal household and court as well as for the use of the **sultan**'s armed retainers. The workforce in these workshops comprised enslaved as well as hired labor.

KARMATHIANS. *See* QARAMITAH.

KASHANI, JALAL AL-DIN. A **Tajik** by origin, Kashani was the grand *qazi* in 1242 under Sultan **Bahram Shah** (1240–1242). He became a party to the conspiracy of slave nobles led by Badr al-Din Sonqur against that **sultan**. After Sonqur's execution, Kashani was dismissed and banished from **Delhi**.

KASHANI, QAZI JALAL. He was serving as an ordinary *qazi* at **Delhi** in 1292 where he was implicated in the affair of **Sidi Maula** and was sent to Badaun as the local *qazi*.

KATEHR. The territory east of **Delhi** across the Ganges that later came to be called Rohilkhand was known in the **Delhi sultanate** as Katehr. It was first subdued by **Iltutmish** in 1227. Roughly until **Balban**'s rise to kingship (1266), Katehr continued to be largely controlled by defiant Hindu chiefs. Several important places located between the Ganges and Ram Ganga had come to be garrisoned with the Delhi sultanate's troops during Nasir al-Din **Mahmud Shah**'s reign (1246–1266). Balban (1266–1286), followed by **Jalal al-Din Firuz Khalji** (1290–1296), conducted sustained military campaigns in the region, leading to its pacification to the point that **'Ala al-Din Khalji** (1296–1316) could include a large part of Katehr, like other less recalcitrant districts, in the region subjected to the land tax based on measurement of land. **Firuz Shah Tughlaq** (1351–1388) had reserved a large tract in Katehr for the royal chase. During the 15th century, under the **Saiyid dynasty**, Katehr was, however, again referred to in history books as a vast *mawas* controlled by local chiefs.

KHAJORAHO. About 220 kilometers southeast of **Gwalior**, it is famous for Hindu and **Jain** temples built under **Chandella** rulers around 1000. The human figures outside the flat ground of the temples are erotic and sensuous. These represent an amalgam of classical and medieval styles of Indian sculpture.

KHALISAH. In the **Delhi sultanate** as well as in the regional sultanates of the 15th century, the income from the *khalisah* or crown lands was reserved for the **sultan**, that is, for the central treasury. The *khalisah* revenues were administered directly by the central *wazir*.

KHALJI DYNASTY. The dynasty founded by **Jalal al-Din Firuz Khalji** (1290–1296) that continued to rule the **Delhi sultanate** until 1220 is known as the Khaljis. The most illustrious ruler of the line was **'Ala al-Din Khalji** (1296–1316). The rise of the Khaljis marked the end of Turkish slaves' rule that had continued since **Iltutmish's** time (1211–1236). *See also* GHAURIDS; QUTB AL-DIN MUBARAK KHALJI; MALIK KAFUR.

KHAMBAYAT. *See* CAMBAY.

KHAN-I JAHAN, QIWAM UL-MULK MALIK MAQBUL (?–1370). Khan-i Jahan Maqbul was a Hindu convert from **Telingana** who was brought to **Delhi** in 1322 as a prisoner. Under **Muhammad bin Tughlaq** (1325–1351), he was entitled Qiwam ul-Mulk and appointed to govern **Multan** in 1327. In 1344, he briefly served in Telingana and then became a deputy governor of Gujarat, where he played a prominent role in the suppression of the *amiran-i sada*. **Firuz Shah Tughlaq** (1351–1388) raised him to the position of principal minister (*wazir*) in the central government, indicated by the new title *Khan-i Jahan*. Much of the peace and prosperity of Firuz's early reign may be ascribed to Maqbul's sage advice to the **sultan** and his efficient handling of finances. After his death in 1370, the office and title were transferred to his son.

KHANQAH. A hospice or monastery where **Sufis** belonging to a particular order would reside or assemble. The organization of a *khanqah* was headed by a senior member of the order authorized by his preceptor to do so. The expenses of the organization, which often included a mosque, residential spaces, and a free kitchen, would ordinarily be met from voluntary contributions and occasionally also from income yielded by land grants made by rulers or nobles.

KHARAJ. The land tax collected in an Islamic state. In the **Delhi sultanate**, it was often called *kharaj-i jiziya*, denoting that the land tax was treated as the equivalent to the *jiziya* prescribed for non-Muslim subjects. **'Ala al-Din Khalji** (1296–1316) collected the *kharaj* at the rate of one half of the produce by measurement of land under cultivation and fixation of yield per standard unit (*wafa'-i biswa*).

KHAZAIN UL-FUTUH. This book contains an account written by **Amir Khusrau** of **'Ala al-Din Khalji**'s military campaigns. It also furnishes a reliable narrative of developments at the court. The *Khazain ul-futuh* represents Khusrau's prose in its most organized and elegant form. The first passage refers to the conquest of **Ranthambhor** (1301).

KHIZR KHAN (?–1316). Ala al-Din Khalji's eldest son, he was appointed heir apparent after the conquest of **Chitor** (1303). Then only seven years old, Khizr Khan was appointed to govern Chitor with the help of a senior noble, Malik Shahin. Khizr fell in love with and married **Deval Rani**, the daughter of Rai Karan Baghela, in 1307. Deval Rani was then staying in the royal harem with her mother, Kamla Devi. During 'Ala al-Din's fatal illness in 1315, Khizr Khan and his mother fell out of favor with **Malik Kafur**, the *na'ib*. Malik Kafur obtained orders from 'Ala al-Din for imprisonment of Khizr Khan in the fort of **Gwalior**. In 1316, Khizr Khan was executed on the order of **Qutb al-Din Mubarak Khalji** (1316–1320).

KHIZR KHAN, SULTAN (?–1421). The first ruler of the **Saiyid dynasty**, he was the son of Sulaiman, the commandant of **Multan** under **Firuz Shah Tughlaq** (1351–1388). Succeeding his father at Multan, he was entitled first Nasir ul-Mulk and later, in 1389, Khizr Khan. In the beginning of Sultan **Mahmud Shah Tughlaq**'s reign (1394–1412), the *muqti'* of **Dipalpur**, Sarang Khan, occupied Multan, taking Khizr Khan a prisoner. Escaping from imprisonment, he joined Amir **Timur**, who confirmed him as the commandant of Multan and Dipalpur. He was practically an independent ruler of these places following Timur's invasion. In 1405, Khizr Khan defeated **Mallu Iqbal Khan**, who had usurped authority at **Delhi**. On Mahmud Tughlaq's death (1412), Khizr Khan came to rule from Delhi in 1414. Subsequently, he firmly suppressed the local chiefs in **Katehr**, Etawa, **Gwalior**, and Mewat for collecting revenue in the form of tribute. He recruited many **Afghan** chiefs into his army who were mostly stationed in the Punjab, and Sultan Shah, an uncle of **Bahlul Lodi** (1451–1489), was one of them.

KHOKHARS. A Rachnao Doab tribe inhabiting the large tract that had cooperated with Muizz al-Din **Muhammad Ghauri** when he came to besiege **Lahore** in 1180. They were later suppressed by him harshly. In 1206, Muhammad Ghauri was assassinated by a Khokhar tribesman.

KHUSRAU MALIK (?–1186). The last **Ghaznavid** ruler who came to the throne at **Lahore** in 1160. In 1180, **Muhammad Ghauri** evicted Ghaznavid troops from Peshawar and then besieged Lahore, forcing Khusrau Malik to submit. Ghauri also established an outpost at Sialkot after suppressing the **Khokhars**. Subsequently, Khusrau Malik besieged Sialkot with the help of the Khokhars, provoking Ghauri to return to the Punjab in 1186. After a brief siege, Khusrau Malik surrendered and Lahore was annexed to the Ghaurid Empire. Khusrau was executed the same year at Firuz Koh.

KHUSRAU SHAH, SULTAN NASIR AL-DIN (?–1320). Originally known as Hasan, he was a neo-Muslim belonging to the warrior clan of **Parwaris** present in large numbers in the royal contingent under **Qutb al-Din Mubarak Khalji** (1316–1320). He became a favorite of Mubarak Khalji, who gave him the title Khusrau Khan. In 1320, Khusrau Khan killed Mubarak Khalji and ascended the throne with the title Nasir al-Din Khusrau Shah. In staging this coup d'état, Khusrau Khan was helped by his fellow clansmen. During his rule of two months or so, an impression was created that the Hindu officers related to Khusrau Khan were being favored. Some of them were also accused of offending the religious susceptibilities of the Muslims. However, many of the senior nobles of the previous regime, all of them Muslims, continued to side with Khusrau Shah until he was eventually overthrown. Even Shaikh **Nizam al-Din Auliya** did not feel any harm in accepting a present of five lac *tankas* from him, which the *shaikh* distributed among the needy. Ghazi Malik (**Ghiyas al-Din Tughlaq**), however, projected his revolt against Khusrau Shah as a religious war. Within two months of his rise to the throne, Khusrau Shah was defeated by Ghazi Malik near Sirsa. He was captured and executed summarily.

KHWAJA. The designation of an accountant appointed along with the *muqti'* to manage the land revenue of a territory. In the **Delhi sul-**

tanate, this arrangement gained currency from **Balban**'s reign (1266–1286) onward.

KHWAJA JAHAN, AHMAD AYAZ. *See* AHMAD BIN AYAZ KHWAJA JAHAN.

KHWAJA JAHAN, MALIK SARWAR SULTANUS SHARQ. *See* MALIK SARWAR SULTANUS SHARQ.

KHWAJA KHATIR AL-DIN. A prominent **Tajik** noble serving in the finance department during **Balban**'s reign (1266–1286). After **Kaiqubad**'s accession (1287), he was raised to the position of *wazir* but soon lost the coveted position on account of Malik **Nizam al-Din**'s hostility. With **Jalal al-Din Firuz Khalji**'s rise to sovereignty in 1290, Khwaja Khatir once again came to occupy the office of *wazir*. What happened to Khwaja Khatir subsequently is not known. He, like many other nobles of Balban's time, disappeared from the scene after Malik **Chajju**'s revolt.

KILOKHRI. A satellite township established on the bank of the Yamuna River about 6.5 kilometers northwest of **Delhi** (Qila' Rai Pithura) sometime during **Iltutmish**'s reign (1211–1236). In 1259, Nasir al-Din **Mahmud Shah** (1246–1266) received Huleku's envoy at Kilokhri. Sultan Muizz al-Din **Kaiqubad** (1287–1290) formally shifted his residence to this new township. But after the building of fortified townships like **Siri, Jahanpanah**, and **Tughlaqabad** in the vicinity of Delhi in the first half of the 14th century, Kilokhri gradually lost its importance.

KISHLI KHAN, SAIF AL-DIN AIBEK (?–1259). He was the brother of **Balban** and became prominent during Nasir al-Din **Mahmud Shah**'s reign (1246–1266). After **Kushlu Khan** (also known as *Balban-i Kalan* [Elder Balban]) was ousted from Nagaur in 1246, the place was conferred on him. But on Balban's dismissal from the position of *na'ib*, Kishli Khan was deprived of his *iqta'* at Nagaur. His fortunes again brightened with Balban's regaining his position in 1255; he was appointed *amir-i hajib* and *muqti'* of Meerut. On his death in 1259, the position of *amir-i hajib* went to his son 'Ala al-Din Muhammad.

***KITAB AL HIND* (Describing India).** A famous Arabic text written by Abu Rehan **Alberuni** (973–1048) wherein he comments on Indian sciences, Hindu religious beliefs, customs, and social organization. These topics were studied by him from consultation with authoritative Sanskrit texts with the help of scholarly Brahmans then present in the **Ghaznavid** towns of Ghazni and **Lahore**.

KONARAK SUN TEMPLE. Known as the Black Pagoda for its darkish color, this temple is located at Konarak on the Orissa coast 20 kilometers northeast of **Puri**. It was built by the **Ganga** ruler Narasimha I (1238–1264). The temple is designed in the shape of a huge chariot drawn on exquisitely carved wheels by a team of horses. Each part of the structure is harmoniously blended, and the intricate treatment of the walls with figures and decorative motifs vibrates with a unique rhythm.

***KOTWAL*.** Literally meaning the "portal of a fort," the term applied in medieval India to the commandant or magistrate of a township. **Fakhr al-Din**, the *kotwal* of **Delhi** at the time of **Balban**'s demise (1286), played a key role in bringing **Kaiqubad** to the throne.

KRISHNA DEVA RAYA (?–1529). The **Vijayanagar** ruler belonging to the Saluva dynasty who came to the throne in 1509. He was a very cultured man; although a Vaishnava, Krishna Deva was tolerant toward other faiths. He is remembered as a patron of Sanskrit and **Telugu** literature. Krishna Deva defeated a rebellion by the **Ganga** ruler of Ummattur (Mysore) and also captured Udayagiri and several other forts from the ruler of Orissa (1513). He went to war against Bijapur in 1520, forcing Ismail 'Adil Shah to agree to humiliating terms. *See also AMUKTAMALYADA.*

KUMBHA, RANA (?–1468). The son of the **Sisodiya** ruler of **Mewar**, Mokal (1421–1433), he came to the throne in 1433. Kumbha is credited with ending the **Rathor** interference in Mewar and also for forcing the chiefs of Bundi, Kota, Chatsu, Amber, Narwar, Dungerpur, and Sarangpur to submission. Kumbha defeated **Mahmud Khalji** (1436–1469) at Sarangpur in 1437 and built a victory tower at **Chitor** to commemorate this victory. Subsequently, Mewar suffered reverses at the hands of the Malwa ruler, leading to the loss of Gagaraun (1444), **Ranthambhor** (1446), and **Ajmer** (1455). An anti-Mewar alliance of the Malwa and Gujarat sultanates in 1457 aggravated the military challenge faced by Rana Kumbha, who tried to hold his own by adopting a defensive policy. He was assassinated by his son Uda in 1468. Rana Kumbha, an accomplished scholar, was the author of *Rasik priya*, which was a commentry on *Gitagovinda*. He was also known for his command of a number of languages. Several temples, tanks, gateways, and other structures erected by him are extant at Chitor.

KUSHLU KHAN, BAHRAM-I AYBA (?–1327). His father was one of the companions of **'Ala al-Din Khalji** (1296–1316). Kushlu himself was the *muqti'* of Uchch at the time of Ghazi Mulik's revolt against **Khusrau Shah** (1320). For his important role in the overthrow of Khusrau Shah, Kushlu Khan continued to serve in important positions under the first two **Tughlaq** sultans until he revolted against **Muhammad bin Tughlaq** (1325–1351) in 1327. He was then holding a posting in Sind, and Muhammad bin Tughlaq himself marched there to engage and kill him in that year. *See also* GHIYAS AL-DIN TUGHLAQ.

KUSHLU KHAN, 'IZZ AL-DIN BALBAN. A slave noble who played an important role in the factional fights that continued during the reigns of **Iltutmish**'s successors down to 1255. To distinguish him from Baha al-Din Balban (later Sultan Ghiyas al-Din **Balban**), he was often referred to as *Balban-i Kalan* (Elder Balban). Following **Bahram Shah**'s overthrow (1242), he made an attempt to have himself proclaimed a **sultan** but was not successful because a majority of the slave nobles supported **'Ala al-Din Mas'ud**. During Nasir al-Din **Mahmud Shah**'s reign (1246–1266), Kushlu Khan was considered a rival of Baha al-Din Balban, the *na'ib*. He played an active role in the removal of Balban from power in 1252–1253 and secured for himself lucrative *iqta's* in Sind after **Sher Khan** (Balban's cousin) was removed from there. On Balban's restoration (1253), Kushlu Khan continued to defy the *na'ib* in Sind, where he was joined by **Qutlugh Khan**, another influencial opponent of Balban, in 1257. The two tried to seize power at **Delhi** but failed. At this point, Kushlu Khan made common cause with the **Mongols** and turned Sind into a Mongol encampment. Still later, he is reported to have established himself at Uchch and **Multan** as an independent ruler. Kushlu Khan died in Sind sometime during Balban's reign (1266–1286).

– L –

LAHORE. Situated on the bank of the Ravi River, Lahore became the provincial capital of the **Ghaznavids** in the Punjab after **Hindu Shahi** rule was swept aside by **Mahmud of Ghazni** in 1008. It was captured by **Muhammad Ghauri** in 1186. Lahore remained a part of the **Delhi sultanate** until 1388. For a brief period during 1254–1257, it was under **Mongol** occupation but was soon regained. During the 15th century, Lahore came to be controlled from **Delhi** only following the rise of the **Lodi dynasty**.

LAKHNAUTI. Located north of Nadia, near the present day site of Gaur in the Malda district of West Bengal, Lakhnauti was founded by **Lakshamansena** (1175–1206). After sacking Nadia, **Muhammad bin Bakhtiyar** Khalji occupied Lakhnauti and made it his seat of power (1204–1205). From this time onward, until the end of the 14th century, the territory governed from Lakhnauti was bound by Sundarbans on the south, by the Brahmputra River on the east, and by the Kosi River on the West. In the **Delhi sultanate**, the province of Lakhnauti came to be perceived as very rich. As the nobles administering the province had the tendency to rebel, Lakhnauti came to be called *Lughlakpur* (city of insurrection).

LAKSHAMANSENA (?–1206). A Sena ruler of Naida, who came to the throne in 1175, he was famous for his justice and fairness as well as patronage of literature. He was ousted from Nadia by **Muhammad bin Bakhtiyar** Khalji in 1204. Subsequently, Lakshamansena continued to control **Lakhauti** for about two years.

LEKHAPADDHATI (system of accountancy). A collection of model Sanskrit documents from the 9th–15th centuries mostly belonging to presultanate Gujarat. These documents provide information on the administration, particularly the judicial system and taxation, as well as social aspects like the caste system, slavery, and position of women. The name of the compiler is not known.

LODI DYNASTY. It was established by **Bahlul Lodi** (1451–1489), who proclaimed himself a **sultan** at **Delhi** after it had been vacated voluntarily by the last **Saiyid** ruler in 1451. This dynasty continued to rule in a large part of north India until 1526. The second ruler of the dynasty, **Sikandar Lodi** (1489–1517), annexed the **Sharqi** kingdom (1492) and recruited many non-**Afghans**, including several Rajput chiefs, into his nobility. **Ibrahim Lodi**, who had alienated many of his Afghan nobles, was defeated and killed by **Babur** in 1526. *See also* BHUWA, MIAN; UMAR KHAN SARWANI.

– M –

MA'BAR. The name given by Muslim historians to the **Tamil** country south of the Krishna River, which at the time of **Malik Kafur**'s invasion (1310–1311) was ruled by the **Pandya dynasty**.

MAGHRIBI. Name of a particular type of mangonel used in the **Delhi sultanate** that perhaps originated in the western parts of North Africa, called *maghrib* in the Islamic parlance.

MAHIPALA (?–1038). The **Pala** ruler of Bengal, who came to the throne around 988, he is credited with reviving the fortunes of the kingdom. He established Pala authority in eastern Bengal and recovered northern Bihar. Mahipala repaired many **Buddhist** sacred structures at Sarnath and **Nalanda** in 1028. In the west, his kingdom extended up to **Benaras**. It was during his reign that **Rajendra Chola** invaded Bengal. His name is also associated with a large number of tanks and towns in Bengal. On Mahipala's death in 1038, his son, Nayapala, ascended the throne.

MAHMUD BEGARHA (?–1513). Sultan of Gujarat who reigned during 1459–1513. He subdued the nobles and reorganized the administration, creating four regional commands that worked to ensure firm control by the sultan over the local authorities. The hereditary chiefs were forced to accept military service in return for *banth*, a one-fourth share of their original revenues. Several powerful Hindu chieftainships were eliminated, the last of them being Champanir (1484), where the use of gunpowder artillery played a decisive role. The enhanced military clout of the Gujarat sultanate was manifested in its participation in the joint naval expedition of the Mamluks and several Indian states that defeated the Portuguese near Chaul (1508).

MAHMUD GAVAN (?–1481). The famous **Bahmani** minister Mahmud Gavan, an Iranian by origin, emerged by 1464 as the most influential state functionary under Sultan Muhammad Shah (1463–1482). Gavan contributed to removing a threat from the Malwa ruler as well as to the recovery of Balgaon and Goa from **Vijayanagar**. He introduced wide-ranging reforms in the civil and military administration. Gavan was counted among the foreigners (*afaqis*) intensely disliked by local nobles (*deccanis*). In 1481, some of his opponents produced a forged letter containing treasonable matter, which provoked the **sultan** into having him executed. Gavan was a very learned man; his private library at **Bidar** consisted of 3,000 rare books, while his book *Riyaz al-insha* (Garden of Letters) is counted among the excellent specimens of Persian prose.

MAHMUD KHALJI (?–1669). A minister of **Hoshang Shah** (1405–1436) who seized the throne of Malwa after Hoshang's death (1436) and ruled until 1469. Throughout his reign, Mahmud Khalji was constantly at war with the neighboring powers. He is reported to have suffered a defeat at the hands of Rana **Kumbha** of **Mewar** in 1437 but later succeeded in gaining from Mewar important strongholds such as Gagaraun (1444), **Ranthambhor** (1446), and **Ajmer** (1455). Mahmud Khalji's designs to grasp territories in the **Deccan** were thwarted by **Mahmud Gavan**'s tactful invitation to **Mahmud Begarha** (1459–1513) to intervene (1466). The dynasty founded by Mahmud Khalji continued to rule Malwa until 1536.

MAHMUD OF GHAZNI (971–1030). On succeeding his father, Subuktigin (977–998), on the throne in 998, he obtained recognition of his sovereignty by the Abbasid caliph, impelling him to perceive himself in the role of a religious warrior. Between 1000 and 1026, Mahmud carried out 17 plundering raids in India, including the one in which the **Somanath** temple on the seashore in Kathiawar was destroyed (1025). The wealth plundered by Mahmud in India was used for his military campaigns in Central Asia and Persia. Hindu soldiers recruited from among defeated Indians were used in some of these campaigns. He neither established his direct rule in any part of India beyond the Punjab nor did he try to convert defeated Hindu chiefs and their subjects to Islam. There were many among the contemporary Islamic elite, including the famous Abu Rehan **Alberuni**, who did not approve of Mahmud's plundering raids into India.

MAHMUD SHAH, SULTAN NASIR AL-DIN (?–1266). The youngest son of **Iltutmish**, Nasir al-Din Mahmud was brought to the throne by the nobles in 1246. A person of retiring disposition, he left the entire administration to his *na'ib*, Baha al-Din Balban (later Sultan Ghiyas al-Din **Balban**). Throughout his long reign, the pious **sultan** was much preoccupied with his religious and literary hobbies. He died in 1266; there is some basis for suspecting that he was poisoned by his ambitious *na'ib*.

MAHMUD SHAH TUGHLAQ, SULTAN NASIR AL-DIN (?–1412). Mahmud, the son of **Ghiyas al-Din Tughlaq II** (1388–1389), was brought to the throne by the nobles in 1394. At the time of **Timur**'s invasion (1398), Mahmud was the nominal **sultan** at **Delhi** while real power was exercised by the *wazir*, **Mallu Iqbal Khan**. Mahmud escaped to Gujarat but was recalled to Delhi by Mallu Iqbal in 1401. Accepting a pension from Mallu Iqbal Khan, Mahmud retired to **Kanauj** but returned to Delhi after Mallu Iqbal Khan was killed by **Khizr Khan** (1405), and continued to reside there as the nominal **sultan** until his death in 1412.

MAHUAN. An interpreter attached to the Chinese envoy Cheng Ho, who visited Bengal in 1406. In his report of this mission, *Ying-gai-Shang-tan* (1433), Mahuan records interesting information on the socioeconomic conditions of Bengal in the beginning of the 15th century.

MAITHILI. One of the dialects of Bihar that evolved from the **Prakrit** earlier spoken in Magadha. This dialect was associated with the **Vaishnava** cult and *bhakti* literature.

MALAYALAM. Originating as a dialect of **Tamil**, it evolved into an independent language. The infusion of linguistic forms brought from overseas lands and centuries of political isolation from the Tamil region contributed greatly to its development as a distinct language. In the 14th century, **Amir Khusrau** mentions Malayalam as one of major Indian languages.

MALIK KAFUR. *See* KAFUR HAZARDINARI, MALIK.

MALIK SARWAR SULTANUS SHARQ (?–1399). Malik Sarwar, the founder of the **Sharqi dynasty**, was appointed governor in 1394 of the eastern province of **Jaunpur** by Sultan **Mahmud Shah Tughlaq** (1394–1412). He succeeded in subjugating the local chiefs of **Jaunpur** as well as the **Doab** region up to the confines of **Delhi**, which earned him the title *Malikus Sharq* (Ruler of the East). Taking advantage of the collapse of the central authority following **Timur**'s invasion (1398), Malik Sarwar came to rule at Jaunpur in an independent capacity. After his death in 1399, his son and successor Malik Karanfal declared himself a **sultan** with the title **Mubarak Shah Sharqi**.

MALLU, IQBAL KHAN (?–1405). Mallu, entitled Iqbal Khan, was a slave of Nasir al-Din **Muhammad Shah Tughlaq** (1390–1394) who figured prominently in the factional tussle that broke out after **Mahmud Shah**'s accession in 1394. At the time of **Timur**'s invasion (1398), he was controlling **Delhi** as the *wazir* of Mahmud Shah. He was ousted from there by the invader but returned soon after Timur's withdrawal. Mallu Khan was killed in 1405 in a battle with **Khizr Khan**, the then governor of **Multan**.

MANDAHARS. A warrior tribe settled in Kaithal and the surrounding tract during the 13th century. In late 1280, Jalal al-Din Khalji (later

Jalal al-Din Firuz Khalji), then *muqti'* of Kaithal, was wounded while conducting operations against the Mandahars. The Mandahars continued to defy the central authority until the beginning of 16th century.

MANDALAMS. Provinces into which the **Chola** Empire was divided under **Rajaraja** (985–1014). There were in all eight provinces. Each one of them was divided into *valanadus* and *nadus*. The more important *mandalams*, like Vengi, were placed under the charge of princes.

MANDU. An ancient town in the Narbada valley. The ruler of Malwa, **Dilawar Khan** (1401–1405), shifted his capital from Dhar (**Ujjain**) to Mandu, where it remained for the next hundred years or so. Several important buildings erected by Malwa **sultans** survive at Mandu; Jahaz Mahal, a palace, is the most fascinating.

MAPPILAS. The present-day Mappilas (or Malabar) Muslims are descendants of Arab settlers who were welcomed as traders by local rulers. **Ibn Battuta** records the presence of a large Muslim population in Malabar during the 14th century, suggesting that by then the Mappila settlement had become quite noticeable.

MARATHI. The language spoken in the western **Deccan** that flourished under the patronage of the **Yadava** rulers of Deogir. The newly risen *bhakti* cults spreading from the Tamil country to the western Deccan were propagated through the medium of the Marathi language. During the medieval period, new expositions of Puranic texts were also produced in Marathi.

MARCO POLO. The scion of a noble family of Venice who started on his second journey to the east in 1271. He went to China by land route via Hormuz, reaching Kublai's court in 1277. Sailing from China in 1292, Marco Polo reached India and remained there for two years. He visited south India during the latter part of the **Chola** rule and comments on the profit earned by Arab horse traders by supplying warhorses to Indian states. He also refers to the rich trade of Gujarat, then a province of the **Delhi sultanate**. Marco Polo identifies the **Qarauna** Turks (the group to which **Tughlaq dynasty** belonged) as "sons of Indian mothers by Tartar [i.e., **Mongol**] fathers."

MARWAR. The western part of Rajasthan stretching from Bikaner in the north to Mount Abu separated from **Mewar** by the southern spurt of the Aravali range is identified as Marwar. Until the end of the 12th century, southern Marwar was under the control of the **Chaulukyas** of Gujarat, while much of the central parts were under the sway of the **Chahamanas.** Marwar emerged as a distinct state during the 15th century under a **Rathor** ruling clan that claimed descent from the **Gahadavalas** evicted by the **Ghaurids** from **Kanauj** in 1193. From the very beginning, Marwar had to face the hostility of Mewar. **Jodha** (1438–1489) asserted Marwar's independence by expelling Mewar troops from there. He also founded Jodhpur (1459) as the capital of Marwar.

MAS'UD SHAH, SULTAN 'ALA AL-DIN. *See* 'ALA AL-DIN MAS'UD SHAH.

MATHURA. A famous pilgrimage center of the **Vaishnavas**, Mathura was plundered by **Mahmud of Ghazni** in 1017. It came to be controlled by the **Delhi sultanate** in the first half of the 13th century. **Iltutmish** placed Mathura under the charge of the *muqti'* of **Bayana**. This arrangement continued until **Balban**'s reign (1266–1286). The presence of an inscription of '**Ala al-Din Khalji** (1296–1316) at Mathura indicates that by then it had come to be administered from **Delhi**.

MATLA'-I SA'DAIN WA MAJM'-I BAHRAIN **(Ascendance of the Auspicious and Concourse of Waters).** A history of the Timurids from 1304–1305 to 1470 in two parts compiled by '**Abd al Razzaq**. It also contains the author's experiences of his journey to **Calicut** and **Vijayanagar** during 1441–1444. *See also* ZAMORIN OF CALICUT.

MAWAS. A tract inhabited by recalcitrant chiefs and peasants who would not pay land revenue to the officials of the **sultan** without a fight. During the 13th century, one such region was the trans-Ganges tract, where **Balban** campaigned in 1256 pursuing the rural rebels. Often the *mawas* tracts served as a refuge for rebellious nobles of the **Delhi sultanate**.

MEDHATITHI. A 10th-century writer of commentaries on the *Puranas*. His commentaries were subsequently used on a wide scale. Medhatithi regarded handicraft trades as lowly occupations.

MEOS. A warrior tribe inhabiting a vast tract to the south and southwest of **Delhi**. In 1260, **Balban**, then holding the position of *na'ib*, led an expedition against the Meos and captured several of their leading men, who were executed publicly at Delhi. In 1388, the Meo chief **Bahadur Nahir** supported **Abu Bakr**'s efforts to capture the throne of Delhi.

MEWAR. Southeastern Rajasthan demarcated in the north by the Banas River and on the west by the southern extension of Aravalli range is known as Mewar, with Udaipur and Chitor as its important strongholds. The **Guhilas** ruled over the region as early as the eighth century. The Guhila dynasty, evicted from **Chitor** by 'Ala al-Din Khalji in 1303, was reestablished there by Rana **Hammir**, who belonged to the **Sisodiya** branch of the ruling family.

MINGBARNI, JALAL AL-DIN (?–1231). The son of 'Ala al-Din Khwarazm Shah. He was posted at Ghazni at the time **Chingez Khan** overran Khwarazmi territory up to Herat. In 1221, Jalal al-Din Mingbarni vacated Ghazni and moved toward the Indus River with the idea of seeking refuge inside the **Delhi sultanate**. He was hotly pursued by Chingez. Being overwhelmed by the **Mongols**, Mingbarni plunged his horse into the Indus and swam to the other side. During the years that Mingbarni was in the Punjab and Sind, he tried to establish himself there as an independent ruler but was not successful. **Iltutmish**, on his part, politely indicated that Mingbarni was not welcome to his court. Finally, he proceeded to Iran, marching through Kirman, Isfahan, and Tabrez. Mingbarni was killed in western Iran by Kurd bandits in 1231.

MINHAJ SIRAJ JUZJANI (1193–?). A well-known historian who wrote his *Tabaqat-i Nasiri* during the reign of Nasir al-Din **Mahmud Shah** (1246–1266). His father held the high ecclesiastical offices of *qazi* and *khatib* under Sultan Baha al-Din Sam. Minhaj was born in 1193 and was brought up by Mah-i Mulk, a daughter of Ghiyas al-Din Muhammad b. Sam (**sultan** of Ghaur 1162–1202). In 1226, Minhaj left Ghaur for India. In Uchch he was appointed by Nasir al-Din **Qubacha** as the head of a school and worked in that position until 1227. After Qubacha's overthrow at the hands of **Iltutmish** (1211–1236), he came to **Delhi** with the latter. In 1241–1242, he was made *qazi* of the realm by Sultan **Bahram Shah** (1239–1242). In 1242–1243, Minhaj went to **Lakhnauti** and stayed there for about two years. After his return from Lakhnauti to Delhi, he rose to the position of *sadr-us-sudur* (same as *sadr-i jahan*) under Nasir al-Din Mahmud Shah (1246–1266). During this period, he was closely allied with Baha al-Din **Balban** who, as viceroy (*na'ib*), practically ran the state in the name of Nasir al-Din Mahmud Shah. Minhaj completed *Tabaqat-i Nasiri* (Narrative Dedicated to Nasir al-Din) sometime after Balban's coming to the throne (1266).

MITAKSHARA. One of the two systems of family law that became the basis of civil law relating to property rights in a Hindu joint family. It was formulated by Vijnanesvara at the court of the **Chaulukya** ruler **Vikramaditya VI** (1076–1126). The other system was *dayabhaga*.

MONGOLS. A Mongol (Tartar of European parlance) horde first appeared in India when **Chingez Khan** came up to the western bank of the Indus River in pursuit of Jalal al-Din **Mingbarni** in 1221. After the Mongols had established their control in Central Asia, Khurasan, and Ghazni, they had a tendency to make inroads into the territory of the **Delhi sultanate**. By the middle of the 13th century, the entire Punjab up to **Lahore** and **Dipalpur** had become vulnerable to the Mongol threat. **Balban** (1266–1286) tried to check them; his son and heir apparent died fighting Mongols in 1286. The Mongols were repulsed by **'Ala al-Din Khalji** (1296–1316) with great ferocity. Subsequently, internal squabbles within the Mongol Empire combined with increased military might of the Delhi sultanate largely eliminated the threat of Mongol invasions. Many Mongol deserters and those taken prisoners converted to Islam and settled at **Delhi**, some of them joining service as troopers or military officers. Their presence had a visible impact on the political and military institutions of the Delhi sultanate. Mongols are also credited with bringing to India the Chinese expertise of gunpowder-based fireworks.

MUBARAK KHALJI. *See* QUTB AL-DIN MUBARAK SHAH KHALJI.

MUBARAK SHAH, SULTAN (?–1434). The second **sultan** of the **Saiyid dynasty**, Mubarak Shah succeeded on the throne of his father, **Khizr Khan**, in 1421. Mubarak asserted his independence by removing the name of the Timurid ruler Mirza Shah Rukh from the sermon of Friday prayers. He also suppressed the **Khokhar** chief Jasrath, who had become very powerful in the Punjab and was constantly being encouraged by the Timurid prince Shaikh Ali to defy the **Delhi sultan**. Mubarak Shah was murdered in 1434 at the instigation of a disgruntled noble.

MUGHIS, QAZI. A resident of **Bayana** who had access to and conversed with **'Ala al-Din Khalji** (1296–1316) in private. To 'Ala al-Din's reported query as to how the Islamic *shariah* defined the status of Hindus in the **Delhi sultanate**, Qazi Mughis stated that according to the *Hanafi* school they were to be treated as protected people (*zimma*).

MUHAMMAD BIN BAKHTIYAR KHALJI (?–1206). At the head of a band of **Khalji** adventurers, he entered Bihar around 1197. There he destroyed a large **Buddhist** monastery, the ruins of which survive at **Nalanda**. In 1204, he attacked and occupied by surprise Nadia and then **Lakhnauti**, contributing to the collapse of the **Sena dynasty**. For this he gained a robe of honor from **Aibek**. In 1206, Muhammad bin Bakhtiyar led an abortive expedition into the valley of the Brahmputra River but was forced to withdraw by the fierce resistance of the local rulers. During his retreat from Assam, he was killed by one of his lieutenants, Ali Mardan.

MUHAMMAD BIN TUGHLAQ (?–1351). Fakhr al-Din Jauna, the son of **Ghiyas al-Din Tughlaq**, ascended the throne in 1325 with the title Sultan Muhammad Shah bin Tughlaq. He was a very accomplished person and had remarkable proficiency in prose writing and composition as well as in different branches of learning such as mathematics, medicine, and Greek philosophy. Muhammad bin Tughlaq was strict in observing religious rites and abstained from the vices forbidden in the Quran.

These characteristic of his were, however, in contrast to his cruelty and lack of consideration for the common people's difficulties. His whole life was spent pursuing his wild, sometimes visionary, schemes, such as the transfer of the capital and a token currency, actions that often brought immense suffering to his subjects. The strict discipline that he tried to enforce on the nobles combined with his policy of taking the nobles to task for their failure to account for the revenues farmed out to them turned a large number of middle-ranking officers (***amiran-i sada***) hostile, leading to recurring rebellions. One such rebellion gave rise to the **Bahmani kingdom** in the **Deccan** (1347).

Although Muhammad bin Tughlaq tried to strengthen his position by securing a diploma of investiture from the Abbasid caliph, he never allowed the theologians to dictate the state policy. When his own judgment differed from that of a religious doctor, he did not hesitate to overrule the latter. Muhammad bin Tughlaq did not impose on the Hindus any curbs on the observance of their religious rites. A number of new temples were built in the territories of the **Delhi sultanate** during his reign. Muhammad bin Tughlaq participated in the Hindu religious festivals and also mixed frequently with Hindu mendicants. One Hindu practice discouraged by him was that of *sati* (widow burning), which could be performed only with the permission of the **sultan**.

MUHAMMAD GHAURI, SULTAN MUIZZ AL-DIN (?–1206). He was the younger brother of Sultan Ghiyas al-Din Ghauri who handed over the government of Ghazni to him in 1173. Beginning with a campaign against the **Qaramitah** of **Multan** in 1175, Muhammad Ghauri brought the whole of Punjab under his control by ousting the last **Ghaznavid** ruler **Khusrau Malik** from **Lahore** in 1186. In 1192, he occupied **Ajmer** and **Delhi** after defeating the **Chahamana** ruler **Prithviraja III**. By 1204, Bihar and Bengal were overrun by the **Khalji** officers paying allegiance to him. He left the administration of conquered territories in India outside Bengal to his slave Qutb al-Din **Aibek**. Muhammad Ghauri and his brother, Ghiyas al-Din, however, were not very successful against their Turkish adversaries in Central Asia. They suffered a humiliating defeat at Adkhund in 1203. Muhammad Ghauri was assassinated by a **Khokhar** tribesman in 1206.

MUHAMMAD, PRINCE (?–1286). **Balban**'s favorite son, Muhammad, was appointed governor of Sind and stationed at **Multan** some time in the 1270s. He was entrusted with the task of checking the **Mongol** incursions from that side. After the removal of **Bughra Khan** from Samana in 1279, Muhammad was entrusted with the responsibility of protecting the entire western frontier against the Mongols. He was killed in 1286 near **Lahore** in the course of a skirmish with Mongol raiders. Muhammad was fond of learned society; **Amir Khusrau** and **Amir Hasan Sijzi** were in his service at Multan.

MUHAMMAD SHAH BAHMANI (?–1375). The second ruler of the **Bahmani** dynasty who succeeded to the throne in 1358. Within two years, he was recognized by the Abbasid caliph as a **sultan** in his own right. Muhammad Shah's whole reign (1358–1375) was taken up with a continuous war with **Vijayanagar** over the territory of **Telingana**. In one of these campaigns, he routed the Vijayanagar army decisively, forcing **Bukka Raya I** (1356–1377) to agree to terms dictated by him. At the end of this war, Muhammad Shah declared that in the future noncombatants and prisoners of war shall not be molested. One of his noteworthy achievements was the reorganization of the Bahmani state, providing for its division into provinces (*tarafs*), each one of which was placed under a viceroy (*malik na'ib*).

MUHAMMAD SHAH BIN FIRUZ, SULTAN NASIR AL-DIN (?–1394). Muhammad, the only surviving son of **Firuz Shah Tughlaq** (1351–1388), was sought to be sidelined by a faction of the nobles led by the *wazir* in 1380s. They pitted against him **Tughlaq Shah**, a great-grandson of the **sultan**. This led to a sharp struggle that led to Muhammad's emergence as the joint sultan in 1387. On Firuz Shah's death the following year, the slaves of the late sultan present in **Delhi** first brought Tughlaq Shah to the throne and then replaced him by **Abu Bakr** (1388–1390). Muhammad, supported by nobles stationed outside Delhi as well as by many local chiefs, continued to defy Abu Bakr and eventually succeeded in replacing him at Delhi. During Muhammad's short reign, local chiefs in the regions around **Kanauj**, Etawa, Delhi, and those of Punjab were effectively controlled. His death in January 1394, however, disrupted this process.

MUHRDAR. The bearer of the royal seal was an office that carried much prestige in the **Delhi sultanate**. A person holding this office would be regarded as enjoying the **sultan**'s trust. Ghazi Malik (later **Ghiyas al-Din Tughlaq**) occupied this office under **'Ala al-Din Khalji** (1296–1316). The office was held by **Malik Kafur** (not to be confused with **Malik Kafur Hazardinari**) under **Qutb al-Din Mubarak Khalji** (1316–1320) and **Khusrau Shah** (1320).

MU'IN AL-DIN CHISHTI (1114–1236). The founder of the **Chishti Sufic** order in India, Mun'i al-Din Chishti was born in the Persian province of Sistan. Growing up, he traveled widely in Persia, Iraq, and Central Asia and studied with the well-known religious teachers of his time, including Shaikh Abdul Qadir Jilani (1077–1166) and Shaikh Najm al-Din Kubra (1145–1228). He came to India and established his hospice at **Ajmer** toward the end of **Prithviraja Chahamana**'s reign (1180–1192). During his stay at Ajmer, Mu'in al-Din disseminated his mystic ideas couched in a deeply humane language, which earned him the veneration and respect of the common people, including many non-Muslims. After his death in 1236, his mystic mission was carried on in the Ajmer tract by his disciple Shaikh **Hamid al-Din Nagauri**, while outside Ajmer it was carried on by Qutb al-Din Bakhtiyar Kaki (d. 1235) and the latter's disciple, **Farid al-Din Mas'ud Ganj-shikar** (1175–1265).

MUJIR AL-DIN. He belonged to a prominent clan of Central Asian immigrants, the descendants of Abu Rija, who joined service under the **Khaljis** (1290–1320). Mujir al-Din was appointed deputy governor (*na'ib-wazir*) at Deogir by **Mubarak Khalji** (1316–1320), where he continued for a long time. He rose in prominence under **Muhammad bin Tughlaq** (1325–1351), became governor of **Bayana**, and participated in military campaigns against the rebellious nobles **Baha al-Din Garshasp** and **'Ain ul-Mulk Multani**. One of his brothers, Shihab al-Din Abu Rija, the *muqti'* of Nausari, was entitled *Malik al-tujjar* (king of merchants).

MULTAN. Located on the side of the Chenab River about 60 kilometers south of its confluence with Ravi on the northern confines of Sind, Multan was seized by the **Karmathians** toward the end of the 10th century. They were finally overthrown by Muizz al-Din **Muhammad Ghauri** in 1175. Subsequently, and until **Firuz Shah Tughlaq's** reign (1351–1388), Multan remained an important military outpost of the **Delhi sultanate** in the northwest. During this time, it was also important because of the presence of Shaikh **Baha al-Din Zakarya** Suhrawardi's hospice. In the second half of the 15th century, Multan came to be ruled by a local dynasty of Langahs.

MULTANIS. In the **Delhi sultanate**, a large part of the long-distance trade was controlled by a community of traders identified by Ziya' **Barani** as Multanis (i.e., belonging to **Multan**). Some of them also indulged in usury and commerce. Most of the Multanis were probably Hindus, but a few Muslim names are also recorded, **'Ain ul-Mulk Multani** being one of them. The community of Muslim shopkeepers of north India at present identified as Punjabis are believed to be the descendants of Multanis converted to Islam.

MUQTI'. In the **Delhi sultanate**, *muqti'* was the holder of a large territory as his *iqta'*, from where he collected land revenue for maintaining his personal establishment as well as military contingent. The *muqti'* also was responsible for suppressing the local recalcitrants and rebels. Within his *iqta'* a *muqti'* could bestow grants on his retainers and aides.

MUZAFFAR SHAH (?–1411). The founder of the sultanate of Gujarat, he was originally known as Zafar Khan. He was a convert to Islam from a sect of Hindu Khatris known as Tanks. Zafar Khan was governor of Gujarat at the time of **Timur**'s invasion (1398). Taking advantage of the collapse of central authority, Zafar Khan became independent in Gujarat, leading to his declaring himself a sovereign ruler in 1407 with the title Sultan Muzaffar Shah. He died in 1411 and was succeeded on the throne by his grandson **Ahmad Shah**.

– N –

NADU. In the southern kingdoms of medieval India, the *nadu* represented the district administration. Consisting of a group of villages, a *nadu* under the **Cholas** was the subdivision of a *valanadu*.

NAGARAM. Under the **Cholas** (and before them under the Pallavas as well), merchant guilds called *nagarams* existed in many towns. These guilds in turn were affiliated with larger guilds having different specific names.

NAHARWALA. Same as Anhilwara, the capital of the **Chaulukyas** of Gujarat, which was sacked by **Mahmud of Ghazni** in 1026. In the wake of the **Ghaurid** invasion (1192), Naharwala was sacked again in 1197, this time by a Ghaurid army led by Qutb al-Din **Aibek**. In 1242, the Chaulukyas were replaced by the **Vaghelas** as the ruling clan at Naharwala. The town was annexed to the **Delhi sultanate** following the conquest of Gujarat by **'Ala al-Din Khalji** in 1297. In 1345, Naharwala was the seat of the Delhi sultanate's power in Gujarat. In that year, rebellious *amiran-i sada* entered Naharwala and slew the governor. **Muzaffar Shah** (1407–1411), the first ruler of the sultanate of Gujarat, ruled from Naharwala. The capital was shifted to **Ahmadabad** only during the reign of Sultan **Ahmad Shah** (1411–1442).

NA'IB-I SULTANATE. Sometimes also designated as *na'ib-i mamlikat*, he was a viceroy or deputy to the **sultan** who ran the administration on his behalf when he was ill or incapacitated. This was the case in 1315 when Malik **Kafur Hazardinari**, the *na'ib-i mumlikat*, acted on behalf of **'Ala al-Din Khalji** during the latter's illness. Sometimes, when the sultan had no inclination to involve himself in administration for one reason or another, again, the most powerful noble would run the administration as *na'ib*. The authority exercised by **Balban** as *na'ib* under Nasir al-Din **Mahmud Shah** (1246–1266) is an example.

NALANDA. Famous **Buddhist** monastery near Patna that survived until the end of the 12th century. The rulers of the **Pala dynasty** extended patronage and protection to this monastery. It was destroyed by an invading party of **Ghaurid** troops in 1197.

NAMADEVA (1270?–1305?). A Maharastrian saint who was a man of low origin. Born in the latter part of the 13th century (circa 1270), Namadeva preached the unity of God and deprecated idol worship. He is reported to have spent considerable time in the Punjab, which explains his frequent use of Persian and Arabic words. In more ways than one, Namadeva was a precursor of **Kabir**.

NANAK, GURU (1469–1538). The first *guru* of the Sikhs, he was born at Talwandi (District Gurdaspur Gujranwala, Pakistan) into a family of Bedi Khatris in 1469. As a young man, Nanak learned Hindi, Sanskrit, and Persian. He was employed in the establishment of a **Lodi** noble until 1499. At 30, he renounced home, gave up his job, and commenced wandering in the company of the Muslim minstrel Mardana, interacting with the holy men of different faiths. After 40 years of his mission, Nanak passed away in 1538. His teachings, preserved in *Guru Granth Sahib* (Compositions of Gurus), project the concept of one God who is formless (*nirankar*), light (*niranjan*), and a true teacher (*satguru*). He attacked with vehemence what he regarded as superstitious and formal in Islam and Hinduism. Nanak denounced image worship, rejected caste distinctions, and advocated a middle path between extreme asceticism and heedless satisfaction of the senses.

NANAK, MALIK. A Hindu slave officer of **'Ala al-Din Khalji** (1296–1316) who saved the **sultan**'s life when he was attacked by **Akat Khan**. Malik Nanak was *akhur bek* (*amir-i akhur*) and *muqti'* of Samana in 1305 when he defeated a **Mongol** invading army.

NARHARI. One of the 12 disciples of **Ramanand** (1399–1448). He wrote devotional hymns in **Marathi** in praise of God identified with Vishnu. Narhari was a tailor by profession.

NASIR AL-DIN CHIRAGH DEHLI. *See* CHIRAGH DEHLI, SHAIKH NASIR AL-DIN.

NAWAK. A crossbow that Muslim invaders frequently used in India in the 13th and 14th centuries. The term originally denoted a tabular attachment but subsequently came to be applied to the entire weapon. **Malik Kafur** is reported to have used *nawaks* with great effect during his campaigns in south India.

NAYACHANDRA SURI. Author of *Hammira mahakavya* (An Epic on Hammira), compiled possibly in the 15th century, that narrates the heroic deeds of Rana **Hammira Deo Chahamana** of **Ranthambhor**.

NIKITIN, ATHANASIUS. A Russian merchant, resident of Tver, who accompanied Wessili Papin who was sent to the Shah of Shirvan by Grand Duke Ivan III in 1468. He visited **Bidar** in 1470 and returned to Russia in 1474. According to him, the people in India were very poor but the nobles "delight in luxury."

NIZAM AL-DIN AULIYA, SHAIKH (1238–1325). He was born at Badaun (1238) into a family of *khwajas* of Bukhara who had migrated to India following the establishment of **Mongol** rule in Central Asia. Named Muhammad at birth, he later came to be addressed as Nizam al-Din. At the age of 16, he, along with his mother, shifted to **Delhi**. While very young, he became a disciple of Shaikh **Farid al-Din Mas'ud Ganj-shikr**. He eventually came to command great influence and respect in ruling circles as well as among the common people of Delhi. Though Shaikh Nizam al-Din's relations with **'Ala al-Din Khalji** (1296–1316) were cordial, he avoided meeting him. **Qutb al-Din Mubarak Shah** (1316–1320), on the other hand, was throughout very hostile toward Nizam al-Din Auliya and even contemplated his arrest. During **Khusrau Shah**'s short rule (1320), when there were allegations of Islamic sentiments being hurt by the usurper's Hindu supporters, Shaikh Nizam al-Din by and large remained indifferent toward the ruler. Still, he is reported to have accepted a large donation from him that was subsequently distributed among the needy. Shaikh Nizam al-Din is credited with reorganizing the **Chishti order** in India from his hospice at Delhi. Shaikh Nizam al-Din Auliya had among his disciples the well-known poets **Amir Khusrau** and **Amir Hasan Sijzi** (author of *Fawaid al-Fawad*). On his demise in 1325, he was succeeded by **Nasir al-Din Chirgah Dehli** as the head of the Chishti order at Delhi.

NIZAM AL-DIN, MALIK. He served as *wakil-i dar* under **Balban** (1266–1286) and collaborated with Balban's *wazir* in bringing **Kaiqubad** (1287–1290) to the throne. Under Kaiqubad, he became very powerful as *dadbeg*. He brought about the removal of great nobles of the previous regime and also induced the **sultan** to order the execution of **Kaikhusrau**. Eventually Kaiqubad had Nizam al-Din poisoned. *See also* FAKHR AL-DIN KOTWAL, MALIK UL-UMAR; KHWAJA KHATIR AL-DIN.

NUR AL-DIN TURK (?–1237). A man of great piety and mystic leanings, Nur al-Din Turk gathered a large following in the **Delhi sultanate** during the early decades of the 13th century. He condemned Sunni scholars in a derogatory language, which earned him and his followers the charge of being heretics connected with the **Karmathians**. On 5 March 1237, Nur Turk entered the main mosque with his followers and there started a fight between them and others who had come there for Friday prayers. Eventually troops intervened and overcame the rioters. Nur al-Din Turk himself was killed in this fighting. He was remembered with sympathy and admiration in the inner circles of **Chishti Sufis** at **Delhi** until 1325. *See also* QARAMITAH.

NUSRAT KHAN, MALIK NUSRAT JALESARI (?–1300). He was possibly associated with Jalesar (45 kilometers northwest of **Agra**) for a long time or was an Indian noble hailing from that place. Malik Nusrat was entitled Nusrat Khan by **'Ala al-Din Khalji** (1296–1316). He is reported to have become instrumental in amassing great wealth in the treasury from the elimination of the nobles of the previous regime suspected of disloyalty. 'Ala al-Din also made him the *kotwal* of **Delhi**. In 1297, relinquishing the office of *kotwal*, he became *wazir* and was also allotted the prestigious *iqta'* of **Kara**. In 1300–1301, Nusrat Khan was killed while leading the siege operations at **Ranthambhor**.

NUSRAT SHAH (?–1532). Succeeding his father, **'Ala al-Din Husain Shah**, on the throne of Bengal in 1519, Nusrat Shah treated his brother—who was a rival claimant to the throne—with kindness. He maintained friendly relations with the Nuhani chiefs, who had established control in Bihar. In 1529, there was a brief confrontation at Ghoghra between **Babur** and Nusrat Shah, who was encouraged by the Afghan chiefs to resist the eastward advance of the Mughals. Later, he also tried to enter into an anti-Mughal alliance with Bahadur Shah of Gujarat. Before this alliance could materialize, Nusrat Shah was killed by one of his slaves in 1532.

– O –

OGODEI (?–1241). A **Mongol** *khaqan* who succeeded **Chingez Khan** in 1227. As a prince, he overran Firuz Koh in 1222. Like his father, Ogodei believed that he was the ruler of the whole world. It is recorded in the Mongol court chronicle that "the ruler of India" was present at Ogodei's accession, which is perhaps a reference to some Hindu chief of the northwest or to Saif al-Din **Hasan Qarluq**, the ruler of Biban. In December 1241, the Mongols captured **Lahore**. About the same time Ogodei died, leading to the election of his son Guyug (1246–1248) as the next *khaqan*.

– P –

PADMINI. A legendry character who was supposed to be the wise and beautiful wife of Rana Ratan Sen at the time of **'Ala al-Din Khalji**'s attack on **Chitor** (1303). According to this legend, 'Ala al-Din failed to capture the fort despite a siege of eight years. He is eventually supposed to have seized Ratan Sen by deceit and then made a demand for the surrender of Padmini to him. But the **Rajput** warriors, guided and inspired by Padmini, librated the Rana by resorting to the well-known trick of entering the enemy's citadel disguised as secluded ladies. This story, having no historical validity whatsoever, was popularized in the 16th century by Malik Muhammad Jaisi through his versified romance *Padmavat* (1540), which is written in

Awadhi dialect. The earliest manuscript of the book is, however, inscribed in Persian script adapted to Awadhi phonetics.

PAIKS. Hindu infantrymen who served under the **sultans** in medieval India. Under **Balban**, they came to form a royal guard. After **Kaiqubad**'s ouster, the *paiks* rallied around Malik **Chajju**, accepting from him a betel leaf (*tambul*) in their familiar ceremony of pledging support. The royal *paiks* came to play a still more important role under the **Khaljis** (1290–1320). They saved '**Ala al-Din**'s life during the failed attempt to kill him by **Akat Khan**. It was the *paiks* who killed Malik **Kafur** in 1316. **Khusrau Shah**, who had seized the throne after killing **Qutb al-Din Mubarak Shah Khalji** (1316–1320), was originally a *paik*. The *paiks* played an equally important role in the Bengal kingdom. The rise of **Raja Ganesh** (1415–1418) may be attributed to the support of the royal *paiks*.

PALA DYNASTY. The ruling chiefs of Bengal, who were for a long time prey to intrusions by powers located in the Gangetic **Doab** (**Kanauj**) and Kamrupa (Assam), elected in 765 a certain Gopala as their king. The dynasty founded by Gopala came to be called the Palas, who ruled until the beginning of the 12th century. The dynasty collapsed after **Mahipala** (988–1038). A much diminished Pala chieftainship continued to survive even after the rise of the **Senas** (1095) but was extinguished after Muhammad bin Bakhtiyar's invasion (1204). Under the patronage of the Palas, Buddhism continued to survive in Bengal until the end of 12th century at a time when it was disappearing from other parts of the subcontinent under the onslaught of revived Brahmanical faith.

PANDYA DYNASTY. The Pandya kingdom, with its capital at Madurai, controlled the **Tamil** country from very ancient times but lost, in the eighth century, its capital to the **Cholas**, while the Pandya ruler took refuge in Ceylon. The Cholas and their allies retained their hold on the Pandya country for nearly 300 years. At the end of that period, the Pandya prince, Maravaraman Sundar, recovered his ancestral lands by defeating Kotottunga Chola (1178–1216). Toward the end of the 13th century, the Pandyas were weakened by internal dissensions.

Malik Kafur seized Madurai in 1310. Subsequently, the rise of Vijayanagar hastened the downfall of the Pandyas.

PARAMARA DYNASTY. An *agnikula* clan that established its principality at Mount Abu early in the ninth century. For a long time it was subordinate to the Pratiharas of Kanauj. It emerged as an independent power under Vakpati II or Munja Raja (947–997). Raja Bhoja (1020–1060) was the most famous ruler of the dynasty. The Paramara dynasty was overthrown by 'Ala al-Din Khalji (1296–1316).

PARAMARDI, DEVA (?–1203). The Chandella prince who got involved in a prolonged war with the Chahamanas of Ajmer-Delhi, which led to his discomfiture at the hands of Prithviraja III (1180–1192) in 1182–1183. Tradition credits the two heroes of Mahoba, Allha and Udala, for offering heroic resistance to the Chahamanas during this war. When Qutb al-Din 'Aibek advanced against Kalinjar in 1203, Paramardi fought against him with determination but was forced to agree to submit, provoking a Chandella warrior to kill him. *See also* ALLAHKHAND.

PARGANA. In the Delhi sultanate, a unit of 100 villages corresponded to a *pargana* headed by a *chaudhuri*. The term *pargana* is possibly the same as *pratijagaranaka*, used for a territorial unit in Paramara inscriptions. *See also* SARKAR.

PARWARIS. A Hindu warrior clan hailing from Gujarat whose number increased among the royal guards under Qutb al-Din Mubarak Shah Khalji (1316–1320). With the rise of Khusrau Khan, this clan became very influential in the service of that sultan. After Khusrau Shah seized the throne, the Parwaris were accused by elements loyal to the old regime of not respecting the Islamic sensitivities, leading to an uprising culminating in the overthrow of Khusrau Shah and his Parwari followers.

PATWARI. The accountant and record keeper of a village. Along with the *muqaddam* he represented the team of village-level hereditary functionaries in the Delhi sultanate.

PHERU, THAKKURA. *See* THAKKURA PHERU.

PRAKRIT. The popular form of spoken Sanskrit of the post-Vedic times when proper Sanskrit had increasingly become the language of Brahmans. Prakrit continued to be used by **Jain** scholars until medieval times. *See also* APABHRAMSHA.

PRATIHARAS. A branch of the **Gurjaras**. They ruled over **Kanauj** from the middle of the ninth century until 1018. The Pratiharas controlled **Gwalior** until 1234. The last ruler of the dynasty, Mangal Deo, defeated by **Iltutmish** (1211–1236), escaped to Narwar to be ousted from there the next year. Remnants of the Pratihara chiefs in the region were finally subjugated by **Muhammad bin Tughlaq** (1325–1351).

PRITHVIRAJA III (?–1192). The last Chahamana ruler of **Ajmer** who ascended the throne in 1180, he became a romantic hero on account of stories narrated by **Chandbardai**. One of these stories relate to his elopement (1175?) with the daughter of the **Ghahadavala** ruler of **Kanauj, Jaichandra** (1173–1193). Leading an alliance of **Rajput** rajas, Prithviraja defeated Muizz al-Din **Muhammad Ghauri** in the first battle of **Tarain** (1191). The next year (1192), in another contest with Muhammad Ghauri at the same battlefield, Prithviraja was defeated, taken prisoner, and killed.

PRITHVIRAJARASAU (**The Heroic Story of Prithviraja**). A long Hindi poem ascribed to **Chandbardai**, who purportedly lived during the 12th century and was patronized by **Prithviraja Chahamana** (1180–1192). It eulogizes the achievements of the Chahamana ruler. The bulk of the poem, however, has been assigned to the 15th century.

PUNJABI. An Indo-Aryan language spoken in the northwestern parts of the Indian subcontinent, comprising at present the state and province of Punjab in India and Pakistan, respectively. The earliest compositions in Punjabi include the verses attributed to Shaikh **Farid al-Din** and Guru **Nanak** contained in the sacred book of the Sikhs, *Guru Granth Sahib* (Compositions of Gurus).

PURI. The same as present-day Purushottam Khatra on the Orissa coast, south of **Cuttak**. One of Shankara's four *mathas* (monasteries) is located at Puri. It is also famous for the **Jagannath temple** of the Hindu god Purshottama.

– Q –

QA'INI, SHARAF AL-DIN (?–1315). **'Ala al-Din Khalji**'s finance minister Sharaf al-Din Qa'ini held the position of a deputy *wazir*. He enforced the uniform assessment of land revenue based on measurement, together with the grazing and dwelling taxes, over a vast area. Qa'ini is also credited with strict measures to eliminate bribery and embezzlement. During 'Ala al-Din's illness in 1315, Qa'ini came to be perceived by Malik **Kafur**, the *na'ib*, as a threat to his position. The *na'ib* prevailed upon the ailing **sultan** to have Qa'ini executed.

QARAMITAH. The Karmathians, a sect of Shiite Muslims who gained a foothold in Sind in the ninth century. They came to control a greater part of upper Sind, including **Multan** and Uchch. For about three centuries, religious allegiance was owed by the rulers of this tract to the Fatimid caliphs of Egypt. **Mahmud of Ghazni** (997–1030) installed a Sunni ruler in Multan but he was not allowed to continue there for long. Later, Muizz al-Din **Muhammad Ghauri** (1173–1206) had to fight hard to remove the Qaramitah from Multan.

QARAQUSH KHAN, IKHTIYAR AL-DIN AYTEGIN. A slave officer of **Iltutmish** (1211–1236) who was of Kara Khatai origin. In his early career, Qaraqush was appointed as intendant (*shihna*) of royal domains (*khalisah*) at Tabarhind. For some time, he also held **Multan** as his *iqta'*. In 1240, **Raziya Sultan** installed him at **Lahore**. He supported Raziya's attempt to regain the throne in 1240. In the same year, he abandoned Lahore to the **Mongols** but returned on their withdrawal. After the accession of **Mas'ud Shah** in 1242, Qaraqush Khan was made *amir-i hajib*.

QARAUNAS. They were a distinct racial group who came to form a separate *tuman*, that is, a corps of 10,000 in the Timurid armies during the 13th century. They were believed in the 14th century to be the offspring of **Mongols** from non-Mongol mothers. The founder of the Tughlaq dynasty, **Ghiyas al-Din Tughlaq** (1320–1325), was a Qarauna.

QAZI. A judicial magistrate who decided cases in accordance with Islamic law. In most of the towns of the **Delhi sultanate** as well as in each military camp there existed *qazis'* courts. At the center, the **sultan** was advised by the chief *qazi*. One of the advisers of '**Ala al-Din Khalji** (1296–1316) in policy matters was Qazi **Mughis**. The *qazis* at different levels were appointed by the **sultan**.

QILICH KHAN, JALAL AL-DIN MASUD. The son of '**Ala al-Din Jani**, he was the *muqti'* of **Lakhnauti** in 1249. In 1258, Qilich Khan, then the *muqti'* of **Kara**, was again appointed to Lakhnauti, but it is not known if he actually took charge of the place on this occasion.

QUBACHA, NASIR AL-DIN (?–1227). A slave officer of **Muhammad Ghauri** (1173–1206) who was married to two of the daughters of Qutb al-Din **Aibek** (1206–1210). He seized Uchch and **Multan** on Aibek's death (1210). After **Yildiz** was defeated by **Iltutmish** at **Tarain** (1215), Qubacha made an unsuccessful attempt to challenge Iltutmish. Qubacha, who continued to control Sind, was forced to take shelter in the fort of Multan by **Mingbarni** in 1222. In 1227, Iltutmish marched into Sind for the purpose of putting down Qubacha. Pursued by Nizam al-Mulk **Junaidi**, he was killed near Uchch in the same year.

QUTB AL-DIN AIBEK. *See* AIBEK, QUTB AL-DIN.

QUTB AL-DIN HASAN BIN ALI GHAURI (?–1255). One of the freeborn nobles of Ghaur who joined the service under **Qubacha** in 1226. He later held the office of *wakil-i dar* under **Iltutmish** (1211–1236). **Raziya Sultan** (1236–1240) raised him to the position of deputy in command of the army (*naib-i lashkar*). In 1252, when **Balban** was temporarily ousted from power, the office of *na'ib-i sultanate* (viceroy) came to be occupied by him. He was arrested and put to death in 1255 after Balban had regained power at Nasir al-Din **Mahmud Shah**'s court.

QUTB AL-DIN MUBARAK SHAH KHALJI (?–1320). Mubarak was the third son of **'Ala al-Din Khalji** (1296–1316) who escaped being imprisoned and blinded like his elder brother **Khizr Khan** by Malik **Kafur**. After Malik Kafur was assassinated by *paiks* in 1316, Mubarak—then only 17 years old—ascended the throne with the title Qutb al-Din Mubarak Shah. He killed his brothers, including **Khizr Khan** who was then imprisoned in **Gwalior**, and took the widowed **Deval Rani** into his own harem. In the first two years of his reign, Mubarak showed a good deal of competence and energy in dealing with stubborn chiefs and disgruntled nobles as well as with the defiance of the rulers of Deogir and **Telingana** in the **Deccan**. But his career came to an abrupt end in April 1320 when his favorite neo-Muslim noble **Khusrau** Khan killed him and seized the throne with the help of his **Parwari** fellow clansmen.

QUTLUGH KHAN. A Turkish slave noble and one of the rivals of **Balban** who engineered the latter's removal from the position of *na'ib* in 1252–1253. Qutlugh Khan married Sultan Nasir al-Din **Mahmud**'s mother in 1255, which is believed to have alienated the **sultan** from him. After Balban's reinstatement as *na'ib*, Qutlugh and his wife (the sultan's mother) were ordered to take up residence in **Awadh**, which formed Qutlugh's *iqta'*. Subsequently, Qutlugh Khan's relations with the central authorities headed by Balban remained strained. He was accused of encroaching on the territory of Badaun and was replaced in 1256 in Awadh by Arslan Khan, a known supporter of Balban. Qutlugh Khan resisted this order and was driven out of Awadh. He was forced to take refuge with the chief of Simur in Tirhut.

QUWWAT UL-ISLAM **MOSQUE.** Literally meaning "Might of Islam Mosque." This name is a corruption of *Qubbat ul-Islam* Mosque," literally "Dome of Islam Mosque." It is the earliest mosque built after the **Ghaurid** conquest of **Delhi**. According to a surviving inscription, this large complex, which includes the famous *'Alai Darwaza* and *Qutb Minar*, was built out of the material taken from 27 temples. The presence of false arches here is indicative of the use of local architects more familiar with trabeated forms.

– R –

RAJA FARUQI, MALIK (?–1399). He earned **Firuz Shah Tughlaq**'s notice while serving as one of the royal attendants and was appointed in 1371 to Thalner (on the Tapti River) in Khandesh. Subsequently, Raja Faruqi was promoted to the position of a *spahsalar* (commander in chief) of Khandesh, where he raised a large body of troops and started making plundering raids toward Orissa. After Firuz Shah Tughlaq's death (1388), he became independent in Khandesh and established close relations with **Dilawar Khan Ghauri**, who had come to rule Malwa. In the rivalry between Sultan **Muzaffar Shah** of Gujarat and **Dilawar Khan Ghauri**, he sided with the latter, which provoked Sultan Muzaffar to besiege Raja Faruqi in Thalner. Muzaffar was, however, persuaded to withdraw on the promise of good behavior by Raja Faruqi.

RAJA GANESH (?–1418). A local chief of Dinajpur, Raja Ganesh ("Kans" of Persian texts), who was in the employ of the **Ilyas Shahi** rulers of Bengal, captured the throne in 1415 with the help of *paiks* serving as royal guards. On threat of military action by **Ibrahim Shah Sharqi** (1400–1440), Raja Ganesh placed one of his sons on the throne (perhaps with an Islamic title) and wielded authority in his name until 1418. After Raja Ganesh's death in 1418, his son Jadusen ascended the throne with the title Jalal al-Din Muhammad Shah (1418–1431). Raja Ganesh's line continued to rule until 1435.

RAJARAJA I (?–1014). The most illustrious of the **Chola** rulers who came to the throne in 985 and ruled until 1014, Rajaraja I not only contributed to establishing Chola supremacy in south India and northern Ceylon but also extended his sway northward up to Kalinga (modern Orissa).

RAJATARANGINI. A history of Kashmir written by **Kalahana** in Sanskrit in the middle of the 12th century. It is a work of rare quality, displaying remarkable clarity and maturity in historical analysis. Earlier historical works in Sanskrit, such as Bana's *Harshacharitra*

(An Account of Harsha) or Bilhana's *Vikramanka-deva-charita* (An Account of Vikramanka-deva), were biographical in nature. In contrast, *Rajatarangini* is a narrative of the history of a region, Kashmir. The book was translated into Persian at the court of **Zain al-'Abidin** (1420–1470).

RAJENDRA I (?–1044). In 1014, he succeeded his father, Rajaraja I, on the **Chola** throne and ruled for the next 30 years. Rajendra continued the drive of territorial expansion begun by his father. Southern parts of the **Chaulukya** kingdom, representing modern Andhra Pradesh as well as more territories in Ceylon and Kerala, were annexed. Rajendra's forces in the north penetrated up to the valley of the Ganges. His overseas campaigns resulted in the humbling of the Shrivijaya kingdom, from which a number of strategic places along the Malaccan Straits were captured. *See also* MAHIPALA.

RAJPUTS. The origin of the clans identified during the medieval period (1000–1526) as Rajputs may be traced to the groups displaced from Rajputana by newcomers from Central Asia in the wake of the Hun incursions (6th century). In the beginning of 11th century, the Rajputs first appeared in Indian history as ruling clans that were recognized in the contemporary Brahmanical literature as belonging to the warrior (*kshatriya*) caste. The four *agnikula* clans dominated early Rajput activity. Later clans claiming descent from solar and lunar races also established themselves as local kings in different parts of India.

RAMACHANDRA YADAVA (?–1311). Succeeding to the throne in the **Yadava** kingdom of Deogir (later **Daulatabad**) in 1271, Ramachandra extended his domain toward Malwa as well as up to Nagpur and Balaghat. In 1294, Ramachandra submitted to 'Ali Garshasp (later **'Ala al-Din Khalji**), then governor of **Kara**. Subsequently, the Yadava ruler lost much of his territory in the **Deccan** to the **Kakatiyas** and **Hoyasalas**. Around 1307, Ramachandra wavered in his allegiance to **Delhi** but was forced to repent, surrendering the Vaghela princess **Deval Rani**, until then betrothed to his son, to 'Ala al-Din. In 1310, Ramachandra cooperated with **Malik Kafur** when the latter invaded south India. Ramchandra died in 1311, paving the way for the annexation of Deogir to the **Delhi sultanate** in 1317.

RAMANAND (1399–1448?). Born at Prayag (later Allahabad) in 1399, he became a disciple of Raghavananda of **Ramanuja**'s *Sri* sect. To broaden his outlook, he traveled extensively. In his teachings, Ramanand substituted the worship of Rama for that of Vishnu and taught ***bhakti*** to all the four *varnas* (castes). He admitted disciples from all castes, both sexes, and also Muslims. **Kabir**, Raidas, Dhana, and Saindas are included among his disciples.

RAMANUJA (1016–1137). Born in a **Tamil** Brahman family of Turupati, Ramanuja spent a considerable part of his life teaching at the famous temple of Shrirangam. He disagreed with Shankara's view that knowledge was the primary means of salvation. According to Ramanuja, pure devotion was a more effective means. Although Ramanuja accepted special privileges for the higher castes, he was opposed to excluding *shudras* (men of the fourth or lowest caste) from worship in the temple. Accompanied by his disciples, Ramanuja toured different centers of Hindu learning and then settled at Shrirangam to write his treatises *Vedanta sangrah* (A Collection of Vedanta) and *Bhagavad gita* (Divine Song). He died in 1137.

RANAKAS. The title of one of the many lesser feudatories of a king in the period of **Indian feudalism** (800–1200). The kings received military service from them and they in turn conferred estates on their own cavalry commanders called ***rautas*** (Sanskrit, *rajputras*). The *ranakas*, sometimes also called *ranas* and *thakkuras*, were retained in many parts of the **Delhi sultanate** as subordinate chiefs paying tribute to the **sultan**. They headed their own retinues in the service of sultans.

RANAS. A category of Hindu feudatories incorporated in the structure of the **Delhi sultanate** as hereditary chiefs. Their position was akin to that of the ***ranakas*** and ***thakkuras***.

RANTHAMBHOR. A famous fort located northwest of **Chitor** that was ruled by **Chahamanas** in the 12th century. After the defeat of **Prithviraja III** in the battle of **Tarain** (1192), Ranthambhor was occupied by the **Ghaurids**, but soon it was regained by defiant **Rajput** chieftains. **Iltutmish** had to recover this fort from them in 1226–1227. Ranthambhor again came under the control of the Chahamanas toward the end of the 13th century. **'Ala al-Din Khalji** (1296–1316) annexed Ranthambhor to the **Delhi sultanate** in 1301 after defeating and killing **Hammir Deo** at the end of a prolonged siege.

RASTI KHAN (?–1392). A slave officer originally called Malik Mufarrij who was appointed the governor of Gujarat by **Firuz Shah Tughlaq** (1351–1388). In 1387, he killed Sikandar Khan who had been sent to take charge of Gujarat by Prince Muhammad (later **Muhammad Shah bin Firuz**, 1390–1394), then acting as joint *wazir* to the **sultan**. Subsequently, Muhammad's rival, **Ghiyas al-Din Tughlaq Shah**, recognized Malik Mufarrij as the governor of Gujarat and also entitled him Rasti Khan. Rasti Khan, however, transferred his allegiance to **Abu Bakr** (1389–1390). He was killed in Gujarat in 1392 by Muhammad Shah's appointee, **Zafar Khan**.

RATAN (?–1341). One of the Hindu members of the Tughlaq administrative class belonging to the caste of Kayasthas and who was known for his skill in "calculation and writing." He was entrusted by **Muhammad bin Tughlaq** (1325–1351) with the local administration of Sind. Around 1341, Ratan was raised to the position of the *muqti'* but a military officer stationed in Sind, taking advantage of a revolt by Unar, a chief of the Sumra tribe, killed him.

RATHORS. A **Rajput** clan that claimed descent from the **Gahadavalas** of **Kanauj**. The ruling dynasty established by Siha (?–1273) and carried forward by Rawal (14th century) in **Marwar** as well as its branch in Bikaner are identified as Rathors.

RAUTAS. The word "*raut*" is a corruption of Sanskrit *rajaputra* (son of a ruler). In medieval India, the term referred to a cavalry commander who served under local chiefs, the *ranakas* and *thakkuras*, and was paid for his service through a land grant.

RAZIYA SULTAN (?–1240). The daughter of Shams al-Din **Iltutmish** (1211–1236), she was nominated by him to succeed on the throne. The nobles, reluctant to serve under a woman, elevated to the throne one of her brothers, **Rukn al-Din** (1236), who proved incompetent and was removed within a few months. Only then was she invited to ascend the throne. Soon, many nobles, who were not happy that she was seeking to impose firm discipline on them, turned against her. Favor shown by her to the Abyssinian *amir akhur* Malik Jalal al-Din **Yaqat** also offended many nobles. The first to revolt was the governor of **Lahore**, but Raziya promptly chased him out of that province in 1239. While she was busy suppressing the revolt at Lahore, another revolt, this time by the governor of Sirhind, Malik **Altunia**, surfaced. At this point Raziya's Turkish guards betrayed her to the rebels. While a captive in the hands of the rebels, Raziya won over Malik Altunia and married him. Subsequently, she and Altunia marched upon **Delhi**, where the nobles had installed Raziya's brother **Bahram** as the **sultan**. They were defeated twice by the opposing nobles near Kaithal. While fleeing from their enemies, Raziya and Altunia were captured and killed by the local chiefs of the region in October 1240.

ROCKET. A gunpowder-based rocket that was already being used in China as a weapon of war came to India toward the close of the 13th century with its Persian name *hawai*. In the second half of the 14th century, *hawai* were being used in the **Delhi sultanate** as well as **Bahmani kingdom** for military purposes. With its increased effectiveness, this weapon came to be used widely during the 15th century. It subsequently acquired a new name, *ban*, the use of which by Indians in the 18th century is recorded by the officers of the English East India Company. These descriptions were available to Congreve when he designed his rocket. *See also* FIREARMS.

RUDRADEVA II (?–1324). He was the **Kakatiya** ruler of **Warangal** who submitted to **Delhi** when attacked by Malik **Kafur** in 1309. Later, in 1318, when **Khusrau** Khan was deputed by

Mubarak Shah Khalji (1316–1320) to invade **Telingana**, Rudradeva II renewed his allegiance to Delhi. But repudiating the overlordship of the **Delhi sultanate** in 1321, he captured **Bidar**. Subsequently, Warangal was defeated by Ulugh Khan (later **Muhammad bin Tughlaq**). Rudradeva died while being taken to Delhi.

RUKN AL-DIN IBRAHIM. *See* IBRAHIM, SULTAN RUKN AL-DIN.

RUKN AL-DIN KAIKA'US (?–1300?). The son of **Bughra Khan** who succeed to the throne of **Lakhnauti** after his father abdicated in his favor sometime around 1290. He died around 1300.

RUKN AL-DIN SUHRAWARDI (?–1335). A grandson of **Baha al-Din Zakarya**. **Qutb al-Din Mubarak Khalji** (1316–1320) asked him to set up a Suhrawardi hospice at **Delhi** but he declined the suggestion because he did not want to "intrude in the spiritual jurisdiction" of **Nizam al-Din Auliya**. He was given a large grant in **Multan** by **Muhammad bin Tughlaq** (1325–1351).

– S –

SABHA. Under the **Cholas**, the *sabha* was represented by the Brahmans of a village. It was found mostly in villages gifted to the Brahmans. By and large, the *sabha* had the same structure as the *ur*; it had the additional power to set up smaller committees from among its members for specialized tasks. Election to the *sabha* was possibly by lots from among those eligible. *See also* UR.

SADR-I JAHAN. The same as **sadr-us sudur**, it was the highest office in the **Delhi sultanate** to which an Islamic theologian could normally aspire. Ordinarily, the office of chief *qazi* was combined with that of *sadr-i jahan* and the two were held by the same person. The distribution of state patronage to the Islamic elite as well as the maintenance of mosques, *khanqahs*, and so forth was the jurisdiction of the *sadr-i jahan*.

SAHS. Hindu bankers and moneylenders who were quite prosperous during the 14th century. They also acted as moneychangers. In the **Delhi sultanate**, the minting of money was left to them. *See also* MULTANIS; THAKKURA PHERU.

SAIYID DYNASTY. The dynasty established by **Khizr Khan** (1414–1421) that ruled in the **Delhi sultanate** for 39 years. It owed its name to Khizr Khan's claim of being a descendant of the Prophet. The last Saiyid ruler, **'Ala al-Din 'Alam Shah** (1443–1476), left **Delhi** voluntarily in 1451 to take up residence at Badaun, where he died in 1476. Delhi was occupied by **Bahlul Lodi**, who proclaimed himself a **sultan** in 1451. *See also* MUBARAK SHAH.

SALAR MAS'UD. A mythical figure believed to be a soldier of **Mahmud of Ghazni** who carried on a religious war against the Hindu rajas of the Gangetic Plain during the first half of the 11th century. The tomb of Salar Mas'ud in Bahraich was widely venerated in the **Delhi sultanate** during the 14th century.

SALARI, 'IZZ AL-DIN MUHAMMAD (?–1240?). He served in India since **Muhammad Ghauri**'s time (d. 1206), and under **Iltutmish** (1211–1236) he held the position of *barbeg*. Salari initially sided with powerful nobles headed by Nizam ul-Mulk **Junaidi**, who had refused to recognize **Raziya**'s accession. After some negotiations, he crossed to Raziya's side. When Raziya and her husband, **Altunia**, marched on **Delhi** (1240) to suppress **Bahram Shah** (1240–1242), he was with them but disappeared from the scene following Raziya's defeat.

SAMANTA. One of the lesser feudatories of the period of **Indian feudalism** (800–1200) who lived on grants made to them by the kings in perpetuity and also accepted the obligation to supply armed men when required.

SANGA, RANA (?–1528). He came to the throne of **Mewar** in 1508 after the death of his father, Raimal (1473–1508), against the latter's expressed wishes. The nobles, passing over the person nominated by the deceased raja as his successor, invited Sanga from exile to ascend the throne. In 1517, Rana Sanga went to help Medini Rai, who had seized power at **Mandu** after Mahmud Khalji II's escape to Gujarat; he captured a number of strongholds in Malwa. In the ensuing conflict, Mahmud Khalji II was defeated and captured by Sanga at Gagraun but was restored in Malwa after ceding to Mewar the frontier strongholds of **Chanderi** and **Ranthambhor**. Three years later, a conflict arose between Rana Sanga and Muzaffar Shah II of Gujarat, leading to Sanga's advance up to **Ahmadabad** (1520) and the siege of **Chitor** by Muzaffar Shah II and Mahmud Khalji II (1524), which ended only after Sanga agreed to send one of his sons as hostage to Gujarat. Next year, there arose a conflict between Sanga and **Ibrahim Lodi** in the course of which the **Lodis** were defeated at Ghalote.

After **Babur** occupied **Agra** (1526), Rana Sanga mobilized a military alliance of local rulers, including Hasan Khan Mewati and Ibrahim Lodi's brother Mahmud Lodi, that confronted the Mughals at Kanwa (1527). Sanga and his allies were defeated at Kanwa, owing to Babur's superior battlefield management where the use of **firearms** was effectively combined with mounted combat. Following his defeat at Kanwa, Sanga withdrew to Ranthambhor but soon moved out from there with the intention of engaging Babur again, this time near Chanderi. On the way, he was poisoned by his enemies and died at Kalpi on 30 January 1528.

SARA-I 'ADL. A warehouse or market place built by **'Ala al-Din Khalji** (1296–1316) at **Delhi** where the merchants were obliged to bring their wares and sell them to local distributors at fixed prices. It was again at this place that the taxes to be levied on goods brought to market were calculated. The institution continued to function in one form or another until **Firuz Shah Tughlaq**'s time (1351–1388).

SAR-I JANDAR. The commander of the **sultan**'s guards who at times also acted as an executioner.

SAR-I SILAHDAR. The chief of the armor-bearers (*silahdars*) of the **sultan**. The *silahdars* were armed men who waited on the sultan when he gave public audience or rode through the streets. There were generally two *sar-i silahdars*, each guarding one of the flanks.

SARKAR. Fiscal and administrative division comprising several *parganas* that emerged in the **Delhi sultanate** under the **Lodis**. It possibly originated in the territorial assignments held by nobles for long periods during the 15th century. **Babur** has reproduced in *Baburnama* a list of *sarkars* and their estimated revenues that was based on the record of **Sikandar Lodi**'s time available to him.

SATI. The practice of Hindu widows immolating themselves with the dead bodies of their husbands (which is extolled in the Vedic texts) appears to have existed among some of the warrior groups of north India as early as the fourth century BCE. From the beginning of the sixth century onward, this is verified by surviving inscriptions. The **Ghaznavids** as well as the **Delhi sultans** treated sati as a Hindu cultural practice that they were free to continue as long as there was no element of coercion in its observance. In the Delhi sultanate, sati could be performed after informing the authorities. There is nothing on record showing that the Islamic ruling elite of the **Delhi sultanate** ever condemned this barbaric custom; on the other hand, **Amir Khusrau** in one of his verses refers to sati as the proof of Indian women's fidelity to their men. *See also* MUHAMMAD BIN TUGHLAQ.

SENA DYNASTY. The origin of the Sena dynasty of Bengal may be traced to a group of migrant warriors hailing from Karnataka. Sometime in the beginning of the 12th century, one of them, **Vijayasena** (1095–1108), established a principality in west Bengal that with the growing weakness of the **Pala dynasty** became powerful. By the end of the 12th century, it came to control a vast territory extending from **Benaras** to Assam. The last Sena ruler, **Lakshamansena** (1175–1206), was ousted from his capital Nadia by **Muhammad bin Bakhtiyar Khalji** circa 1204.

SHAH MIR, SULTAN SHAMS AL-DIN (?–1342). A pious adventurer with mystic leanings who came to Kashmir from Swat and received from the Hindu ruler Simha Deva (1301–1320) a rich grant at Baramula. After the general destruction brought about by an invading **Mongol** horde in 1320, Shah Mir helped elevate to the throne Rinchan Sadr al-Din (1320–1323), who converted to Islam and appointed Shah Mir his *wazir*. After Rinchan Sadr al-Din was killed in a popular uprising, one of his cousins, Udayna Deva (1323–1339), ascended the throne. During Udayna Deva's reign, Shah Mir became very powerful. In 1340, taking advantage of a renewed Mongol invasion, Shah Mir declared himself the sovereign ruler of Kashmir with the title Sultan Shams al-Din. He ruled for two years. During his short reign, Shah Mir created the structure of the sultanate of Kashmir, including a standing army and the organization of land revenue administration, collecting the state demand at the rate of one-sixth of gross produce. This new sultanate continued to exist until 1561.

SHAIKH UL-ISLAM. Both an office and honorific title in the early phase of the **Delhi sultanate**. The *shaikh ul-Islam*, usually a reputed theologian, enjoyed a special position at the court but was not assigned any duties. He assumed the function of sermonizing the **sultan** and his courtiers on religious issues. The first *shaikh ul-Islam* appointed by **Iltutmish** was Nur al-Din Mubarak Ghaznavi. According to Ziya' al-Din **Barani**, he urged the **sultan** to be harsh with the Hindus. The next *shaikh ul-Islam* of Iltutmish is accused in the **Chishti** texts of being rude to Shaikh **Mu'in al-Din Chishti**.

SHANKARADEVA (1449?–1568). He was born to Shaivite parents of the Kayastha caste in Ranpur district of Assam. Educated in Sanskrit, he became famous as a poet, musician, singer, and painter. Having met **Chaitanya** at **Puri**, he was attracted to **Vaishnava** doctrines. He was influenced by the teachings of the Madhavacharya sect of Puri. Shankaradeva's idea of *bhakti* was opposed to *karma-marga* (selfless activity), and his beliefs were a sort of revolt against the monism of *advaita* and agnosticism of *samkhya*. He used short plays on Puranic themes for disseminating his ideas in the Assamese language.

SHARF AL-DIN QA'INI. *See* QA'INI, SHARAF AL-DIN.

SHARQI DYNASTY. It was established by **Khwaja Jahan Sultan-us Sharq**, who was appointed to **Jaunpur** in 1394 by Sultan **Mahmud Tughlaq** (1394–1412). His adopted son, Malik Karanfal, declared himself an independent **sultan** at Jaunpur with the title **Mubarak Shah Sharqi** in 1398. The most illustrious ruler of the dynasty was **Ibrahim Shah Sharqi** (1401–1440). **Husain Shah Sharqi**, the last ruler of the line, was ousted from Jaunpur by **Sikandar Lodi** (1489–1417).

SHER KHAN, NUSRAT AL-DIN SANJAR (?–1270) One of the *chihilganis* who was a cousin of **Balban**. In 1242, Sher Khan was stationed in Sind, where he occupied **Multan** after ousting **Hasan Qarluq**. Following Balban's removal from the position of *na'ib* in 1252, Sher Khan lost his extensive *iqta'* covering Uchch, **Multan**, and Tabarhind. He subsequently went away to the **Mongol** court. After Balban returned to power (1254), Sher Khan came back from the Mongol court and was assigned an extensive *iqta'* in the Punjab that included **Lahore**. Throughout the remaining years of Nasir al-Din **Mahmud Shah**'s reign (1246–1266) as well as in the early years of Balban's rule (1266–1286), Sher Khan, not trusting his cousin fully, did not come to **Delhi**. Balban had him poisoned in 1269–1270.

SHIQ. A territorial division cutting across the old revenue divisions introduced in the beginning of the 14th century. Under **Muhammad bin Tughlaq**'s (1325–1351) regulations enforced in the 1340s, *shiqs* were created all over the empire. Marhatta country in the **Deccan** was, for example, divided into four *shiqs*, each headed by a commandant (*shiqdar*) who was instructed to deal with disaffected *amiran-i sada* harshly.

SIDI MAULA (?–1292?). An immigrant dervish from Central Asia whose hospice at **Delhi** started attracting numerous visitors after **Jalal al-Din Firuz Khalji**'s accession (1290). Khan-i Khanan Mahmud, the eldest son of the **sultan**, became an ardent follower of Sidi Maula. On Khan-i Khanan's death in 1292, many grandees from **Balban**'s era, including the Hindu chiefs Hatya Paik and Brinjin the *kotwal*, engaged in a conspiracy to bring Sidi Maula to the throne. The conspiracy was betrayed by a newly recruited **Mongol** noble. Sidi Maula was interrogated in open court, where he was injured by a group of Haidari mendicants and trampled under the feet of an elephant on the order of the sultan's son **Arkali Khan**. Hatya Paik and Brinjin Kotwal were also executed. Others involved were exiled and their properties confiscated.

SIKANDAR LODI (?–1517). Bahlul Lodi's son Nizam ascended the throne with the title Sultan Sikandar Ghazi (popularly called Sikandar Lodi) in 1489. He is credited with annexing **Jaunpur**, Bihar, and **Gwalior**. Unlike his father, Sikandar Lodi imposed firm control on the nobles and also sought to recruit into the nobility many non-**Afghans**, including a number of **Rajput** chieftains. He is known to have patronized the learned and devout at his court. He loved justice but his religious intolerance often led him to be unfair toward Hindus. As a prince, he wanted to demolish temples at Kurukshetra but desisted from taking that step when told by a respected theologian (Miyan '**Abd Allah Ajodhani**) that such a step would violate Islamic *shariah*.

SIKANDAR SHAH (?–1413). The son of Sultan Qutb al-Din who came to the throne of Kashmir in 1393 with the title Sultan Sikandar Shah. One of his senior nobles, Rai Maduri, who contributed to stabilizing his position on the throne, was dismissed and imprisoned by Sikandar soon after his accession. Subsequently, Siya Butt, a Brahman converted to Islam who was Sikandar's new *wazir*, urged him to embark on a policy of forced conversions and wholesale destruction of temples. Sikandar Shah is also reported to have offered his services to **Timur** when the latter invaded the **Delhi sultanate** in 1398. He is remembered in history as an intolerant breaker of idols and also as a ruler who exempted his subjects, Hindus as well as Muslims, from the tax on import (*tamgha*). His patronage of Islamic learning attracted to his court many dignitaries from Iran and Central Asia.

SIRAT-I FIRUZ SHAHI **(Qualities of Firuz Shah).** A panegyrical text by an anonymous author on the achievements of **Firuz Shah Tughlaq** (1351–1388) that was compiled around 1370. It focuses on Firuz Shah's intolerant measures against Hindus and his wars with non-Muslim rulers as well as his supposed acts of piety.

SIRHINDI, YAHYAH BIN AHMAD. Author of *Tarikh-i Mubarak Shahi* (History of Mubarak Shah), a general history of the **Delhi sultanate** that he dedicated to the second ruler of the **Saiyid dynasty**, Muizz al Din **Mubarak Shah** (1421–1433). His book ends rather abruptly in 1434 in the first year of Muhammad Shah's reign

(1434–1443). He was possibly attached in some capacity to the court of Mubarak Shah.

SIRI. A fort built by **'Ala al-Din Khalji** around 1301 at a short distance (three kilometers) northeast of old **Delhi** (Qila'i Rai Pithora). It came to be referred to as *hisar-i nao* (new fort).

SISODIYAS. A branch of the **Guhila** ruling family of Mewar. It was founded by Rahapa son of Karna. Sisodiya supremacy was established at **Chitor** by **Hammira** (1326–1364).

SOLANKIS. *See* CHAULUKYAS.

SOMADEVA. Author of a Sanskrit anthology of stories written in versified form under the title *Kathasaritsagara* (The Ocean of the Stream of Stories). These stories, recorded in the 11th century, have become a part of popular memory. To this day, some of these stories are narrated by ordinary folk in different parts of India.

SOMANATH. An important seaport of Gujarat in the 11th century, located on the southern part of Kathiawar coast. A famous temple devoted to the Hindu deity Somanath gave this city its name. Somanath was plundered by **Mahmud of Ghazni** in 1025. He gave vent to his religious bigotry by destroying the great temple and its main idol.

SUFIS. Muslim mystics who generally lived an isolated life in their hospices devoting themselves to prayers and other forms of perceiving God. Many of the Sufis regarded devotional music as a means of perceiving divinity. In medieval India, there existed several orders of Sufis; the more important ones were the **Chishtis** and **Suhrawardiyas**. The Chishtis often did not approve proximity to men in authority, though many of them are known to have accepted patronage from rulers.

SUHRAWARDIYA ORDER. This order was founded by Najib al-Din 'Abdul Qadir Suhrawardi. It was brought to India by Shihab al-Din Suhrawardi's disciple **Baha al-Din Zakarya**, who established his *khanqah* at **Multan**. The Suhrawardiya order flourished in Sind and

Punjab, with **Multan** and Uchch being principal centers. Several of Shihab al-Din Suhrawardi's disciples, other than Baha al-Din Zakarya, also migrated to India. Among them were included Jalal al-Din Tabrizi and Qazi **Hamid al-Din Nagauri**. Jalal al-Din, who established a *khanqah* in Assam, is supposed to have converted a large number of local people to Islam. **Sufis** of the Suhrawardiya order emphasized compliance with orthodox *shariah* and unlike those of the **Chishti** order did not see any harm in amassing wealth or seeking state patronage. Baha al-Din Zakarya's son and successor, Sadr al-Din 'Arif, however, had a different attitude: he did not approve of acquiring wealth. A disciple of Baha al-Din Zakarya, Sayyid Jalal al-Din Makhdum-i Jahanian (1308–1383) had his *khanqah* at Uchch. Shahbaz Qalandar of Sind also claimed spiritual authority from Baha al-Din Zakarya.

SULTAN. The monarchs in the **Ghaznavid** and **Ghaurid** empires, as well as in states ruled by Muslim dynasties in India until 1526, were generally referred to with the royal title "sultan." These sultans, though sovereign rulers, often maintained the fiction of paying allegiance to the Abbasid caliphs, whose line, after the sack of Baghdad by the **Mongols** in 1258, continued at Cairo on the sufferance of Mamluk rulers. The sultan was the head of state and its chief military commander. The nobles serving under him were deemed his slaves.

SWARGADWARI. A township established by **Muhammad bin Tughlaq** (1325–1351) on the bank of the Ganges River near present-day Thana Daryaoganj (District Etah, Uttar Pradesh) in 1339. The place chosen for the purpose was, as is suggested by its name Swargadwari ("Gate to Heaven"), already a pilgrimage center of Hindus. Muhammad bin Tughlaq stayed at Swargadwari and ran his empire from there between 1339 and 1341.

– T –

TABAQAT-I NASIRI **(Stories about the Deliverer).** A general history within the framework of Islamic tradition written by **Minhaj Siraj**

Juzjani in 1260s. It was dedicated to Sultan Nasir al-Din **Mahmud Shah** (1246–1266). It is the most important source of information for the history of the **Delhi sultanate** prior to 1260.

TAHQIQ AL-HIND. *See* KITAB AL-HIND.

TAJIKS. In the early phase of the **Delhi sultanate**, Persian-speaking freeborn nobles, including those belonging to **Ghaurid** ruling clans, were generally identified as Tajiks or Taziks to distinguish them from Turkish slaves promoted to high positions.

TAMIL. The earliest non-Aryan language of the extreme south, Tamil was first committed to writing in the third or second century BCE when Brahmi script was introduced from north India. Tamil devotional cults contributed during 500–900 to the popularization of the Tamil language. It emerged as a well-developed language during the ascendancy of the **Cholas** (900–1300). Its vocabulary was enriched by association with Sanskrit. Writing in the beginning of the 11th century, **Abu Rehan Alberuni** lists Tamil as a distinct Indian language, calling it Dravidi.

TANKA. Originally, it was the name of a silver coin weighing 168.24 grams current in northwest India prior to the annexation of the Punjab to the **Ghaznavid** Empire (1009). Under the Ghaznavids, this name was transferred to their *dirham*, which weighed 45 grains. In the **Delhi sultanate**, a new silver *tanka* weighing 172 grains was introduced by **Iltutmish**.

TARAF. In the early phase of the **Delhi sultanate**, *tarafs* were subdivisions of the larger territories of *vilayats*. In the **Bahmani kingdom**, this term applied to provinces. It was divided into four *tarafs* administered by provincial commandants designated *tarafdars*.

TARAIN. A place close to the fort of Sirsa (Sarsati of Persian texts) in the district of Bhatinda (the Punjab). It is famous for battles fought between **Muhammad Ghauri** and **Prithviraja III** in 1191 and 1192.

TARIKH-I FIRUZ SHAHI **OF 'AFIF (History of Firuz Shah by 'Afif).** A history dealing with the life and achievements of **Firuz Shah Tughlaq** (1351–1388) by Siraj 'Afif, who was a clerk in the office of the *wazir* sometime after **Timur**'s invasion (1398).

TARIKH-I FIRUZ SHAHI **OF ZIYA'BARANI (History of Firuz Shah by Ziya' Barani).** A history of the **Delhi sultanate** from **Balban's** accession (1266) to the sixth year of **Firuz Shah Tughlaq**'s rule (i.e., 1357), by **Ziya' Barani**. It forms a continuation of **Minhaj Siraj's** account in *Tabaqat-i Nasiri*.

TATAR KHAN (?–1404). The son of the governor of Gujarat **Zafar Khan**, who joined Nusrat Shah on the latter's being proclaimed a rival **sultan** at Firuzabad (near **Delhi**) after the accession of Nasir al-Din **Mahmud Shah Tughlaq** at Delhi in 1394. On being outmaneuvered in the tussle that ensued, Tatar Khan returned to Gujarat (1397) and tried to persuade his father to march on Delhi. Sometime around 1403, Tatar Khan, with the reluctant connivance of his father, declared himself an independent ruler in Gujarat. He died while proceeding to Delhi purportedly for the purpose of ousting **Mallu Iqbal** from there in 1404.

TELINGANA. The **Telugu**-speaking region immediately to the south of Godavari with **Warangal** as its political center was ruled by the **Kakatiya** dynasty until 1321, when it was annexed to the **Delhi sultanate**. After the rise of the **Bahmani kingdom** (1347), Telingana territory—which had again come to be ruled by independent chieftains— obstructed its advance toward the eastern coast. The ruler of Warangal was supported and encouraged by **Vijayanagar** to defy the Bahmanis. **Ahmad Shah Bahmani** (1422–1435) forced the chief of Telingana to become a tributary of the Bahmani **sultan** in 1324.

TELUGU. It evolved as a separate language in the Andhra region during the 9th century. Mentioning Telugu as one of the Indian languages in the beginning of the 11th century, **Alberuni** calls it Andhri. Like **Tamil** and **Malayalam**, Telugu was evolved from Dravidian roots but carried a deeper imprint of Sanskrit vocabulary.

THAKKURA. One of the titles of lesser feudatories of early medieval India (800–1200). In the **Delhi sultanate**, the term applied to the hereditary chiefs of the category represented by *ranas* and *ranakas*.

THAKKURA PHERU. A mint master in the service of **Qutb al-Din Mubarak Shah Khalji** (1316–1320) who describes in his 1318 treatise, *Dravya Pariksha* (Test of Substance), in detail all the contemporary issues of coins and working of the mints.

TIMUR (1334–1405). Born in the Barlas tribe of Mongolid Turks, Timur rose to kingship at Samarqand in 1370. With the help of his Turk-Mongol corps of military officers, he established a vast empire that soon came to include the whole of Khwarazm and Turkistan as well as Persia and Mesopotamia. This was followed by his invasion of Ottoman territories in Anatolia and the conquest of the entire territory up to the Sulaiman range in the east.

In 1396–1397, Timur's grandson, Pir Muhammad, besieged the garrison stationed by the **sultan** of **Delhi** at **Multan**. The next year (September 1398), Timur crossed the Indus River near Bannu and advanced toward Delhi, passing through **Dipalpur** and Ajodhan. Muslims as well as Hindus of this tract fought stoutly against the invaders, which prompted the Timurid historian Sharaf al-Din 'Ali Yazdi to describe the Indian Muslims opposing Timur's advance as "faithless ones," faithless Hindus" "hyprocrites." **Mallu Iqbal Khan,** a minister of Sultan **Mahmud Shah Tughlaq** (1394–1412), came forward to check Timur but was defeated. Subsequently, outside Delhi, Timur massacred the 100,000 men (many of them Muslims) made captives during his march to Delhi. Sultan Mahmud Shah Tughlaq himself was defeated outside Delhi on 18 December 1398 and fled from the capital; a general pillage followed. The city was systematically plundered for five days. A surviving inscription in a Delhi mosque cursing Timur testifies to the people's resentment over this atrocity. After a stay of a fortnight at Delhi, Timur proceeded to besiege Meerut and Hardwar. He left India via Kangra and Jammu, leaving the **Delhi sultanate** in total anarchy. Timur carried away a huge treasure as well as a large number of Indian artisans and masons as slaves, contributing to the dissemination of Indian handicrafts in Central Asia.

TOGHRIL (?–1282?). One of the slave nobles of **Balban** (1266–1286) who was appointed governor of Bengal in 1266–1267. He rebelled, assuming the sovereign title Sultan Mughis al-Din in 1279–1280. Balban marched to **Lakhnauti**, took Toghril prisoner, and put him to death in 1281–1282.

TOMARAS. A **Rajput** clan that ruled over **Delhi** and the neighboring territory during the 12th century. Toward the middle of the 12th century, the Tomaras of **Delhi** were subjugated by the **Chahamanas** of **Ajmer**. The occupation of Delhi (1193) by the **Ghaurids** put an end to the Tomara principality there. After the subjugation of **Pratihara** chiefs in the **Gwalior** region by **Muhammad bin Tughlaq** (1325–1351), there emerged a Tomara chieftainship at Gwalior that until 1380 rendered military service to **Firuz Shah Tughlaq (1351–1388)** but tended to be independent of the Delhi **sultan**'s authority after 1401. The Tomaras controlled Gwalior until the middle of the 15th century.

TUGHLAQ DYNASTY. The dynasty established by **Ghiyas al-Din Tughlaq** (1320–1325) in the **Delhi sultanate** continued until 1412. It originated as a family of **Qarauna** Turks in the service of **Khalji** rulers (1290–1320). The nobles' revolt against **Khusrau Shah** (1320) led to the rise of the Tughlaqs to power. The apex of Tughlaq rule was represented by the reigns of Ghiyas al-Din Tughlaq and his two successors (1320–1388). This period witnessed important developments like **Muhammad bin Tughlaq**'s attempt to establish greater control on regions and the resulting local revolts, the rise of the **Vijayanagar** and **Bahmanis**, and an extension of agriculture and the accompanying promotion of irrigation facilities. While Ghiyas al-Din rose to power as a defender of Islam, Muhammad bin Tughlaq promoted Hindus in his service and also extended state patronage to non-Muslim religious institutions. **Firuz Shah Tughlaq**, on the other hand, tried to impose *jiziya* on the Hindus. **Timur**'s invasion (1398) resulted in the fragmentation of the Tughlaq Empire, leading to its end in 1412.

TUGHLAQ SHAH I, GHIYAS AL-DIN. *See* GHIYAS AL-DIN TUGHLAQ SHAH.

TUGHLAQABAD. A fortified township built by **Ghiyas al-Din Tughlaq** (1320–1325) about five kilometers east of **Delhi** (Qil'a Rai Pithora). Ghiyas al-Din Tughlaq's tomb, an important landmark in the development of Indo-Muslim architecture, is located close to Tughlaqabad.

TURUSHKAS. The Sanskrit name for Turks frequently found in Hindu inscriptions of the period 1000–1526. In these inscriptions, this term often connotes Muslim invaders as well as those settled in the territories ruled by Hindu rajas.

– U –

UJJAIN. Some 121 kilometers west of Bhopal, the capital of Madhya Pradesh, it is an important Hindu pilgrimage center. It was also a major administrative center and entrepot where trade routes converged under the Mauryas (322–184 BCE) and Guptas (320–500 CE). At the time of the **Ghaurid** conquest of north India (1192–1206), Ujjain was a part of the **Paramara** kingdom of Malwa with its capital at Dhar. It was plundered by **Iltutmish** in 1235. Ujjain was annexed to the **Delhi sultanate** in 1305. Subsequently, Ujjain and Bhilsa together constituted the *iqta'* of **Ain ul-Mulk Multani** (1320).

'ULAMA. The Muslim theologians who were considered competent to interpret the holy Quran and Sunnah (traditions of the Prophet Muhammad). **Sultans** in medieval India often allowed the *'ulama* to act as religious and legal arbiters.

ULUGH KHAN (?–1315?). **'Ala al-Din Khalji**'s brother who was originally known as Almas Beg. He was made *barbeg* and entitled on his brothers accession (1296) as Ulugh Khan. After he defeated a large **Mongol** invading horde in the Punjab (February 1298), Ulugh Khan was appointed to the prestigious *iqta'* of **Bayana**. In 1301, Ulugh Khan was appointed to the newly acquired **Ranthambhor**, which he continued to command until the time of his sudden death, possibly from poisoning, in 1315.

'UMAR KHAN SARWANI (?–1500?). *Wazir* of **Bahlul Lodi** (1451–1489). At the latter's demise (1489), he is reported to have played a crucial role in ensuring the accession of **Sikandar Lodi** (1489–1517). In 1493, Sikandar Lodi imprisoned his brother Barbak Shah for showing incompetence in the fight against the **Sharqis** and gave him into the joint custody of Haibat Khan and 'Umar Khan Sarwani; the latter was then holding a large *iqta'* at Sirhind. Umar Khan had close relations with Shaikh **'Abd al-Quddus Gangohi** and had provided the *shaikh* a lucrative grant at Shahabad.

UR or *URAR*. Informal gathering of an entire village that coordinated with the *sabha*, the assembly representing formally the population of a village in southern kingdoms of early medieval India. The *ur* was open to all the male adults of a village but the older members took a more prominent part.

– V –

VAGHELA DYNASTY. The Vaghelas replaced the **Chaulukyas** as the ruling dynasty of Gujarat sometime toward the end of the 12th century. At the time **'Ala al-Din Khalji** (1296–1316) invaded Gujarat (1397), it was being ruled by Vaghelas. Following the defeat of the last Vaghela ruler, Karna Deva, and occupation of a large part of Gujarat by the invaders that year, the territory around Vadodara continued to be controlled by the Vaghelas. They were finally driven out of Gujarat in 1310.

VAISHNAVAS. Worshipers of Vishnu perceived as one of the trinity of gods (Brahma, the creator; Vishnu, the preserver; and Shiva, the destroyer) representing the Absolute or the universal soul postulated in the *Upanishads*. The Vaishnavas, present in large numbers in north India during 1000–1526, worshiped Vishnu mainly in his two incarnations—namely, Rama, the warrior king, and Krishna, the sage charioteer, jovial herdsman, and friend of Radha.

VALLABHACHARYA. Like **Ramanuja**, he was a *bhakti* teacher from the south. Vallabhacharya is regarded as the founder of the *bhakti* school identified with Krishna in north India. It was mostly in the first half of the 16th century that the traders (*vaishyas*) of Gujarat were converted to the Vallabhacharya sect of **Vaishnavism**.

VASCO DA GAMA (1460–1524). Born in 1460 at Sine, he entered the service of the Portuguese court. King Emanuel I sent him in command of a fleet sailing to India in 1497. He rounded the Cape of Good Hope and arrived at **Calicut** on 22 May 1498. Vasco da Gama returned to Calicut in 1504 and proclaimed the king of Portugal lord of the seas. He bombarded Calicut and established a factory at Cochin.

VEDANTA. Shankaracharya, the proponent of *vedanta*, lived in the eighth or ninth century. His teachings continued to be a major intellectual current in medieval Hindu thought. The *vedanta* reduces the realities of soul and matter to one absolute reality that manifests itself in the multiplicity of names and forms of the phenomenal universe. It suggests that the soul is not only conscious but one and the same in all beings and is identical with God (Brahma).

VETTI. Forced labor that the peasants were sometimes made to perform for the state authorities. In the **Chola** Empire, a tax equivalent in value to the expected forced labor was also realized.

VIDYAPATI THAKKURA. The author of the Sanskrit text *Purushapariksha* (The Test of a Man) was attached to the Mithila (north Bihar) rulers Deva Simha (?–1412) and his successors. Vidyapati Thakkura wrote another book, *Shaiva-sarvasva-sara* (Quintessence of Shaiva), on the order of Queen Visvasa Devi. The *Purushapariksha* is a collection of tales that often refer to historical characters, including rulers of the **Delhi sultanate**. These stories throw interesting sidelights on the social norms and ethical values of the period. Interestingly enough, these tend to show that religious hatred or differences did not figure prominently in the conflicts that frequently cropped up between the **sultans** and Hindu chiefs. Among Vidyapati's writings in **Apabrahmsha**, *Kirti-lata* (The Creeping Glory) is well known. His songs in the **Maithili** dialect dealing with the legend of Krishna and Radha are still popular in eastern India.

VIJAYANAGAR EMPIRE. Founded by **Harihara** and **Bukka** who claimed to be the descendents of **Yadava** rulers of Deogir. They were originally in the service of the **Kakatiya** ruler of **Warangal**, **Rudradeva**, and were carried to **Delhi** as prisoners along with him in 1324. On being released from captivity in 1336, they established a new state with its capital at Vijayanagar, the newly built city on the southern bank of the Tungbhadra River. This new state became famous as the Vijayanagar Empire. It was constantly at war with the **Bahmani kingdom** and successors, but was dismantled after its defeat in the battle of Talicota (1565). The most illustrious ruler of Vijayanagar was **Krishna Deva Raya** (1509–1529). The impress of contacts with the Bahmanis and the **Delhi sultanate** on Vijayanagar's political culture was manifested by the title "Sultan among Hindu kings" used for the ruler and also by the presence of a large contingent of Muslim horsemen in his army.

VIJAYASENA (?–1108). A Kanara by origin, Vijayasena (grandson of Samantasena) established a small principality in southwest Bengal around 1095 and ruled until 1108. Taking advantage of the growing weakness of the **Pala** rule, Vijayasena consolidated and extended his principality, which came to control a vast territory.

VIKRAMA ERA. An Indian system of reckoning historical chronology that was established in 58 BCE by Vikramaditya, who ruled over Malwa from his capital **Ujjain**. This era fell in disuse after Vikramaditya but was revived by Chandra Gupta II in 389. It continued to be used during the medieval period.

VIKRAMADITYA VI (?–1126). The **Chaulukya** ruler of Kalyani who came to throne in 1076. As prince, he had invaded Bengal and Malwa. On his accession, Vikramaditya VI assumed the title *Tribhuvanamalla* and also started a new era. Already by 1100 the **Yadavas** of Narmada were his feudatories. He seized Kanchi (1085) and wrested Andhra from **Cholas** (1118–1124). Vikramaditya VI also subdued the **Hoyasalas**, annexing **Dorasamudra** in 1120. He was patron to the poet Bilhana and to Vijnanesvara, the author of *mitakshara*.

VILAYAT. A regular province as distinct from the area of a military command (*iqta'*) in the **Delhi sultanate**. A *vilayat* was sometimes divided into *shiqs*. The formal designation of the head of a *vilayat* was *vali*.

– W –

WAJAHDARS. Under **Firuz Shah Tughlaq** (1351–1388), troops who were paid their salaries through assignments were called *wajahdars* as opposed to those who were paid cash or in drafts on the revenues of the provinces. By the time **Babur** established himself at **Agra** (1526), the term had come to connote the assignment holders in general.

WAKIL-I DAR. The head of the department of the royal household, which included a large number of production centers and stores that supplied the court as well as different central establishments with provisions and equipment. In the **Delhi sultanate**, this office was generally occupied by a very senior noble. Under **Iltutmish** (1211–1236), the office of *wakil-i dar* was held by 'Izz al-Din **Salari**.

WARANGAL. The same as Arangal, capital of the **Kakatiya** principality of **Telingana** until 1321. Malik **Kafur** defeated Warangal in 1310 after a long siege, forcing the Kakatiya ruler to agree to pay tribute to **Delhi**. Warangal was annexed to the **Delhi sultanate** in 1321. The local defiance at Warangal continued throughout the 14th and 15th centuries; its chiefs often sided with **Vijayanagar** against the **Bahmani kingdom** during the 15th century.

WAZIR. He headed the civil administration in the medieval sultanates. The w*azir's* special domain in the **Delhi sultanate** was financial organization. When the **sultan** was weak, the *wazir* tended to usurp his powers. The position of **Khan-i Jahan Maqbul** in **Firuz Shah Tughlaq's** reign (1351–1388) is an example. Most of the *wazirs* in the Delhi sultanate were men of culture and taste; even the ill-educated Khan-i Jahan Maqbul was considered very wise and capable. *See also* MUHAMMAD SHAH BIN FIRUZ, SULTAN NASIR AL-DIN.

– Y –

YADAVA DYNASTY. The Yadavas of Deogir emerged as local rulers in their own right only in the late 12th century. Before that, they were there as understudies of the western **Chaulukyas**. The Yadava ruler Bilhala III, who asserted his independence in 1185, may be regarded as the founder of dynasty that ruled from Deogir until 1317. The Yadavas were uprooted in that year by **'Ala al-Din Khalji**'s general Malik **Khafur**. *See also* RAMACHANDRA YADAVA.

YAQUT, JAMAL AL-DIN (?–1240). A slave military officer of Abyssinian origin who already enjoyed a considerable position by the time **Raziya** (1236–1240) ascended the throne. Impressed by Yaqut's ability, Raziya promoted him to the position of *amir-i akhur* and also entitled him *amir al-umara* (chief amir). This was resented by senior slave officers, in particular by **Ikhtiyar al-Din Aitegin**, who, jointly with **Altunia**, the governor of Tabarhind, started a revolt while Raziya was campaigning against the rebellious governor of **Lahore**. The rebels seized Yaqut and put him to death in 1240.

YILDIZ, TAJ AL-DIN (?–1216). Yildiz was a slave of **Muhammad Ghauri**. He proclaimed himself a **sultan** at Ghazni on his master's death in 1206. Yildiz adopted a conciliatory attitude toward Qutb al-Din **Aibek** (1206–1210), who had made himself the independent ruler of the conquered territories in India. Yildiz gave one of his daughters in marriage to Aibek. After **Iltutmish**'s rise to the throne of **Delhi** in 1211, Yildiz refused to acknowledge his sovereignty. In 1214, when a Khwarazmian incursion ousted Yildiz from Ghazni, he came to the Punjab with the idea of carving out a territory for himself there but was overtaken and defeated by Iltutmish in 1216. Yildiz was taken prisoner and executed.

YINALTEGIN, TAJ AL-DIN. A noble who was in the service of Nasir al-din **Qubacha** until 1221. On the arrival of Jal al-Din **Mingbarni** in the Salt Range region, he joined the Khwarazmi prince. Subsequently, Yinaltegin established himself as the ruler of Sistan. One of his cousins, Saif al-Din Firuz, was in **Iltutmish**'s service. Yinaltegin possibly belonged to the category of freeborn Turks hailing from

Khwarazm. He was overthrown in Sistan by an invading **Mongol** force in 1235.

– Z –

ZAFAR KHAN. *See* MUZAFFAR SHAH.

ZAFAR KHAN, HIZABR AL-DIN YUSUF (?–1300). A maternal nephew of **'Ala al-Din Khalji** (1296–1316). On 'Ala al-Din's accession (1296), he was made *'ariz* and entitled Zafar Khan. In 1298, Zafar Khan, along with **Ulugh Khan**, commanded **Delhi**'s forces against the **Mongols** led by Qutlugh Qocha. In a battle near Delhi, Zafar Khan defeated the Mongols, pursuing them for nearly 48 kilometers.

ZAFAR KHAN, TAJ AL-DIN MUHAMMAD LUR FARSI. His family came possibly from southwest Persia. During the Bengal campaign of 1360, **Firuz Shah Tughlaq** (1351–1388) had agreed to withdraw from Sonargaon on the condition that his client, Zafar Khan, would be installed there. But Zafar Khan chose instead to return to **Delhi**.

ZAIN AL-'ABIDIN, SULTAN (?–1473). He succeeded his elder brother, Ali Shah, on the throne of Kashmir in 1423 and ruled for the next 50 years. He was a pious, orthodox, and learned Muslim and is known to have reversed the intolerant religious policy of his father, Sultan **Sikandar** (1393–1413), who is known to have destroyed temples and persecuted non-Muslims. While encouraging leading men of Islam, Zain al-'Abidin also showed the same kindness to the Hindu religious elite, extending many facilities to them. Hindus who had been earlier evicted from their houses were brought back and provided protection. Hindus and Muslims were encouraged to participate in each others' religious celebrations. Zain al-'Abidin is also known to have patronized the arts and crafts. Under his encouragement, the manufacture of **firearms** as well as the use of paper was introduced in Kashmir. He is also known for his measures of public welfare like the digging of irrigation canals and the establishment of a system of price control and market regulations.

ZAKARYA, SHAIKH BAHA AL-DIN. *See* BAHA AL-DIN ZAKARYA.

ZAMORIN OF CALICUT. The rulers of **Calicut** on the Malabar coast from the 15th century onwards were known as Zamorins. Mirza Shah Rukh's (1405–1448) envoy **'Abd al-Razzaq**, who calls this ruler Samurai, visited his court at Calicut in 1443.

ZIYA' BARANI. *See* BARANI, ZIYA' AL-DIN.

ZOROASTRIANISM. Religion based on the teachings of the sixth-century BCE Persian sage Zoroaster where divinity is perceived in two predominant spirits: of light and good and of darkness and evil. The followers of the Zoroastrian faith, popularly known as Parsis, came to the western coast of India after they were evicted from Iran in the wake of the Islamic conquest (in the early eighth century). In Gujarat, they were given protection by the **Chaulukyas**. In the medieval period, many of them took to trade, which tended to identify them as a community of traders.

Bibliography

The following book list aims at enabling lay readers as well as professional historians to access more significant publications that carry varied interpretations of the history of medieval India (1000–1526) and the source material on which these are based.

For classifying this literature in a proper sequence, the medieval period of Indian history is divided into three phases: (1) early medieval India (1000–1200); (2) the Delhi sultanate (1200–1412); and (3) regional states (1412–1526). It goes without saying that such a periodization roughly corresponds to features of state systems in the subcontinent at different points of time. During the early medieval Indian period, the entire subcontinent with the exception of parts of the Punjab controlled by Ghaznavids and, perhaps, the Chola kingdom of the extreme south was divided into semifeudal Hindu monarchies; on the other hand, the Delhi sultanate and the regional states phases are identified with the highly centralized Delhi sultanate and regional kingdoms of the 15th century respectively.

For each one of the above phases, books as well as important items of periodical literature are divided under the following subheadings: (a) Sources, (b) Political History, and (c) Social and Cultural History.

The Sources sections include English translations of contemporary and near-contemporary Arabic, Persian, Sanskrit, and other literary texts that furnish information for each phase. There are also listed translations of original documents and epigraphs as well as commentaries on the nature of available source material. While books and articles included in Political History sections generally relate to dynastic changes as well as to the growth of political structures contributing to state formation at different planes, the Social and Cultural History sections deal with trade, commerce, agrarian economy, currency system, production technology, weapons of war, and so forth. Studies included in this latter section also note the state of cultural hiatus as well as adjustments flowing from the emergence of new ethnocentric groups, particularly those identified as followers of Islam. Some of them also reflect on new religious attitudes (*bhakti* and Sufism, for example) as well as changes in literary tastes, music, architecture, and other fine arts.

In selecting books and articles for this bibliography, I attempted to make it as representative of different views and approaches as are present among historians on medieval Indian history—which has always been a controversial subject. But due care is taken to exclude much of the ideological pamphleteering that has gone on since the late 19th century that projected English colonialist, Hindu nationalist, or Islamic visions in the garb of school or college textbooks or popular history books. At the same time, all-important writings—having a bearing on different aspects of medieval Indian history, irrespective of any biases these betray—are included. The basic criterion for judging the viability of a writing on the subject has consistently been if it was rooted in the available source material. However, it is obvious that writings revealing a critical approach to sources are rated as more reliable.

The original source materials on medieval Indian history, which are mainly available in the form of Persian and Sanskrit texts, may be consulted in the collections of the British Library (London), India Office Library (London), Khuda Bakhsh Oriental Public Library (Patna), and similar locations. For epigraphical material, one may consult the files of *Epigraphia Indica* (Calcutta/Delhi) and *Epigrahia Indo-Moslemica* (Calcutta/Delhi; now *Epigraphia Indica, Arabic and Persian Supplement*, Delhi). Most of the modern publications on the subject, including periodical literature, should be available at the British Library (London), Library of Congress (Washington, D.C.), National Library of India (Calcutta), Research Library of the Centre of Advanced Study in History (Aligarh Muslim University, Aligarh), and similar other collections at important centers in India, Pakistan, Great Britain, and the United States where medieval Indian history is taught and researched.

1. EARLY MEDIEVAL INDIA: (1000–1200)

Sources

Agarwala, V. S. "The Sanskrit Legend on the Bilingual Tankas of Mahmud Ghazni." *Journal of Numismatic Society of India* 5 (1943): 155–61.

Al-Idrisi. *Nuzhat al-Mushtaq.* Portion relating to India. Ed. and trans. S. Maqbul Ahmad, *India and Neighbouring Territories as Described by the Sharif al-Idrisi.* Part (1) Arabic text, Aligarh, 1954; Part (2) translation and commentary. Leiden: E. J. Brill, 1960.

Choudhary, Gulab Chandra. *Political History of Northern India from Jain Sources (c.650 A.D. to 1300 A.D.).* Amritsar: Sohanlal Jaindharma Pracharak Samiti, n.d.

Cunningham, A. *Coins of Medieval India from the 7th Century Down to the Muhammadan Conquests.* Reprint. Delhi: Oriental Books, 1967.

Desai, Z. A. "Arabic Inscriptions of the Rajput Period from Gujarat." *Epigraphia Indica: Arabic and Persian Supplement* (1961): 1–24.

Diskalkar, D. B. "Inscriptions of Kathiawad." *New Indian Antiquary* 1 (1938–1939): 686–96.

Dikshit, M. G. *Selected Inscriptions from Maharashtra (Fifth to Twelfth Century A.D.).* Poona: n.p., 1947.

Jonaraja. *Rajatarangini (1459). Kings of Kashmir.* Trans. J. C. Dutt. Reprint. Delhi: Low Price, 1986.

Kalhana. *Rajatarangini.* Trans. M. Stein. Reprint. Delhi: Motilal Banarsidas, 1979.

Karashima, N. *South Indian History and Society: Studies from Inscriptions, A.D. 850–1800.* Delhi: Oxford University Press, 1984.

Karashima, N., and B. Sitaraman. "Revenue Terms in Chola Inscriptions." *Journal of Asian and African Studies* 5 (1972): 81–117.

Karashima, N., Y. Subbarayulu, and T. Matsui. *A Concordance of the Names in the Chola Inscriptions.* 3 vols. Madurai: n.p., 1978.

Marco Polo. *Book of Ser Marco Polo: The Venetian, Concerning the Kingdoms and Marvels of the East.* Trans. Henry Yule, rev. by Henry Cordier. 3rd ed. Reprint. New Delhi: Munshiram Manoharlal, 1993.

Nilakanta Sastri, K. A. *Sources of Indian History with Special Reference to South India.* Bombay: Asia Publishing House, 1964.

Reynolds, James. *Kitab-i Yamini: Historical Memoirs of Amir Subaktagin and the Sultan Mahmud of Ghazna.* Reprint. Lahore: Qausain, 1975.

Rodgers, C. J. *Catalogue of Coins in the Government Museum, Lahore.* Calcutta: Baptist Mission Press, 1891.

Sachau, E. C. *Alberuni's India.* 2 vols. Reprint. Delhi: Atlantic, 1979.

Sircar, D. C. *Indian Epigraphical Glossary.* Reprint. Delhi: Motilal Banarsidas, 1966.

Stein, M. A. *Kalhana's Rajatarangini.* Translation with an introduction, commentary, and appendixes. 4 vols. Reprint. Delhi: Munshiram Manoharlal, 1960.

Sewell, R. "Dates of Chola Kings." *Epigraphia Indica* 11, no. 23 (1911–1912): 241–51.

Thomas, Edward. *On the Coins of Ghazna.* London: n.p., 1848.

Wright, H. Nelson. *Catalogue of the Coins of Indian Museum, Calcutta.* Vols. 2–3. Oxford: Clarendon Press, 1907.

Political History

Abdur, Rehman. *Last Two Dynasties of the Sahis: An Analysis of Their History, Archaeology, Coinage and Palaeography.* Delhi: Renaissance, 1988.

Acharyya, N. N. *The History of Medieval Assam.* Gauhati: Omsons, 1984.

Altekar, A. S. *Rashtrakutas and Their Times.* Poona: Oriental Book Agency, 1934.

Baqir, Muhammad. "Lahore during the Pre-Muslim Period." *Islamic Culture* 22, no. 3 (1948): 295–306.

Bhandarkar, D. R. "The Chahamanas of Marwar." *Epigraphia Indica* 11, no. 4 (1911–1912): 26–85.

Bhatia, Pratital. *The Paramaras (c.800–1305 A.D.).* New Delhi: Munshiram Manoharlal, 1970.

Bosworth, C. E. *The Ghaznavids: Their Empire in Afghanistan and Eastern Iran 994–1040.* Edinburgh: Edinburgh University Press, 1963.

———. *The Later Ghaznavids, Splendour and Decay: The Dynasty in Afghanistan and Northern India 1040–1186*. Edinburgh: Edinburgh University Press, 1977.

Chowdhuri, Abdul Momin. *Dynastic History of Bengal (c.750–1200 A.D.)*. Dacca: Asiatic Society of Pakistan, 1967.

Derrett, J. Duncan M. *The Hoyasalas: A Medieval Indian Royal Family*. Madras: Oxford University Press, 1957.

Dikshit, G. S. *Local Self Government in Medieval Karntaka*. Dharwar: Karnatak University, 1964.

Dikshit, R. K. *The Candellas of Jejakabhukti*. New Delhi: Abhinav, 1977.

Elphinstone, Mount Stuart. *The History of India: The Hindu and Muhhometan Periods*. E. B. Cowell. 6th ed. London: Murray, 1874.

Friedmann, Yohanan. "A Contribution to the Early History of Islam in India." In *Studies in Memory of Gaston Wiet*. Edited by M. Rosen-Ayalon. Jerusalem: Institute of Asian and African Studies, Hebrew University, 1977.

Ganguli, D. C. *History of the Paramara Dynasty*. Dacca: n.p., 1943.

Islam, Riazul. "The Rise of the Sammas in Sind." *Islamic Culture* 22, no. 4 (1948): 359–83.

Habib, M. *Sultan Mahmud of Ghazni*. Reprint. Delhi: S. Chand, 1967.

Karashima, Noboru. *Kingship in Indian History*. New Delhi: Manohar, 1999.

Khuhro, Hamida, ed. *Sind through the Centuries*. Karachi: Oxford University Press, 1981.

Majumdar, A. K. *The Chaulukyas of Gujarat*. Bombay: Bhartiya Vidya Bhavan, 1956.

Majumdar, R. C., H. C. Ray Chaudhri, and Kalikinkar Datta. *Advanced History of India*. Madras: Macmillan India, 1981.

Misra, Binayak. *Medieval Dynasties of Orissa*. Calcutta: Chatterji, 1934.

Mishra, V. B. *Gurjaras-Pratiharas and Their Times*. Delhi: S. Chand, 1966.

Moreland, W. H., and A. C. Chatterjee. *Short History of India*. 2nd ed. London: Longmans, 1944.

Nazim, Muhammad. *The Life and Times of Sultan Mahmud of Ghazna*. Reprint. New Delhi: Munshiram Manoharlal, 1971.

Nilakanta, Sastri, K. A. *Cholas*. Madras: University of Madras, 1955.

———. *A History of South India*. London: Oxford University Press, 1955.

———. *History of South India from Prehistoric Times to the Fall of Vijayanagar*. 3rd ed. London: Oxford University Press, 1966.

———. *South Indian Influence in the Far East*. Bombay: Hind Kitabs, 1949.

Niyogi, Roma. *The History of Gahdavala Dynasty*. Calcutta: Calcutta Oriental Book Agency, 1959.

Petech, Luciano. *Medieval Nepal (c.750–1480)*. Rome: Rome Serie Orientale, 1958.

Prasad, Ishwari. *New History of India, from the Earliest Times to the Present Day*. Rev. ed. Allahabad: Indian Press. 1978.

Raychaudhuri, H. C., and K. K. Datta. *An Advanced History of India*. 4th ed. Madras: Macmillan, 1981.

Ray, H. C. *Social, Cultural and Economic History of India: Medieval Age.* Delhi: Surjeet, 1978.

Rosen, Stephen Peter. *Societies and Military Power: India and Its Armies.* Delhi: Oxford University Press, 1996.

Sharma, D. *Early Chauhan Dynasties.* Delhi: S. Chand, 1959.

Sharma, R. S., and K. M. Shrimali, eds. *Colas, Calukyas and Rajputs, A.D. 985–1206.* New Delhi: Peoples Publishing House, 1992.

Singh, R. B. *The History of the Chahamanas.* Varanasi: N. Kishore, 1964.

Smith, V. A. *The Early History of India from 600 B.C. to the Muhammadan Conquest.* Ed. S. M. Edwardes. Oxford: Clarendon Press, 1957.

———. *The Oxford History of India.* Oxford: Clarendon Press, 1958.

Srivastva, Balam. *Rajendra Chola.* Reprint. New Delhi: National Book Trust, 1994.

Tripathi, R. S. *History of Kanauj.* Delhi: Motilal Banarsidas, 1964.

Vaidya, C. V. *Downfall of Hindu India.* Delhi: Gian Publishing House, 1986.

Wink, Andre. *Al-Hind: The Making of Indo-Islamic World.* Vol. 1, *Early Medieval India and the Expansion of Islam, 7th–11th centuries.* Delhi: Oxford University Press, 1990.

———. *Al Hind: The Making of the Indo-Islamic World.* Vol. 2, *The Slave Kings and the Islamic Conquest, 11th–13th centuries.* Delhi: Oxford University Press, 1990.

Social and Cultural History

Chanda, Ramaprasad. *Medieval Indian Sculpture.* Varanasi: Indological Book House, 1972.

Chandra, M. "Indian Costumes and Textiles from the 8th to the 12th century." *Journal of Indian Textile History* 5 (1960): 2–41.

Chattopadhyaya, Brajadulal. *Making of Early Medieval India.* Delhi: Oxford University Press, 1994.

Chauhan, Gian Chand. *Economic History of Early Medieval North India.* New Delhi: Atlantic, 2003.

Choudhary, A. K. *Early Medieval Village in North Eastern India, 600–1200.* Calcutta: Punthi Pusak, 1971.

Cousens, H. *The Antiquities of Sind with Historical Outline.* Calcutta: Archaeological Survey of India, 1929.

De Bary, W. T., ed. *Sources of Indian Tradition.* New York: Columbia University, 1958.

Deloche, Jean. *The Ancient Bridges of India.* New Delhi: Sitaram Bhartia Institute of Scientific Research, 1984.

Deyell, John S. *Living without Silver: The Monetary History of Early Medieval India.* Delhi: Oxford University Press, 1990.

Foekema, Gerard. *Hoysala Architecture: Medieval Temples of South Karnataka Built during Hoysala Rule.* 2 vols. New Delhi: Books and Books, 1994.

Friedmann, Y. "The Temple of Multan: A Note on Early Muslim Attitude to Idolatry." *Israel Oriental Studies* (1972): 176–82.

———. "Qissat Shakarwati Farmad: A Tradition Concerning the Introduction of Islam to Malabar." *Israel Oriental Studies* 5 (1975): 233–58.

Gopal, Lallanji. *Economic Life of North India (c. A.D. 700–1200).* Delhi: Motilal Banarsidas, 1965.

Hourani, George F. *Arab Seafaring in the Indian Ocean in Indian Ancient and Early Medieval Times.* Revised and expanded by John Carswell. Princeton, NJ: Princeton University Press, 1995.

Jha, D. N. "Early Indian Feudalism: A Historical Critique." *Proceedings of Indian History Congress* 40 (1979): 15–45.

———. *Society and Ideology in India; Essay in Honour of Prof. R. S. Sharma.* New Delhi: Munshiram Manoharlal, 1996.

———. "Temples as Landed Magnates in Early Medieval South India (c. A.D. 700–1300)." In *Indian Society: Historical Problems.* Edited by R. S. Sharma and Vivekanand Jha. New Delhi: Peoples Publishing House, 1974: 202–216.

Karashima, N., and Y. Subbarayalu. "A Statistical Study of Personal Names in Tamil Inscriptions." *Computational Analysis of Asian and African Languages,* no. 3 (1976): 15.

Khan, Iqtidar Alam. "Concept of India in Alberani." *In India-Studies in History of an Idea.* Edited Irfan Habib. New Delhi: Munshivan, 2005: 110–121.

Kuppuswamy, G. R. *Economic Conditions in Karnataka A.D. 973–1336.* Dharwar: Karnatak University, 1975.

Liceria, M. "Emergence of Brahmanas as Landed Intermediaries in Karntaka (A.D. 1000–1300)." *Indian Historical Review* 1 (1974): 28–36.

Mahalingam, T. V. *South Indian Polity.* Rev. ed. Madras: University of Madras, 1967.

———, ed. *Mackenzie Manuscripts: Summaries of the Historical Manuscripts in the Mackenzie Collection.* Vol. 1. Madras: University of Madras, 1972–1976.

Mazumdar, B. P. *The Socio-Economic History of Northern India (Eleventh and Twelfth Centuries).* Calcutta: Firma K. L. Mukhopadhyay, 1960.

Nesar Ahmad, Syed. *Origins of Muslim Consciousness in India: A World System Perspective.* New York: Greenwood, 1991.

Nilakanta Sastri, K. A. *South Indian Influence in the Far East.* Bombay: Hind Kitabs, 1949.

Niyogi, P. *Contribution to the Economic History of North India: From the Tenth to the Twelfth Century, A.D.* Calcutta: Progressive, 1962.

Shanmugam, P. *The Revenue System of the Cholas 850–1279.* Madras: New Era, 1987.

Sharma, R. S. *Indian Feudalism, c.300–1200 A.D.* Calcutta: University of Calcutta, 1965.

———. *Social Changes in Early Medieval India (Circa A.D. 500–1200).* New Delhi: Peoples Publishing House, 1993.

———. *Urban Decay in India: c.300–c.1000.* New Delhi: Munshiram Manoharlal, 1987.

Sharma, Sunil. *Persian Poetry of the Indian Frontier: Mas'od Sa'd Salman of La-hore.* Delhi: Permanent Black, 2000.

Sivaramamurti, C. *Chola Temples: Thanjavur, Gangaikonda Cholapuram and Darasuram.* 3rd ed. New Delhi: Archaeological Survey of India, 1979.

Tara, Chand. *Influence of Islam on Indian Culture.* Allahabad: Indian Press, 1963.

Tibbetts, G. R. *Arab Navigation in the Indian Ocean.* London: Royal Asiatic Society, 1971.

Toy, S. *The Fortified Cities of India.* London: Heinemann, 1965.

———. *The Strongholds of India,* London: Heinemann. 1964.

Yadava, B. N. S. *Society and Culture in Northern India in the Twelfth Century.* Allahabad: Central Book Depot, 1973.

DELHI SULTANATE (1200–1412)

Sources

Abdul Waheed Khan, Mohamad, ed. *Andhra Pradesh State Museum, Hyderabad. Gold and Silver Coins of Sultans of Delhi in Andhra Pradesh State Museum, Hyderabad by Muhammad Abdul Wali Khan.* Hyderabad: Government of Andhra Pradesh, 1974.

Abdur Rashid, Shaikh. "Khwaja Zia ul Millat wad Din Zia ud Din Barni." *Muslim University Journal* (March 1942): 248–78.

———. "Insha'-i-Mahru or Tarassul-i Ain-ul-Mulk." *Islamic Culture* 16 (1942): 279–90.

———. "Dastur-ul-albab fi 'ilm-il-hisab." *Medieval India Quarterly.* 3–4 (1954?): 59–99.

Ahmad, Q., ed. *Corpus of Arabic and Persian Inscriptions of Bihar (AH 640–1200).* Patna: K. P. Jayaswal Research Institute, 1973.

Askari, S. M. "Material of Historical Interest in I'jaz-i Khusravi." *Medieval India: A Miscellany* 1 (1969): 1–21.

———. *Amir Khusrau as a Historian.* 5 vols. Patna: Khuda Bakhsh Oriental Public Library, 1988.

Barani, Ziyauddin. *Reign of Alauddin Khilji (Ta'rikh-i Firuz Shahi).* Trans. by A. R. Fuller and A. Khalique. Calcutta: Pilgrim, 1967.

———. *Political Theory of the Delhi Sultanate (Fatawa-i Jahandari).* Trans. by Mohammad Habib and Afsar U. S. Khan. Allahabad: Kitab Mahal, n.d.

Basu, K. K. "An Account of Firoz Shah Tughlaq." *Journal of Bihar and Orissa Research Society* 22 (1936); 23 (1937).

———. "An Account of Firoz Shah Tughluq and His Bengal Campaign." *Journal of Bihar and Orissa Research Society* 27 (1941): 97–112.

Bihamadkhani, Muhammad. *Ta'rikh-i Muhammadi.* Partial trans. (from 735/1354) by Muhammad Zaki. Aligarh: Department of History, Aligarh Muslim University, 1972.

Boyle, J. A. *History of World-Conqueror.* 2 vols. Manchester: University of Manchester, 1958.

Briggs, John. *History of the Rise of Mahomadan Power in India till the Year A.D. 1612, Translated from the Original Persian of Mohammad Kasim Firishta.* 4 vols. Calcutta: Camray, 1910.

Buhler, G. "A Jaina Account of the End of the Vaghelas of Gujarat." *Indian Antiquery* 26, (1897): 194–95.

Chandbardai. *Prithvirajarasau.* Edited by S. S. Das. Banaras: n.p., 1904.

Cunningham, A. *Coins of Medieval India.* Reprint. Delhi: Oriental Books, 1967.

Desai, P. B. "Kalyana Inscription of Sultan Muhammad, Saka 1248." *Epigraphia Indica* 32, (1957–1958): 165–70.

Desai, Z. A. "The Inscriptions of 'Alau'd-din Khalji from Chitorgadh." *Epigraphia Indica: Arabic and Persian Supplement* (1959–1960): 69–74.

———. "Khalji and Tughluq Inscriptions from Gujarat." *Epigraphia Indica: Arabic and Persian Supplement* (1962): 1–40.

———. "Inscriptions of Mamluk Sultans of Delhi." *Epigrahia Indica: Arabic and Persian Supplement* (1966): 4–18.

———. "The Jalor 'Idgah Inscription of Qutb-u'd-din Mubarak Shah Khalji." *Epigraphia Indica: Arabic and Persian Supplement* (1972).

Edward, Thomas. *The Chronicles of the Pathan Kings of Delhi.* Reprint. Delhi: Munshiram Manoharlal, 1967.

Elliot H. M., and Dowson, J. *The History of India as Told by Its Own Historians.* 8 vols. Reprint. Allahabad: Kitab Mahal, 1964.

Firuz Shah b. Rajab (Sultan). *"Futuhat-i Firuz Shahi* [The Victories of Sultan Firuz Shah of Tughluq Dynasty]." Trans. by N. B. Roy. *Islamic Culture* 15 (1941).

Ghaznawi, 'Abd al-Hamid Muharrir. *"Dastur al-Albab fi 'Ilmi'l-Hisab* (1231)." Partial trans. Shaikh Abdur Rashid. *Medieval India Quarterly* 1, 3–4 (1950): 59–99.

Gibb, H. A. R. *The Travels of Ibne Battuta A.D. 1325–1354.* London: Routledge & Kegan Paul, 1969.

Hardy, P. "Some Studies, in Pre-Mughal Muslim Historiography." In *Historians of India, Pakistan and Ceylon.* Edited by C. H. Philips. London: Oxford University Press, 1961: 115–127.

Habib, Muhammad. "The Campaigns of 'Alauddin Khalji: Being the English Translation of the *Khazainul Futuh* of Amir Khusrau." In *Collected Works of Professor Muhammad Habib, Politics and Society during the Early Medieval Period.* Edited by K. A. Nizami. Vol. 2. New Delhi:. Peoples Publishing House, 1981: 149–270.

Hodivala, S. H. *Studies in Indo-Muslim History.* Bombay: Popular Book Depot, 1939.

Hultzsch, E. "The Coinage of the Sultans of Madura." *Journal of Royal Asiatic Society* (1909): 667–83.

Husain, A. M. "Six Inscriptions of Sultan Muhammad bin Tughluq Shah." *Epigraphia Indica: Arabic and Persian Supplement* (1957–1958).

Ibn Battuta. *Travels in Asia and Africa, 1325–135.* Trans. and selected by H. A. R. Gibb. London: Routledge & Kegan Paul, 1969.

'Isami, 'Abd al-Malik. *Futuh ul-Salatin.* Trans. A. M. Husain. 3 vols. Bombay: Asia Publishing House, 1967–1977.

Juwaini, 'Ala al-Din 'Ata Malik. *Ta'rikh-i Jahan–Gusha (The History of the World—Conqueror).* Trans. J. A. Boyle. 2 vols. Manchester: University of Manchester, 1958.

Juzjani, Minhaj al-Din Abu 'Umar b. Siraj al-Din. *Tabaqat-i Nasari.* Trans. H. G. Raverty. In *Tabaqat-i Nasiri: A General History of the Muhammadan Dynasties of Asia.* 2 vols. Reprint. Delhi: Oriental Books, 1970.

Khan, M. S. "An Undiscovered Arabic Source of the History of Sultan Muhammad bin Tughlaq." *Islamic Culture* 53 (1979): 187–205.

Khusrau, Amir. *Khaza'inul Futuh.* Trans. Muhammad Habib. Bombay: Taraporevala, 1931.

Lane-Poole, Stanley. *The Coins of the Sultans of Delhi in the British Museum.* Edited by Reginald Stuart Poole. London: Trustees of British Museum, 1884.

Levy, R. "The Letters of Rashid al-Din Fazl Allah." *Journal of Royal Asiatic Society* (1946): 74–78.

Moneer, Q. M. "Two Unpublished Inscriptions of the Time of Sultan Muhammad bin Tughluq." *Epigraphia Indo-Moslemica* (1939–1940): 23–26.

Nelson Write, H. *Coinage and Metrology of the Sultans of Delhi.* Delhi: Manager Publications, Government of India, 1936.

Neog, Mahaeswar, ed. *Prachya-Sasanavali: An Anthology of Royal Charters etc., of Kamperupa, Asam, Saumara, Koch–Behar, etc. from 1205 A.D. to 1847 A.D.* Gauhati: n.p., 1974.

Nizami, K. A., ed. "Some Documents of Sultan Muhammad bin Tughluq." *Medieval India: A Miscellany* 1 (1969): 301–14.

Nurul Hasan, S. "*Sahifa-i Na't-i Muhammadi* of Zia-ud-din Barani." *Medieval India Quarterly* 1, 3–4 (1950): 100–106.

Page, J. A. "A Memoir on Kotla Firoz Shah." *Memoirs of the Archaeological Survey of India* 52, (1937): 33–42.

Paul, Horn. "Muhammadan Inscriptions from the *Suba* of Delhi." *Epigraphia Indica* 2 (1894): 130–60.

Philips, C. H. *Historians of India, Pakistan and Ceylon.* London: Oxford University Press, 1961.

Prasad, Pushpa, ed. *Sanskrit Inscriptions of Delhi Sultanate 1191–1526.* Delhi: Oxford University Press, 1990.

Rashid al-Din Tabib. *Successors of Chinghis Khan.* Trans. J. Andrew Boyle. New York: Columbia University Press, 1971.

Raverty, Major H. G. *Tabaqat-i Nasari: A General History of the Muhammadan Dynasties of Asia Including Hindustan.* 2 vols. Reprint. Delhi: Oriental Books, 1970.

Rose, H. A. "Notes on Raverty's Translation of *Tabaqat-i Nasari.*" *Journal of Punjab History Society* 1 (1911–1912): 176–77.

Roy, N. B. "The Victories of Sultan Firuz Shah of Tughluq Dynasty." *Islamic Culture* 15 (1951).

Siddiqui, I. H., trans. *Masalik al-absar: 14th Century Arab Accounts of India under the Sultan Muhammad bin Tughlaq.* Aligarh: Siddiqui Publishing House, 1971.

———. "Historical Information in a Thirteenth-Century Collection of Persian Poems." *Studies in Islam* 19 (1982): 47–76.

———. "Fresh Light on Diya' al-Din Barani: The Doyen of the Indo-Persian Historians of Medieval India." *Islamic Culture* 63 (1989): 69–84.

Sirat-i Firuz-Shahi. "An Account of Firoz Shah Tughlaq." Extracts trans. K. K. Basu. *Journal of Bihar and Orissa Research Society* 22 (1936): 96–107; 23 (1937): 97–112.

Spies, O. *An Arab Account of India in the Fourteenth Century.* Aligarh: Aligarh Muslim University, 1936.

Wright, H. Nelson. *The Coinage and Metallurgy of the Sultans of Delhi.* Oxford: Clarendon Press, 1907.

Yazdani, Ghulam Husain. "Inscriptions of the Turk Sultans of Delhi-Mui'izzu-d-din Bahram, 'Ala'uddin Mas'ud, Nasiru-d-din Mahmud, Ghiyathu-d-din Balban and Mu'izzu-d-din Kaiqubad." *Epigraphia Indo-Moslemica* (1913–1914): 13–46.

———. "Inscriptions of the Khalji Sultans of Delhi and Their Contemporaries in Bengal." *Epigraphia Indo-Moslemica* (1917–1918): 8–42.

Yule, H. *The Book of Ser Marco Polo: The Venetian Concerning the Kingdoms and Marvels of the East.* 2 vols. London: Murray, 1921.

Political History

Abdul Aziz. *Early Turkish Empire of Delhi.* Lahore: Shaikh Muhammad Ashraf, 1949.

Abdur Rashid. *Jalal al-Din Firuz Khilji.* Aligarh: Muslim University Press, n.d.

Abdur Rashid, Shaikh. "Firoz Shah's Investiture by the Caliph." *Medieval India Quarterly* 1 (1950): 66–72.

Abdur Rashid, Shaikh. "Price Control under Alauddin Khilji." *Proceedings of the All-Pakistan History Conference. First Session, held in Karachi.* Karachi: n.p., n.d.

Ahmad, Aziz. "Mongol Pressure in an Alien Land." *Central Asian Journal* (1961): 182–93.

———. "The Sufis and Sultan in Pre-Mughal Muslim India." *Islam* 38 (1962): 142–53.

Ahmad, Muhammad Aziz. *Political History and Institutions of Early Turkish Empire of Delhi, 1206–1290.* New Delhi: Oriental Books Reprint, 1972.

Aiyangar, S. K. *South India and Her Muhammadan Invaders.* Madras: S. Chand, 1921.

Banerjee, Jamini Mohan. *History of Firoz Shah Tughluq.* Delhi: Munshiram Manohar-lal, 1967.

Boyle, J. A. "The Mongol Commanders in Afghanistan and India According to the Tabaqat-i Nasiri of Juzjani." *Islamic Studies* 2 (1963): 235–47.

Chandel, L. S. *Early Medieval State: A Study of Delhi Sultanate.* New Delhi: Commonwealth, 1989.

Choudhary, Radhakrishna. *History of Muslim Rule in Tirhut: 1206–1765 A.D.* Varanasi: Chowkhamba, 1970.

Day, U. N. *Administrative System of Delhi Sultanate (1206–1413 A.D.).* Delhi: Kitab Mahal, 1959.

———. "The North-West Frontier under the Khalji Sultans of Delhi." *Islamic Culture* 39 (1963).

Digby, Simon. "Iletimish or Iltutumish? A Reconstruction of the Name of the Delhi Sultan." *Iran* 8 (1970): 57–64.

———. *War-horse and Elephant in the Delhi Sultanate: A Problem of Military Supplies.* Oxford: Orient Monographs, 1971.

———. "The *Sufi Shaykh* and the Sultan: A Conflict of Claims to Authority in Medieval India." *Iran* 28 (1990): 71–81.

Ernst, Carl W. *Eternal Garden, Mysticism, History and Politics at a South Asian Sufi Centre.* Albany: State University of New York Press, 1992.

Gupta, Hari Ram, ed. *Essays Presented to Sir Jadunath Sarkar.* Sir Jadunath Sarkar Commemoration Vol. 2. Hoshiarpur: Department of History, Punjab University, 1958.

Gupta, Satya Prakash. "Jhain of the Delhi Sultanate." *Medieval India: A Miscellany* 3 (1975): 209–16.

Habib, Irfan. "Barani's Theory of the History of the Delhi Sultanate." *Indian Historical Review* 7 (1980–1981): 99–115.

———. "Formation of the Sultanate Ruling Class of the Thirteenth Century." In *Medieval India 1: Researches in the History of India 1200–1750.* Edited by I. Habib. Delhi: Oxford University Press, 1992: 1–21.

———, ed. *Medieval India 1: Researches in the History of India 1200–1750.* Delhi: Oxford University Press, 1992.

———. "The Price Regulations of 'Ala'uddin Khalji: A Defence of Ziya' Barani." *Indian Economic and Social History Research* 21 (1984): 393–414.

Habib, M. "Shahab-ud-Din of Ghor." *Muslim University Journal* 1 (1930): 10–55.

———. *Some Aspects of the Foundation of the Delhi Sultanate.* Delhi: Ashraf Memorial Committee, 1966.

———. *Politics and Society during the Early Medieval Period: Collected Works of Professor Mohammad Habib.* Edited by K. A. Nizami. 2 vols. New Delhi: Peoples Publishing House, 1974.

Habib, Muhammad, and Khaliq Ahmad Nizami, eds. *The Delhi Sultanate (A.D. 1206–1526): A Comprehensive History of India*. Vol. 5. New Delhi: Peoples Publishing House, 1982.

Habibullah, A. B. M. *Foundation of Muslim Rule in India*. Allahabad: Central Book Depot, 1961.

Haig, Wolseley. *The Cambridge History of India* (1937). Vol. 3, *Turks and Afghans*. Reprint. Delhi: S. Chand, 1965.

———. "Five Questions in the History of the Tughluq Dynasty of Delhi." *Journal of the Royal Asiatic Society* (1922): 319–72.

Hambly, Gavin R. G. "Who Were the Chihilgani, the Forty Slaves of Sultan Shams al-Din Iltutmish of Delhi?" *Iran* 10 (1972): 57–62.

Hardy, Peter. *Historians of Medieval India*. London: Luzak, 1960.

———. "Force and Violence in Indo-Persian Writing on History and Government in Medieval South Asia." In *Islamic Society and Culture. Essays in Honour of Professor Aziz Ahmad*. Edited by Milton Israel and N. K. Wagle. Delhi: Manohar, 1983: 165–208.

———. "Didactic Historical Writing in Indian Islam: Ziya' al-Din Barani's Treatment, of the Reign of Sultan Muhammad Tughluq (1324–1351)." In *Islam in Asia*. Edited by Yohanan Friedmann. Yeroshalam: n.p., 1984.

———. "The Growth of Authority over a Conquered Political Elite: The Early Delhi Sultanate as a Possible Case Study." In *Kingship and Authority in South Asia*. Edited by John S. Richards. Delhi: Oxford University Press, 1998: 216–241.

———. "The *Orato Recta of Barani's Ta'rikh-i Firuz Shahi:* Fact or Fiction?" *Bulletin of School of Oriental and African Studies* 20 (1957): 315–21.

Hodivala, S. H. *Studies in Indo-Muslim History*. 2 vols. Bombay: Popular Book Depot, 1939–1957.

Husain, A. Mahdi. *The Rise and Fall of Muhammad bin Tughluq*. Delhi: Idara-i Adbiyat, 1972.

Husain, Wahid. *The Administration of Justice during the Muslim Rule in India*. Calcutta: n.p., 1934.

Islam, Zafarul. "Firuz Shah's Attitude towards Non-Muslims." *Islamic Culture* 64, no. 4 (1990): 65–79.

Jackson, Peter. "The Mongols and Delhi Sultanate in the Reign of Muhamad Tughlaq (1325–1351)." *Central Asian Journal* 19 (1975): 118–57.

———. "Jalal al-Din, the Mongols and Khwarazmian Conquest of the Punjab and Sind." *Iran* 28 (1990): 45–54.

———. "The Fall of the Ghurid Dynasty." In *Festschrift for Professor Edmund Bosworth*. Edited by Carloe Hillenbrand. Edinburgh: n.p., n.d.

———. "The *Mamluk* Institution in Early Muslim India." *Journal of Royal Asiatic Society* (1990): 340–58.

———. *The Delhi Sultanate: A Political and Military History*. Cambridge: Cambridge University Press, 1999.

Joshi, P. M., and Agha Mahdi Husain. "Khaljis and Tughluqs in the Deccan." In *History of Medieval Deccan (1295–1724)*. Edited by H. K. Sherwani and P. M. Joshi. Vol. 1. Hyderabad: The Government of Andhra Pradesh, 1973: 29–55.

Kehrer, Kenneth C. "The Economic Policies of 'Ala-ud-Din Khalji." *Journal of the Punjab University Historical Society* 16 (1963): 55–66.

Khan, Iqtidar Alam. "Origin and Development of Gunpowder Technology in India, A.D. 1250–1500." *Indian Historical Review* 4, no. 1 (1977): 20–29.

———. "Coming of Gunpowder to the Islamic World and North India: Spotlight on the Role of the Mongols." *Journal of Asian History.* 30, no. 1 (1996): 27–45.

———. "The Role of the Mongols in the Introduction of Gunpowder and Firearms in South Asia." In *Gunpowder: The History of an International Technology.* Edited by Brenda J. Buchanan. Bath: Bath University Press, 1996: 33–44.

———. "The Indian Response to Firearms (1300–1750)." Presidential Address. *Proceedings of the Indian History Congress* 39 (1997): 1–29.

———. *Gunpowder and Firearms: Warfare in Medieval India.* New Delhi: Oxford University Press, 2004.

Lal, K. S. "Sultan Nasir al-Din Khusrau Shah (1320 A.D.)." *Journal of Indian History* 23 (1944): 169–78.

———. *History of the Khaljis.* 3rd ed. New Delhi: Munshiram Manoharlal, 1980.

Lane-Poole, S. *Medieval India from the Mahommedan Conquest to the Reign of Akbar the Great.* Reprint. New Delhi: Asian Educational Service, 1987.

Majumdar, R. C., ed. *History and Culture of the Indian People.* Vol. 5, *The Struggle for Empire.* Bombay: Bharti Vidya Bhawan, 1955.

Makhdoomee, M. Akram. "Gunpowder Artillery in the Reign of Sultan Eltutmish of Delhi." *Journal of Indian History* 15, no. 2 (1936): 185–88.

Mill, James. *The History of British India.* 9 vols. London: James Madden, 1840.

Mirza, Muhammad Wahid. *Life and Works of Amir Khusraw.* Calcutta: Baptist Mission, 1932.

Moinul Haq, S. "Was Muhammad Bin Tughlaq a Parricide?" *Muslim University Journal* 5, no. 2 (1938): 17–49.

———. "The Deccan Policy of Sultan Muhammad bin Tughlaq." *Proceedings of the Indian History Congress* (1944): 269–76.

Nadvi, Abu Zafar. "The Use of Cannon in Muslim India." *Islamic Culture* 12, no. 4 (1938): 405–18.

Nigam, S. B. P. *Nobility under the Sultans of Delhi A.D. 1206–1398.* Delhi: Munshiram Manoharlal, 1968.

Nizami, K. A. "Early Indo-Muslim Mystics and Their Attitude towards the State." *Islamic Culture* 22 (1948): 387–398; 23 (1949): 13–21, 312–21; 24 (1950): 60–71.

———. *Studies in Medieval Indian History.* Aligarh: Cosmopolitan, 1956.

———. *Some Aspects of Religion and Politics in India in the Thirteenth Century.* Aligarh: Department of History, Aligarh Muslim University, 1961.

——. *Supplement to Elliot and Dowson's History of India.* Vols. 2 and 3. Delhi: Idarah-i Adbiyat, 1981.

Pal, Dharam. "Ala'-ud-Din's Price Control System." *Islamic Culture* 18 (1944): 44–52.

——. "Ala'-ud-Din Khilji's Mongol Policy." *Islamic Culture* 21 (1947): 255–63.

Prasad, Ishwari. *History of Medieval India.* Allahabad: Indian Press, 1966.

——. *A History of the Qaraunah Turks in India.* Allahabad: Central Book Depot, 1974.

Qurieshi, I. H. *The Administration of the Sultanate of Delhi.* Lahore: Muhammad Ashraf, 1942.

Riazul, Islam. "A Review of the Reign of Firoz Shah (1351–1388 A.D.)." *Islamic Culture* 23 (1949): 281–97.

——. "The Age of Firoz Shah." *Medieval India Quarterly* 1, no. 1 (1950): 25–41.

Ray, H. C. *Dynastic History of Northern India, Early Medieval Period.* 2 vols. 2nd ed. Delhi: Munshiram Manoharlal, 1973.

Roy, Atul Chandra. *History of Bengal: Turko-Afghan Period.* New Delhi: Kalyani, 1987.

Roy, N. B. "The Transfer of Capital from Delhi to Daulatabad." *Journal of Indian History* 20 (1941): 159–80.

——. "Jajnagar Expedition of Sultan Firoz Shah." *Journal of Asiatic Society of Bengal, Letters* 8 (1942): 57–98.

Sabahuddin, S. "Conduct of Strategy and Tactics of War during the Muslim Rule in India." *Indian Culture* 20 (1946): 154–64, 291–96, 345–52; 21 (1947): 7–15, 123–34.

Saran, P. *Studies in Medieval Indian History.* Delhi: Ranjit Printers, 1952.

Sharma, G. N. *Glories of Mewar.* Agra: Shiva Lal Agarwala, n.d.

Sherwani, H. K., and P. M. Joshi, eds. *History of Medieval Deccan, 1295–1724.* 2 vols. Hyderabad: Government of Andhra Pradesh, 1973, 1974.

Siddiqi, I. H. "The Nobility under Khalji Sultans." *Islamic Culture* 37 (1963): 52–66.

Siddiqi, M. Y. Z. "Arzdasht of Badr Hajib." *Medieval India: A Miscellany* 2 (1975): 291–97.

Stapleton, H. E. "Contributions to History and Ethnology of North-Eastern India IV. Bengal Chronology during the Period of Independent Muslim Rule. Part I, 686–735 H.H. (1286–1334 A.D.)." *Journal of Asiatic Society of Bengal* 18 (1922): 407–30.

Thomas, Edward. *The Chronicles of the Pathan Kings of Delhi.* Reprint. Delhi: Munshiram Manoharlal, 1967.

Tripathi, R. P. *Some Aspects of Muslim Administration.* Allahabad: Central Book Depot, 1950.

Vaidya, C. V. *History of Medieval Hindu India.* 3 vols. New Delhi: Cosmopolitan, 1979.

Venkataramanayya, N. "The Date of the Rebellions of Tilang and Kampila against Sultan Muhammad bin Tughluq." *Indian Culture* 5 (1938–1939): 135–46, 261–69.
———. *The Early Muslim Expansion in South India*. Madras: n.p., 1942.
Wahid Husain. *Administration of Justice during the Muslim Rule in India with a History of the Origin of the Islamic Legal Institutions*. Calcutta: Calcutta University, 1934.

Social and Cultural History

'Abdul-Ghani, Muhammad. *Pre-Mughal Persian in Hindustan: A Critical Survey of the Growth of Persian Language and Literature in India from the Earliest Times to the Advent of Mughal Rule*. 2 vols. Allahabad: n.p., n.d.
Abdul Mannan, Qazi. *Emergence and Development of Dobhasi Literature in Bengal up to 1855 A.D*. Dacca: University of Dacca, 1966.
Abdul Rehman, et al., ed. *Seminar on the Sultanate Period Architecture in Pakistan: Proceedings*. Lahore: Anjuman-i Mimaran, 1990.
Abha Rani. *Tughluq Architecture of Delhi*. Varanasi: Bharat Prakashan, 1991.
Ahmad, Aziz. *Studies in Islamic Culture in the Indian Environment*. Oxford: Clarendon Press, 1964.
Ahmad, Laiq. "Kara: A Medieval Indian City." *Islamic Culture* 55 (1981): 83–92.
Ashraf, K. M. *Life and Conditions of the People of Hindustan*. Reprint. Delhi: Jiwan Prakashan, 1959.
Askari, S. H. "Risail-ul-Ijaz, of Amir Khusrau: An Appraisal." *Dr. Zakir Husain Presentation Volume*. Delhi: n.p., 1968.
Athar Ali, M. "Capital of Sultans: Delhi during the Thirteenth and Fourteenth Centuries." In *Delhi through the Ages: Essays in Urban History, Culture and Society*. Edited by R. E. Frykenberg, Delhi: Oxford University Press, 1986: 34–44.
Brown, P. *Indian Architecture—Islamic*. Reprint. Mumbai: D. P. Taraporevala, 1997.
Burton-Page, J. "A Study of Fortifications in the Indian Sub-continent from the Thirteenth to the Eighteenth Century A.D." *Bulletin of Oriental and African Studies* 23, no. 3 (1960): 86–98.
Chandra, M. "Costumes and Textiles in the Sultanate Period." *Journal of Indian Textile History* 6 (1961): 5–61.
Codrington, O. "On a Hoard of Coins Found at Broach." *Journal of Bombay Branch of Royal Asiatic Society* 15 (1882–1883).
Currie, P. M. *Shrine and Cult of Muin al-Din Chishti of Ajmer*. Delhi: Oxford University Press, 1989.
Deloche, Jean. *Transport and Communication in India Prior to Steam Locomotion*. Trans. by James Walker. Delhi: Oxford University Press, 1993.
Digby, Simon. "The Literary Evidence for Painting in the Delhi Sultanate." *Bulletin of American Academy of Benaras* I (1967): 47–58.

———. "The Currency System." In *Cambridge Economic History of India*. Edited by Tapan Raychaudhuri and Irfan Habib. Vol. 1, *c.1200–1750*. Cambridge: Cambridge University Press, 1982: 93–101.

———. *War-horse and Elephant in the Delhi Sultanate: A Problem of Military Supplies,* Oxford: Orient Monographs, 1971.

Fergusson, James. *History of Indian and Eastern Architecture.* 2 vols. Rev. and ed. James Burgess and R. Phene Spiers. Reprint. Delhi: Low Price, 1994.

Friedmann, Yohanan. "Medieval Muslim Views of Indian Religions." *Journal of the American Oriental Studies* 95 (1975): 214–21.

Gode, P. K. *Studies in Indian Cultural History.* 3 vols. Reprint. Hoshiarpur: Vishreshvanandan Vedic Research Institute, 1961.

Habib, Irfan. "Distribution of Landed Property in Pre-British India." *Enquiry* 2, no. 3 (1965).

———. "Technological Changes and Society, 13th and 14th Centuries." *Proceedings of Indian History Congress* (1969): 139–61.

———. "Economic History of the Delhi Sultanate: An Essay in Interpretation." *Indian Historical Review* 4 (1977): 287–303.

———. "Non-agricultural Production and Urban Economy." In *The Cambridge Economic History of India.* Vol. 1, *c.1200–1750.* Edited by T. Raychaudhuri and I. Habib. Cambridge: Cambridge University Press, 1982: 76–93.

———. "The Peasant in Indian History." Presidential Address. *Proceedings of Indian History Congress* 43 (1982): 1–53.

———. "Changes in Technology in Medieval India." *Studies in History* 2, no. 1 (1986): 45–62.

Habib, Muhammad. *Hazrat Amir Khusrau.* Calcutta: Karim Bux Brothers, 1927.

———, trans. *Khaza'inul Futuh* [Treasures of Victory]. Bombay: Taraporevala, 1931.

———. "Indo-Muslim Mystics." *Muslim University Journal* 4, no. 1 (1937): 25–61; 5, no. 2 (1938): 1–17.

———. "Shaikh Nasir-uddin Mahmud Chiragh-i Dehli as a Great Historical Personality." *Islamic Culture* 20 (1946): 129–53.

———. "Chishti Mystics' Records of the Sultanate Period." *Medieval India Quarterly* 1 (1950): 1–42.

Hambly, Gavin R. G. "Twilight of Tughluqid Delhi." In *Delhi through the Ages: Essays in Urban History, Culture and Society.* Edited by R. E. Frykenberg. Delhi: Oxford University Press, 1986: 45–62.

Havell, E. B. *Ancient and Medieval Architecture of India: A Study of Indo-Aryan Civilization.* Reprint. Delhi: S. Chand, 1972.

Husain, A. B. M. *The Manara in Indo-Muslim Architecture.* Decca: Asiatic Society of Pakistan, 1970.

Husain, A. Mahdi. "The Social Life and Institutions with Special Reference to Hindus in the Days of Muhammad Bin Tughliq." *Proceedings of Indian History Congress* 10 (1947): 297–305.

Hussaini, Shah Khusro. *Sayyid Muhammad Ali Husayni-i Gisudiraz (721/1321–825/1422) on Sufism.* Delhi: Idarah-i Adbiyat, 1983.

Islam, Riazul. "Some Aspects of the Economy of Northern South Asia during the Fourteenth Century." *Journal of Central Asia* 11, no. 2 (1988): 5–39.

Islam, Zafarul. "The *Fatawa Firuz-i Shahi* as a Source for the Socio-economic History of the Sultanate Period." *Islamic Culture* 60, no. 2 (1986): 97–117.

Jackson, Paul. *Way of a Sufi, Sharafuddin Maneri.* Delhi: Idarah-i Adabiyat, 1987.

Khan, Yusuf Husain. "Origin and Growth of Urdu Language in Medieval India." *Islamic Culture* 36, no. 4 (1956): 351–60.

Law, N. N. *Promotion of Learning in India during Muhammadan Rule by Muhammadans.* London: Longman, 1915.

Moosvi, Shireen. "Numismatic Evidence and the Economic History of the Delhi Sultanate." *Proceedings of the Indian History Congress* 50 (1989): 207–14.

Moreland, T. *Agrarian System of Muslim India.* Reprint. Delhi: Oriental Books Reprint, 1968.

Mujib, M. "The Urdu Language and Indian Muslim Culture." *Islamic Culture* 1 (1937): 341–53.

Nath, R. *History of Sultanate Architecture.* New Delhi: Abhinav, 1978.

Nizami, K.A. "Early Indo-Muslim, Mystics and Their Attitude towards the State." *Islamic Culture* 22, 4 (1948): 387–99.

———. *Some Aspects of Religion and Politics in India during the Thirteenth Century.* Aligarh: Department of History, Aligarh Muslim University, 1961.

———. *The Life and Times of Shaikh Farid-ud-din Ganj-i-Shakar.* Dehli: Idara-i-Adbiyat, 1975.

———. "The Impact of Ibn Taimiyya on South Asia." *Journal of Islamic Studies* 1 (1990).

———. *Life and Times of Shaikh Nizam-ud-din Auliya.* Delhi: Idarah-i-Adabyat, 1991.

———. *Life and Times of Shaikh Nasir-ud-din Chiragh-i-Dehli.* Delhi: Idarah-i-Adabiyat, 1991.

Prasad, Pushpa. "Hindu Craftsmen in the Delhi Sultanate (An Epigraphic Study)." *Indica* 21, no. 1 (1984): 11–15.

Rani, Abha. *Tughluq Architecture of Delhi.* Varanasi: Bharati Prakashan, 1991.

Rashid, A. *Society and Culture in Medieval India.* Calcutta: Firma, 1969.

Raychaudhury, Tapan, and Irfan Habib, eds. *The Cambridge Economic History of India.* Vol. 1, *c.1200–1750.* Cambridge: Cambridge University Press, 1982.

Sharma, Krishna. *Bhakti and the Bhakti Movement, a New Perspective: A Study in the History of Ideas.* New Delhi: Munshiram, 1987.

Siddiqi, I. H. "Social Mobility in the Delhi Sultanate." In *Medieval India I: Researches in the History of India, 1200–1750.* Edited by Irfan Habib. Delhi: Oxford University Press, 1992: 22–48.

Simkin, C. G. F. *The Traditional Trade of Asia.* London: n.p., 1968.

Smart, E. S. "Some Fourteenth-century Chinese Porcelain from a Tughlaq Palace in Delhi." *TQCS* (1975–1977).

Srivastava, A.L. "Hindu-Muslim Relations during the Sultanate Period (1206–1526 A.D.)." *Journal of Indian History* 41 (1963): 577–93.

Stein, B. *Peasant and Society in Medieval South India.* New Delhi: Orient Longmans, 1980.

——. "The Economic Function of a Medieval South Indian Temple." *Journal of Asian Studies* 19 (1960).

——. "The State, the Temple and Agricultural Development: A Study in Medieval South India." *Economic Weekly Annual* (February 1961).

——. "Devi Shrines and Folk Hinduism in Medieval Tamilnad." In *Studies in the Language and Culture of South Asia.* Edited by Edwin Gerow and Margery D. Lang. Seattle: n.p., 1973.

Troll, Christian W., ed. *Muslim Shrines in India.* Delhi: Oxford University Press, 1989.

Verma, H. C. *Harvesting Water and Rationalization of Agriculture in North Medieval India (13th–16th Centuries).* New Delhi: Anamica, 2001.

Watt, G. *Indian Art at Delhi, 1903, London, 1904.* Calcutta: Superintendent of Government Printing, 1904.

Welch, Anthony, and Howard Crane. "The Tughluq: Master-builders of the Delhi Sultanate." *Muqarnas* 1 (1983).

Welch, Stuart Cary. *India: Art and Culture, 1300–1900.* New York: Mapin, 1985.

REGIONAL STATES (1412–1526)

Sources

'Abdallah Muhammad Al-Makki Al-Asafi Hajji-u'd-Dabir Ulughkhani. *Zafar ul-Walih bi Muzaffar wa alih.* Trans. M. F. Lokhandwala. 2 vols. Baroda: Oriental Institute, 1970, 1974.

Abdul Karim. *Corpus of the Muslim Coins of Bengal: Down to A.D. 1538.* Dacca: Asiatic Society of Pakistan, 1960.

Abdul Karim, ed. *Corpus of the Arabic and Persian Inscriptions of Bengal.* Dacca: Asiatic Society of Bangladesh, 1992.

Ahmad Shah. *Bijak of Kabir.* (English trans.) New Delhi: Asian Publication Services, 1977.

Agrawala, V. S. "A Unique Treatise on Medieval Indian Coins." In *Ghulam Yazdani Commemoration Volume.* Edited by H. K. Sherwani. Hyderabad: Maulana Abul Kalam Azad Oriental Research Institute, 1966: 87–101.

Ayyangar, Krishnaswami. *Sources of Vijayanagar History: Selected and Edited for the University of Madras.* Madras: University of Madras, 1919.

Barbosa, Duarte. *The Book of Duarte Barbosa: Account of the Countries Bordering on Indian Ocean and Their Inhabitants.* Trans. Longworth Dames. 2 vols. London: Hakluyt Society, 1918, 1921.

Basu, K. K., trans. *Yahya Bin Ahmad Abdullah Sirhindi's Tarikh-i Mubarak Shahi Translated into English from Original Persian etc.* Karachi: Karim & Sons, 1977.

Bayley, E. C. *The Local Muhammadan Dynasties: Gujarat.* London: W. H. Allen, 1886.

Bendrey, V. S. *Study of Muslim Inscriptions.* Bombay: Karnatak, 1944.

Chakravarti, Monmohan. "Notes on Gaur and Other Old Places in Bengal." *Journal of Asiatic Society of Bengal* (New Series) 5 (1909): 199–235.

Chattopadhyaya, B. D. "Irrigation in Early Medieval Rajasthan." *Journal of the Economic and Social History of the Orient* 16, nos. 2–3 (1973): 298–316.

Commissariat, M. S. *History of Gujarat.* 2 vols. Bombay: Longmans, 1938.

Dani, Ahmad Hasan. *Muslim Inscriptions of Bengal.* Appendix to *Journal of Asiatic Society of Pakistan* 2 (1957).

———. "Shamsuddin Ilyas Shah-i-Bangalah." *Essays Presented to Sir Jadunath Sarkar.* Edited by H. R. Gupta, Hoshiarpur, Punjab University, 1958: 50–71.

Desai, Z. A. "Inscriptions of the Gujarat Sultans." *Epigraphia Indica: Arabic and Persian Supplement* (1963): 5–50.

———. "Three Inscriptions of the Auhadis." *Epigraphia Indica: Arabic and Persian* (1961): 59–63.

Duyvendak, J. *Ma-Huan Re-examined.* Amsterdam: n.p., 1933.

Forbes, Alexander Kinlock. *Hindu Annals of Western India with Particular Reference to Gujarat.* New Delhi: Heritage, 1973.

Forbes, Alexander Kinloch. *Ras Mala.* Edited by H. G. Rawlinson. London: n.p., 1924.

Gait, E. *History of Assam.* 2nd ed. Calcutta: Thaker-Spink, 1926.

Hira Lal. *Descriptive List of Inscriptions in Central Provinces and Berar.* Nagpur: Government Press, 1939.

Imamuddin, S. M. "The Tarikh-i Khan-i Jahani wa Makhzan-i Afghani." *Islamic Culture* 22, nos. 2–3 (1948): 128–42, 280–90.

Khare, G. H. *Sources of the Medieval History of the Dekkan.* Vol. 1. Poona: n.p., 1930.

Krishnadeva Raya. "Political Maxims of the Emperor Poet, Krishnadeva Raya." Trans. A. Rangasvami Sarasvati. *Journal of Indian History* 6 (1925).

Ma Huan (1433). *Ying-yai Sheng-lan: "The Over-all Survey of the Ocean's Shores."* Trans. J. V. G. Mills. London: Hakluyt Society, 1970.

Major, R. H. *India in the 15th Century.* London: Hakluyt Society, 1857.

Majumdar, N. G., ed. *Inscriptions of Bengal.* Vols. 1–3. Rajshahi: Varendra Research Society, 1929.

Mushtaqui, Shaikh Rizqullah. *Waqiat-e-Mushtaqi.* Trans. and ed. Iqtidar Husain. Siddiqui, New Delhi: Indian Council of Historical Research/Northern Book Centre, 1993.

Niamatullah, Khwaja. *History of Afghans.* Trans. by Nirodbhusan Roy and B. Dorn. Santiniketan: Santiniketan Press, 1958.

Nilakanta Sastri, K. A. *Further Sources of Vijayanagara History.* Madras: University of Madras, 1946.

———. *History of South India from Pre-Historic Times to the Fall of Vijayanagar.* London: Oxford University Press, 1966.

Patil, D. R. *Mandu.* New Delhi: Archaeological Survey of India, 1971.

Rahim, S.A. "Some More Inscriptions from Khandesh." *Epigraphia Indica: Persian and Arabic Supplement* (1962): 62–86.

Salim, Ghulam Husain. *Riyaz-us salatin.* Trans. Abdus Salam. Delhi: *Idarah-i Adabiat,* 1975.

Sikandar b. Muhammad, alias Manjhu. *Mir'at-i Sikandari.* Trans. E. C. Bayley. *The Local Muhammadan Dynasties: Gujarat.* London: W. W. Allen, 1886.

Srivara. *Jaina Rajatrangini.* Ed. and trans. Kashi Nath Dhar, New Delhi: Peoples Publishing House, 1994.

Subrahmanya Sastry, Sadhu, and V. Vijayraghavacharya. *Early Inscriptions.* 7 vols. Delhi: Sri Satguru, 1984.

Tod, James. *Annals and Antiquities of Rajasthan.* Edited with an Introduction and Notes by William Crooke. 3 vols. Oxford: Oxford University Press, 1920.

Varthema, Ludovic de. *Travels in Egypt, Syria, Persia, India, Ethiopia (1503–8).* Trans. John Winter James. Edited by G. P. Badger. 1st ed. London: Hakluyt Society, 1863; 2nd ed., edited by R. C. Temple, 1928.

Yazdani, G. "Some Inscriptions of Musulman Kings of Bengal." *Epigraphia Indo-Moslemica* 12–13 (1929–1930): 9–13.

Political History

'Abdul Halim. *History of the Lodi Sultans of Delhi and Agra.* Delhi: Idarah-I Adbiyat, 1974.

'Abdul Karim. "Aspects of Muslim Administration in Bengal Down to A.D. 1538." *Journal of Asiatic Society of Bengal* 3 (1958): 67–103.

Aijaz, Bano. "The Zamindars of the Sultanate of Gujarat: 1407–1572." *Proceedings of the Indian History Congress* 45 (1984): 37–40.

Boxer, C. R. *Portuguese Seaborn Empire.* London: Hutchinson, 1969.

Commissareat, M. S. "A Brief History of Gujarat Sultanate." *Journal of Bombay Branch of Royal Asiatic Society* (1917–1921): 82–133, 246–321; 26 (1921–1926): 99–157.

———. *History of Gujrat Sultanate.* 2 vols. Bombay: Longmans, 1938–1957.

Dodwell, H. H. *Cambridge History of India.* Vol. 5, *British India, 1497–1858.* Reprint. Delhi: S. Chand, New Delhi.

Haig, T. W. "The Chronology and Genealogy of the Muhammadan Kings of Kashmir." *Journal of Royal Asiatic Society* (1978): 451–68.

———. "The Faruqi Dynasty of Khandesh." *Indian Antiquery* 47 (1918): 113–24, 141–49, 178–86.

Hasan, M. *Kashmir under the Sultanate.* Calcutta: Iran Society, 1959.

Husain, Syed Ejaz. *The Bengal Sultanate: Politics, Economy and Coins (A.D. 1205–1576).* Delhi: Manohar, 2003.

Imamuddin, S. M. "Raja Ganesh of Bengal." *Proceedings and Transactions of All India Orientalist Conference* 13 (1946), part II: 438–43.

Khan, Iqtidar Alam. "Early Use of Cannon and Musket in India, A.D. 1442–1526." *Journal of the Economic and Social History of Orient* 24, no. 2 (1980): 146–64.

King, J. S. *History of the Bahmanid Dynasty (Based on Burhan-i Maathir).* London: n.p., 1900.

Krishnaswami, A. *The Tamil Country under Vijayanagar.* Annamalainagar: Annamalai University, 1964.

Lal, Kishori Saran. *Twilight of the Sultanate.* Bombay: Asia Publishing House, 1963.

Mahalingam, T. V. *Administration and Social Life under Vijayangar.* Madras: University of Madras, 1969.

———. *Reading of South Indian History.* Delhi: B. R. Publishing, 1977.

Majumdar, R. C., ed. *History of Bengal.* Dacca: University of Dacca, 1943.

Neog, Maheshwar. *Socio-Political Events in Assam Leading to the Militancy of the Mayamria Vaisnavas.* Calcutta: Centre for Studies in Social Sciences/Bagchi, 1982.

Misra, S. C. *The Rise of Muslim Power in Gujarat: A History of Gujarat from 1298 to 1442.* Delhi: Munshiram Manoharlal, 1982.

Pannikar, K. M. *Malabar and the Portuguese.* Bombay: n.p., 1929.

———. *A History of Karala 1499–1801.* Annamalainagar: Annamali University, 1960.

Qanungo, K. R. "Origin of the Bahamani Sultans of Deccan." *Dacca University Studies* 3 (1936): 137–44.

Ramanayya, N. V. *Studies in the History of the Third Dynasty of Vijayanagra.* Madras: n.p., 1941.

Ross, E. Denison. "The Portuguese in India and Arabia between 1507 and 1538." *Journal of the Royal Asiatic Society* (1921): 1–18.

Sewell, R. *A Forgotten Empire (Vijayanagar).* New Delhi: National Book Trust, 1962.

Shmasuddin, M. 'The Rise and Fall of the Sharqi Kingdom of Jaunpur." *Proceedings of Pakistan History Conference* 6 (1965): 267–73.

Sherwani, H. K. *The Bahmanis of the Deccan.* Hyderabad: Manager of Publications, 1955.

———. *The Great Bahmani Wazir Mahmud Gavan.* Allahabad: Kitabistan, 1942.

———. "The Independence of Bahmani Governors." *Proceedings of the Indian History Congress* (1944): 256–62.

Sherwani, H. K., and P. M. Joshi, eds. *History of Medieval Deccan, 1295–1724.* Hyderabad: Publications Bureau, Government of Maharashtra, 1973–1974.

Siddiqui, I. H. *Some Aspects of Afghan Despotism in India.* Aligarh: T. M. Publications, 1969.

Sinha, S. K. *Medieval History of the Deccan.* Edited by Muhammad Abdul Waheed Khan. Hyderabad: Andhra Pradesh Government, 1964

Swaminathan, K. D. *The Nayakas of Ikkeri.* Madras: n.p., 1957.

Tarafdar, M. R. *Husain Shahi Bengal 1494–1538 A.D.: A Socio-Political Study.* Decca: Asiatic Society of Pakistan, 1965.

Venkataramanayya, N. *Studies in the History of the Third Dynasty of Vijayanagara.* Reprint. Delhi: Gian, 1986.

Social and Cultural History

'Abid Ali Khan, M. *Memoirs of Gaur and Pandua.* Edited and rev. by H. E. Stapleton. Calcutta: Bengal Secretariat Book Depot, 1931.

'Abdul Karim. *Social History of the Muslims in Bengal (Down to A.D. 1538).* Dacca: Asiatic Society of Pakistan, 1959.

'Abdul Latif, S. K. *Muslim Mystic Movements in Bengal, 1301–1550.* Calcutta: K. P. Bagchi, 1993.

'Ali Ashraf, Syed. *Muslim Tradition in Bengali Literature.* Dacca: Islamic Foundation Bangladesh, 1983.

Burgess, Jas. *On the Muhammadan Architecture of Bharoch, Cambay, Dholka, Champanir, and Mahmudabad in Gujarat.* New Delhi: Archaeological Survey of India, 1896.

Das Gupta, T. C. *Aspects of Old Bengal Society from Old Bengali Literature.* Calcutta: n.p., 1935.

Digby, Simon. "The Maritime Trade of India." In *The Cambridge Economic History of India.* Vol. 1, *c.1200–1750.* Edited by Tapan Raychaudhuri and Irfan Habib. Cambridge: Cambridge University Press, 1982: 125–162.

Eaton, Richard M. *Rise of Islam and the Bengal Frontier, 1204–1760.* Delhi: Oxford University Press, 1994.

Fuhrer, A. *The Sharqi Architecture of Jaunpur.* Edited by J. Burgess. Reprint. Varanasi: Indological, 1971.

Gillion, K. L. *Ahmadabad, a Study in Indian Urban History.* Berkeley: University of California Press, 1968.

Gholam Rasool, Muhammad. *Chishti—Nizami Sufi Order of Bengal, till Mid-15th Century and Its Socio-Religious Contributions.* Delhi: Idarah-i Adbiyat, 1990.

Habib, Irfan. "Agrarian Economy." In *The Cambridge Economic History of India.* Vol. 1, *c.1200–1750.* Edited by T. Raychaudhuri and I. Habib. Cambridge: Cambridge University Press, 1982: 48–76.

Kameswara Rao, V. *Select Vijayanagara Temples of Rayalseema.* Hyderabad: Government of Andhra Pradesh, 1976.

Kennedy, M. T. *Chaintanya—A Study of the Vaishnavism of Bengal.* London: Oxford University Press, 1925.

Kenneth, L. *Ahmadabad: A Study in Indian Urban History.* Berkeley: University of California Press, 1968.

Khandalavala, K., and M. Chandra. *New Documents of Indian Painting: A Reappraisal, Prince of Wales Museum of Western India.* Bombay: Trustees of the Prince of Wales Museum, 1969.

Mahalingam, T. V. *Administrative and Social Life under Vijayanagara.* 2nd ed. Madras: Madras University, 1969.

Michell, George, ed. *Islamic Heritage of the Deccan.* Bombay: Marg, 1986.

———. *Vijayanagra Country Style: Incorporation and Synthesis in the Royal Architecture of Southern India, 15th–16th Centuries.* New Delhi: Manohar, 1992.

Michell, George, and Sneha Shah, eds. *Ahmaadabad.* Bombay: Marg, 1988.

Michell, George, and M. Zebrowski. *Architecture and Art of the Deccan Sultanates.* Cambridge: Cambridge University Press, 1999.

Nurul Hasan, S. "Agra." In *Encyclopaedia of Islam.* Vol. 1. 2nd ed. Leiden: E. J. Brill, 1965.

Pearson, M. *Merchants and Rulers in Gujarat.* New Delhi: Munshilal Manoharlal, 1976.

Sadanandan, P. "Islamic Influence in Vijayanagara Capital." *Journal of Andhra Historical Research Society* 30 (1964–1965): 85–88.

Saletore, B.A. *Social and Political Life in the Vijayanagara Empire.* 2 vols. Madras: B. G. Paul, 1934.

Sarkar, Jadu Nath, *Chaitnaya's Life and Teachings.* Calcutta: Sarkar, 1932.

Sen, Dinesh Chandra. *Chaitanya.* Calcutta: Calcutta University, 1922.

Soundara Rajan, K. V. *Ahmadabad.* New Delhi: Archaeological Survey of India, 1980.

Verghese, Amila. *Religious Traditions at Vijayanagara; As Revealed through Its Monuments.* New Delhi: Manohar, 1995.

Verma, H. C. *Dynamics of Urban Life in Pre-Mughal India.* New Delhi: Munshiram Manoharlal, 1986.

About the Author

Iqtidar Alam Khan retired as a professor of history from Aligarh Muslim University in 1994. His early research concerned the political process within the Mughal Empire, leading to two monographs, *Mirza Kamran: A Biographical Study* (Bombay, 1963) and *The Political Biography of a Mughal Noble: Life of Mun'im Khan, Khan-i Khanan* (New Delhi, 1973), and a large number of papers published in leading journals. Later, he widened the area of his research to cover themes like the concept of India in Alberuni, Abdul Qddus Gangohi's relations with state authorities, medieval archaeology, the role of middle classes in Mughal India, gunpowder technology in South Asia, and so forth. His latest book, *Gunpowder and Firearms: Warfare in Medieval India* (2004), attempts to provide a new comprehension of the impact of gunpowder on Indian polity and society during the medieval period. Iqtidar Alam Khan was the general president of the Indian History Congress's 59th session held at Bangalore in 1997.